INSTITUTE FOR RESEARCH ON PUBLIC POLICY

IRPP

INSTITUT DE RECHERCHE EN POLITIQUES PUBLIQUES

Founded in 1972, the Institute for Research on Public Policy is an independent, national, nonprofit organization. Its mission is to improve public policy in Canada by promoting and contributing to a policy process that is more broadly based, informed and effective.

In pursuit of this mission, the IRPP

- identifies significant public policy questions that will confront Canada in the longer term future and undertakes independent research into these questions;
- promotes wide dissemination of key results from its own and other research activities;
- encourages non-partisan discussion and criticism of public policy issues in a manner which elicits broad participation from all sectors and regions of Canadian society and links research with processes of social learning and policy formation.

The IRPP's independence is assured by an endowment fund, to which federal and provincial governments and the private sector have contributed.

Créé en 1972, l'Institut de recherche en politiques publiques est un organisme national et indépendant à but non lucratif.

L'IRPP a pour mission de favoriser le développement de la pensée politique au Canada par son appui et son apport à un processus élargi, plus éclairé et plus efficace d'élaboration et d'expression des politiques publiques.

Dans le cadre de cette mission, l'IRPP a pour mandat :

- d'identifier les questions politiques auxquelles le Canada sera confronté dans l'avenir et d'entreprendre des recherches indépendantes à leur sujet;
- de favoriser une large diffusion des résultats les plus importants de ses propres recherches et de celles des autres sur ces questions;
- de promouvoir une analyse et une discussion objectives des questions politiques de manière à faire participer activement au débat public tous les secteurs de la société canadienne et toutes les régions du pays, et à rattacher la recherche à l'évolution sociale et à l'élaboration de politiques.

L'indépendance de l'IRPP est assurée par les revenus d'un fonds de dotation auquel ont souscrit les gouvernements fédéral et provinciaux, ainsi que le secteur privé.

thomas a. hutton

the transformation of canada's pacific metropolis:

a study of vancouver

series edited by

france st-hilaire

IRPP

Printed in Canada

Bibliothèque nationale du Québec
Dépôt légal 1998

Canadian Cataloguing in Publication Data

Hutton, Thomas A.
The transformation of Canada's Pacific metropolis :
a study of Vancouver

(Monograph series on cities ; 4)

ISBN 0-88645-172-8

1. Vancouver Metropolitan area (B.C.) – Economic
conditions. 2. Cities and towns – Canada – Growth – Case
studies. I. Institute for Research on Public Policy.
II. Title. III. Series.

HC118.V35H88 1998 338.9711'33 C98-900085-0

Suzanne Ostiguy McIntyre
Administrative Director

Copy Editor
Francesca Worrall

Editorial Assistance
Sylvana Frangosia
Chantal Létourneau

Design and Production
Studio Duotone inc.

Cover Illustration
Tanya Johnston

Published by
The Institute for Research on Public Policy (IRPP)
L'Institut de recherche en politiques publiques
1470 Peel Street, Suite 200
Montreal, Quebec H3A 1T1

Distributed by
Renouf Publishing Co. Ltd.
5369 Canotek Road, Ottawa, Ontario K1J 1J3
Tel.: 613-745-2665 Fax: 613-745-7660

Contents

List of Tables and Figures

Tables

Figures

Foreword

City-regions are key transmission points in the global economy. They are home to skilled labour, extensive communications and transportation networks and the most flexible and innovative firms. Yet the importance of city-regions and their role in driving the economy is poorly recognized in Canada. Local government structures are often unwieldy; tax and transfer systems are unadapted to the form and function of modern city-regions and government policies, in general, seldom address their particular needs.

In what way has the role of city-regions evolved over the past 20 years of structural change? How should government policy be altered to reflect the importance of city-regions in the new economy? What particular institutional or fiscal arrangements are best suited to address the current needs and realities of metropolitan areas and enhance the efficiency and effectiveness of their local governments? These are some of the questions the contributors to IRPP's City-Regions series seek to answer.

In the first volume, William Coffey examines the impact of globalization and restructuring on Canada's urban areas and describes the new sectoral, occupational and spatial realities that are transforming our metropolitan economies. In the second study, Andrew Sancton compares governance structures and institutions in a number of Canadian city-regions and questions the objectives of recent municipal reforms and the conventional means of achieving them. The third volume in the series is a collection of essays by six experts on local government finance. The authors examine a broad range of issues related to local governance and finance in larger metropolitan areas and look at the implications of alternative financing and expenditure arrangements in achieving greater efficiency, equity and accountability.

In the present volume, Thomas Hutton of UBC's Centre for Human Settlements documents the extraordinary economic and socio-cultural transformation of Vancouver over the last decade. The study is a comprehensive analysis of the city's distinctive growth trajectory since the mid-1980s. It describes how, over a relatively short period of time, Vancouver has undergone a complex series of demographic, economic and socio-cultural changes that have given the city a radically different profile. Vancouver is no longer simply Canada's third largest city or British Columbia's urban core. It has assumed a new identity or new identities, as it were, as the country's gateway to the Pacific; a vibrant, multi-cultural metropolis; a preferred destination for Asian immigrants; and an integral part of new regional entities such as the Vancouver-Seattle urban development corridor and the emerging Cascadia ecological/economic zone.

IRPP is extremely pleased to be bringing this important work to a wider audience. While Vancouver's recent experience is in many ways the outcome of a unique interplay of economic, demographic and cultural factors, it is also a revealing and instructive example of contemporary urban change from which a wide range of policy lessons can be drawn. Finally, it should be noted that the opinions expressed in this volume are the responsibility of the author and do not necessarily reflect the views of IRPP or its Board of Directors.

Monique Jérôme-Forget
President, IRPP

Editor's Introduction

Medium-sized cities are playing an increasingly important role in the global economy. While they may not qualify as "world cities" or "global cities," many second- and third-tier cities (cities with populations in the one- to three-million range) are distinguishing themselves as regional and international gateways and as centres of innovation and technology-intensive production. In some cases, they have even outpaced the largest cities in terms of new investment and growth potential. Identifying the factors that explain this enviable economic performance is naturally of great interest to urban scholars, policy specialists and public officials.

Conventional models of urban development have proved inadequate in providing a full account of these recent urban success stories. For instance, the standard economic factors (i.e., capital, labour and natural resource endowments, location, market size and infrastructure) are still important, but their role has changed. Moreover, other elements that used to be regarded as merely contextual have become major influences on urban development and transformation. Natural and cultural amenities, entrepreneurship, human capital, foreign and domestic immigration and niche-market opportunities, combined with information technologies that reduce the impediment of distance, are increasingly identified as determinants of contemporary urban growth and change.

In many ways Vancouver is the ideal case through which to explore these issues. The city has undergone a dramatic transformation in the past decade or so. Having shed its long-standing primary role as urban core to British Columbia's resource-based hinterland, it has become a dynamic, rapidly changing, multi-cultural metropolis whose economy is increasingly linked to international trade and finance networks. But the most dominant and visible aspect of this metamorphosis has been the city's deepening engagement with the markets and societies of the Asia-Pacific. Indeed, much of the growth and change experienced by Vancouver since the mid-1980s has been fuelled by large inflows of Asian immigrants and capital, to the point where the city has been called the most Asian city in Canada. Between 1991 and 1996, Vancouver's immigrant population grew more rapidly than that of any other Canadian city. Today more than one-third of the city's population is foreign-born, and the majority of recent arrivals are of Asian origin. To many observers, the choice of Vancouver to host the 1997 meeting of the Asia-Pacific Economic Cooperation (APEC) forum confirmed its rising status in the Pacific Rim.

These cursory observations, however, do not convey the complexity and the extent of the demographic, economic, and socio-cultural changes that have taken place in Canada's third largest city over the last 15 years. For Thomas Hutton, determining the impetus behind Vancouver's rapid growth and the impact of this growth on the city is more than an intriguing research question, it also provides the basis for a comprehensive and instructive framework through which to analyse and understand contemporary urban change in all its dimensions. As the author points out, the usual explanations of urban growth do not apply to Vancouver; the city "lacks the large and diversified manufacturing base characteristic of the industrial city and possesses neither the major complex of corporate head offices that define the services city, nor the world-scale high-technology sector that is associated with the 'urban technopoles' of the knowledge or information era." (p. 9) Despite these "deficiencies," Vancouver is alone among Canada's largest cities to have achieved sustained growth since the mid-1980s. (Although recent events in Asia are likely to have an impact on the city's economy, it is too soon to tell how extensive this impact will be.)

This book presents a wide-ranging analysis of Vancouver's distinctive growth trajectory. Using his framework of urban transformation, Hutton documents the restructuring of the city's economy, the shift in its traditional relationship with British Columbia's resource-based hinterland and the expansion and diversification of the service sector. While rapid service-sector growth is a feature that Vancouver shares with other Canadian cities, the author finds important differences in the city's industrial and occupational structures, growth patterns, business cycles and market orientation which suggest that the overall trend is one of divergence and gradual disengagement from the rest of the Canadian urban system.

Hutton describes how the city's regional context is being redefined as new regional entities emerge (i.e., the Vancouver-Seattle urban development corridor, the Georgia Basin bioregion and the Cascadia ecological/economic zone) and as its role in the Asia-Pacific evolves. He explores key aspects of Vancouver's new "Pacific destiny" and how the dramatic economic, demographic and socio-cultural changes of the last decade have left their imprint on the city. Urban mega-projects, reconstructed inner-city industrial districts, major new cultural and entertainment amenities and changing residential housing styles are some of the physical manifestations of Vancouver's new identity.

Since the early 1990s, Canada's largest cities have undergone profound change. Toronto is in many ways still recovering from the severe economic downturn it experienced during the last recession. Montreal finally appears to be making real headway in key sectors of the new economy after decades of painful restructuring. Calgary has become a real contender for corporate head offices, and Ottawa's high-tech sector has reached critical mass. For its part, Vancouver is poised for yet more change. The next few years will demonstrate what the city can make of its newly acquired assets and external linkages. In the short term its continued prosperity will depend on whether its economy is sufficiently diversified and whether the new class of immigrant entrepreneurs is able to take advantage of its foothold in North America to withstand the current economic turmoil in Asia. As Hutton points out, the city also faces a longer-term challenge; that is, to develop and implement a sustainable development strategy. Hutton's study is an important contribution to our understanding of these ongoing processes of urban growth and change.

France St-Hilaire
Series Editor

Acknowledgements

This project has been undertaken in response to an invitation to contribute to IRPP's City-Region series. The findings presented herein represent considerable new research, but also build on almost two decades of inquiry into economic restructuring and transformation within Canadian cities. In this endeavour I have been fortunate indeed to work with two outstanding colleagues, Professor Craig Davis, of the UBC School of Community and Regional Planning, and Professor David Ley, of the UBC Department of Geography. This current work has also been inspired by the seminal scholarship of my mentor, the late Professor Jean Gottmann, FBA. I am happy to acknowledge the significant influence of numerous colleagues within the Canadian urban studies community, notably Bill Coffey, of the University of Montreal, and Larry Bourne, of the University of Toronto.

There is a formidable list of individuals who have assisted greatly in the preparation of this volume, including two anonymous reviewers who offered many useful and constructive comments. Here at CHS, I am deeply grateful to Ms. Karen Zeller and Ms. Christine Evans, who provided many hours of highly professional (and unfailingly patient) assistance in the preparation of the text, tables and diagrams, through several drafts, and in the face of innumerable deadlines. Mr. Eric Leinberger, of the UBC Department of Geography, provided cartographic advice and most of the maps in this volume.

Finally, I want to acknowledge the quite indispensable roles of three individuals. France St-Hilaire was not only an unusually dedicated, careful and supportive editor, but also a source of many insights and ideas that helped me clarify and refine my observations and findings. My wife, Lesley Wood Hutton, contributed the photographic plates, as well as constant support and encouragement. To Lesley, and to our daughter Siena (who contributed in ways only an active three-year old can!), I am very pleased to dedicate this volume.

Tom Hutton
CHS-UBC, Vancouver
June 1998

Introduction and Overview

As we approach the end of the twentieth century, change has become as important as growth to the development of many cities and city-regions in industrialized, industrializing, and post-industrial societies. Change here includes not only increases in population, employment and economic activity and the familiar vagaries of cyclical change, but also more fundamental transformation or restructuring. Economic restructuring is characterized by dramatic shifts in the industrial mix of metropolitan cities that generally favours services and technology-intensive production over basic manufacturing. It sets the stage for the wider aspects of urban transformation, including the interconnected processes of occupational, social, cultural, spatial and physical change. Together, these trends have been described by the eminent geographer Jean Gottmann as a "metamorphosis of the modern metropolis," a term that connotes rapid and far-reaching change rather than evolution.[1]

Over the past three decades, studies of restructuring have tended to focus on the experiences of the largest metropolitan areas – the so-called "world cities"[2] or "global cities."[3] There are, of course, important reasons for this emphasis: world cities with populations of five to 10 million or more represent giant markets and centres of production and account for significant proportions of GDP, both nationally and globally. World cities such as New York, London, Tokyo and Los Angeles have also attracted the headquarters of many corporations, information- and knowledge-based firms, leading banks and financial institutions and sophisticated business-service firms. As a result, the influence of these cities projects far beyond their localized hinterlands into global markets. These massive conurbations also suffer from severe planning problems, such as congestion, pollution and housing shortages, which attract the attention of urban scholars, policy specialists and public officials.[4] It is in these large world cities, too, that the fundamental restructuring processes of de-industrialization and the rapid growth of service industries were first observed, along with the resulting dislocation of employment and loss of income, revenue and social welfare.

As important as these mega-urban regions are, the growth trajectories and restructuring processes of dynamic medium-sized (or second- and third-tier) cities, with populations ranging between one and three million, now merit more attention. Many of these medium-sized cities are playing increasingly important roles as regional and international gateways, locations of specialized knowledge industries and institutions, technology-intensive production zones and centres of innovation. In the United States, second-tier cities like Boston, Atlanta, Minneapolis and Denver have fared better than New York and Chicago in maintaining employment and investment levels,[5] while in Europe the most dynamic urban regions include second-tier cities such as Bristol, Toulouse, Florence and Stuttgart.[6] Cities such as Seattle and Munich house propulsive world-scale corporations (Microsoft and Boeing in Seattle and BMW in Munich), while others, such as Brisbane and Vancouver, which have attracted relatively large amounts of foreign capital, are being visibly transformed both by foreign direct investment (FDI) and immigration.

To some extent, of course, the growth of these dynamic medium-sized cities can be attributed to the familiar mix of Weberian (least-cost) locational factors, natural resources, agglomeration and scale economies and proximity to large markets. But many are also responding to new dynamics such as amenities (natural and cultural), entrepreneurship, human capital, immigration (foreign and domestic), information technologies and systems (which reduce the impediment of distance), opportunities in niche markets and local governance factors. Many have been able to prosper through induced rather than natural comparative advantages, such as prudent investment decisions (e.g., transportation and communications infrastructure) and progressive planning. More importantly, second- and third-tier cities are also subject to the imperatives of economic globalization and market integration and are thus increasingly part of extensive urban networks, markets and cultural systems.

Another distinguishing characteristic of many of these dynamic medium-sized cities is the presence of specialized service industries and a highly tertiarized labour force (i.e., one that is dominated by service occupations). In Canada, for example, there has been a strong correlation between the growth of services and urban expansion which has resulted in cities being repositioned in the national urban hierarchy.[7] Over the past decade or so, highly service-oriented cities such as Toronto, Vancouver, Ottawa-Hull, Calgary, London and Quebec City have benefited most from these trends, while major manufacturing centres like Montreal, Winnipeg and Hamilton have declined, in relative terms. Manufacturing is still an important part of the nation's economy, but the economic structures (industrial mix) and space-economies (patterns of economic activity)[8] of Canadian city-regions are increasingly dominated by interactive ensembles of specialized service industries, institutions and firms.

This monograph presents a case study of Vancouver, Canada's third-largest city and a metropolis that has experienced high rates of growth (in terms of population, employment, investment and trade) over the past decade, in contrast with the decidedly mixed fortunes of most other Canadian cities during

figure 1

Population Growth in Toronto, Montreal and Vancouver CMAs, 1961-1996 (1961=100)

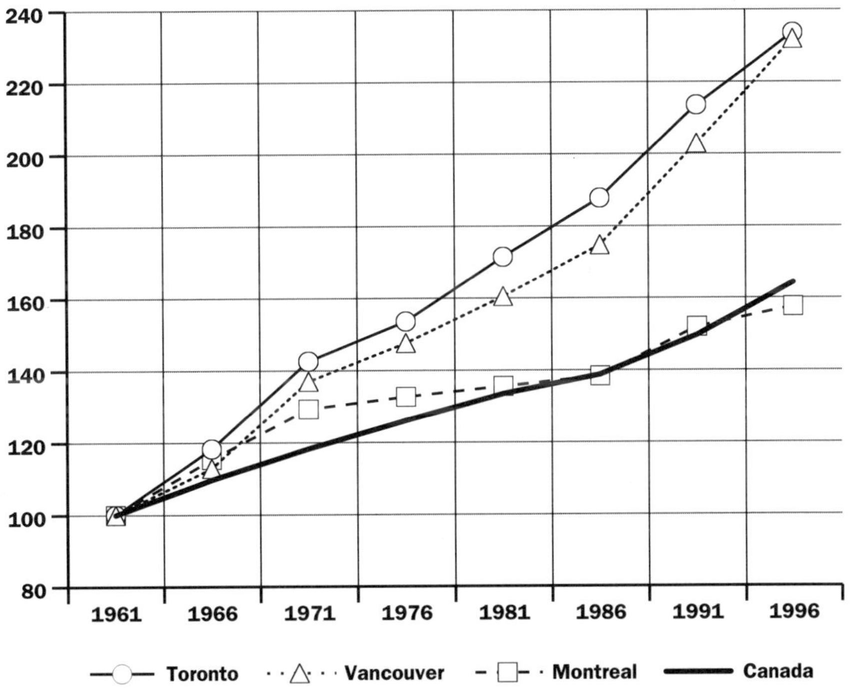

Source: Statistics Canada, Census of Canada, 1961-1996.

this period. Vancouver's population growth rate has been significantly higher than the Canadian average over the past three decades and has recently even surpassed Toronto's (Figure 1). Not only is its status enhanced within the Canadian urban hierarchy, but since the early 1980s Vancouver also ranks prominently among the fastest-growing metropolitan cities in North America (Table 1).[9] As the northern pole of the Vancouver-Seattle development corridor, it is located within an increasingly important urban economic zone and a key development axis in the dynamic Pacific Basin. More importantly, Vancouver has become a significant node of the Pacific Basin urban system, a network of city-regions linked by flows of capital, technology, commodity trade, tourism and culture.[10]

table 1
Population Growth in Selected Canadian and American Metropolitan Areas, 1980–1990

Metropolitan Area	Growth Rate (%) 1980-1990
Phoenix	40.6
San Diego	34.2
Atlanta	32.6
Dallas-Fort Worth	32.5
Tampa-St. Petersburg-Clearwater	28.1
Los Angeles-Anaheim-Riverside	26.4
Vancouver	25.2
Seattle-Tacoma	22.3
Toronto	22.1
Miami-Fort Lauderdale	20.8
Washington	20.7
Houston-Galveston-Brazoria	19.7
San Francisco-Oakland-San Jose	16.5
Minneapolis-St. Paul	15.3
Montreal	9.6
Baltimore	5.0
Boston-Lawrence-Salem	5.0
Philadelphia-Wilmington-Trenton	3.8
New York-Northern New Jersey-Long Island	3.1
St. Louis	2.8
Chicago-Gary Lake County	1.6
Detroit-Ann Arbor	-1.9
Cleveland-Akron-Lorain	-2.6
Pittsburgh-Beaver Valley	-7.4

Source: Groupe SECOR based on data from Statistics Canada and the US Bureau of the Census.

table 2

Population Rankings and 1991-1996 Growth Rates for Canada's Twenty-five Largest Metropolitan Areas

	Rank	Population	% change
CMA	1996		1991-96
Toronto	1	4,263,757	9.4
Montreal	2	3,326,510	3.7
Vancouver	3	1,831,665	14.3
Ottawa-Hull	4	1,010,498	7.3
Edmonton	5	862,597	2.6
Calgary	6	821,628	9.0
Quebec	7	671,889	4.1
Winnipeg	8	667,209	1.0
Hamilton	9	624,360	4.1
London	10	398,616	4.5
Kitchener	11	382,940	7.4
St. Catharines – Niagara	12	372,406	2.2
Halifax	13	332,518	3.7
Victoria	14	304,287	5.7
Windsor	15	278,685	6.3
Oshawa	16	268,773	11.9
Saskatoon	17	219,056	3.8
Regina	18	193,652	1.0
St. John's	19	174,051	1.3
Sudbury	20	160,488	1.8
Chicoutimi – Jonquière	21	160,454	-0.3
Sherbrooke	22	147,384	4.7
Trois-Rivières	23	139,956	2.7
Saint John	24	125,705	-0.1
Thunder Bay	25	125,562	0.5

Source: Statistics Canada, Census of Canada, 1996.

After a period of rapid population and employment growth in the 1980s, Vancouver's growth rate was higher than those of all Canadian cities during the first half of the present decade. Its population grew by 14.3 percent between 1991 and 1996 (Table 2), a growth rate exceeding that of Canada's 25 largest census metropolitan areas (CMAs) and a full five percentage points higher than that of Toronto (9.4 percent), the city at the peak of Canada's urban hierarchy. It was almost four times as high as Montreal's (3.7 percent) and nearly double Ottawa-Hull's (7.3 percent).

In general, Canada's largest CMAs grew considerably faster than the medium-sized ones. The 12 largest experienced population growth averaging 5.8 percent between 1991 and 1996, compared with the group that ranked 13th to 25th, whose population growth averaged only 3.3 percent. Among the economic, demographic and policy factors that underlie this trend toward higher growth rates in the largest cities, migration, especially international immigration, is particularly significant. The majority of Canada's new immigrants are attracted to the largest cities by greater employment opportunities, but also for reasons of kinship and for the larger number of services offered to immigrants by various levels of government and by nongovernmental organizations (NGOs).

At a regional level, Vancouver's population growth rate was unsurpassed by any other major western Canadian city-region. In fact, only Calgary (9.0 percent) and Victoria (5.7 percent) experienced population growth rates exceeding five percent in 1991-1996. Population growth rates in other western Canadian cities tended to lag relative to the average for the largest CMAs. This reflects problems in their hinterlands (a theme that will be explored later) and also the emergence of Vancouver and Calgary as the principal western Canadian urban growth centres.[11]

Vancouver's relative dynamism (Table 3) is also manifest in employment trends. Its employment growth rates were considerably higher than those of Toronto and Montreal in most major industrial categories over the period 1984-1994. Most striking is Vancouver's growth in the key finance, insurance and real estate category (47.7 percent) compared with Toronto's (22.7 percent) and Montreal's (11.7 percent) performance; the extraordinary growth in the construction sector, reflecting the sustained construction boom over the past decade; and the city's robust growth in manufacturing (37.7 percent), in contrast to the contractions experienced in both Montreal (-2.1 percent) and Toronto (-13.7 percent).

In his comprehensive analysis of employment change in the Canadian urban system between 1971 and 1994, William Coffey observes that for the most recent period examined (1991-1994) "the performances of Toronto (0.1 percent) and Montreal (0.3 percent) are very weak...In contrast, that of Vancouver (2.3 percent) is only slightly below its 1981-1991 level (2.5 percent)."[12] These data also reflect the widely differing experiences of city-regions in the higher echelons of the Canadian urban hierarchy during a major period of recession.

Vancouver's growth compares favourably with that of Seattle, one of the most dynamic American cities in the 1980s and the fastest-growing American metropolitan area outside the sun-belt (i.e., the south-west and the south-east). Indeed, between 1991 and 1995 Vancouver's population grew by 10.8 percent[13] compared with a growth rate of 9.9 percent for Seattle in 1990-1995.[14]

Vancouver and Seattle have a number of important features in common. Both have strategic gateway functions, export-oriented service industries and entrepreneurial immigrants. The size of their populations is comparable (in the two million range) and both are in the Georgia Basin-Puget Sound metropolitan

table 3
Employment Growth by Sector in Montreal, Toronto and Vancouver CMAs, 1984-1994

	CMAs		
	Montreal	**Toronto**	**Vancouver**
Industry Sector	**percentage change**		
Primary/extractive	37.5	15.3	0.8
Manufacturing	-2.1	-13.7	37.7
Construction	19.2	31.0	122.4
Transportation, communications & other public services	8.7	33.0	11.8
Business services	13.9	32.3	34.0
Finance, insurance & real estate	11.7	22.7	47.7
Other services	45.3	50.8	71.2
Public administration	-1.7	21.7	31.3
Total	19.1	25.2	51.0

Source: Statistics Canada, *Labour Force Annual Averages, 1989-1994* (Ottawa: Minister of Industry, Science and Technology, April 1995) and *Labour Force Annual Averages, 1981-1988* (Ottawa: Supply and Services, March 1989).

bioregion. But there are also significant differences. In particular, the Seattle metropolitan region includes several world-scale multinational corporations (including Boeing and Microsoft) and a large military establishment, for which there are no counterparts in Vancouver. On the other hand, Vancouver has somewhat deeper and more diversified linkages with the markets and societies of the Asia-Pacific. Clearly, high urban growth rates can be associated with distinctive influences, even among cities with similar development trajectories.

A key factor in Vancouver's growth is immigration, particularly international immigration, reflecting Vancouver's attractiveness as a place to work and live. It is also a crucial agent of growth and change. Vancouver has played a prominent role provincially and nationally in receiving new immigrants (Table 4). Between 1991 and 1996, Vancouver attracted about 18 percent of all immigrants to Canada; that is equivalent to three times its share of Canada's population (about six percent). While Vancouver's share of European immigrants is slightly higher than its share of the national population, its share of Asian immigrants is much larger. Four of every five international immigrants that have come to Vancouver in recent years have been from Asia,[15] particularly from Hong Kong. Furthermore, Vancouver attracts a disproportionately large share of "economic" immigrants (i.e., those admitted to Canada as assisted relatives, entrepreneurs, self-employed, investors and other independents).

table 4
Immigrant Landings in Vancouver, British Columbia and Canada, by Country or Region of Origin, 1994-1996

1994

Source	Vancouver Area	Total BC	Canada	Vancouver as a % of Canada
Europe	3,724	5,178	37,581	9.9
Africa	1,483	1,821	13,198	11.2
Asia	33,609	38,132	138,297	24.3
Hong Kong	15,487	16,159	43,651	33.5
India	3,547	5,531	16,685	21.3
Australasia	301	423	1,065	28.3
North & Central America	1,034	1,807	9,281	11.1
United States	760	1,420	6,052	12.6
Caribbean	96	178	9,584	1.0
South America	222	307	7,584	2.9
Oceania	605	683	1,173	51.6
All Areas	41,074	48,529	217,763	18.9

1995

Source	Vancouver Area	Total BC	Canada	Vancouver as a % of Canada
Europe	4,000	5,675	40,914	9.8
Africa	1,148	1,378	14,369	8.0
Asia	30,155	34,066	128,351	23.5
Hong Kong	11,366	11,807	31,705	35.8
India	3,470	5,158	16,141	21.5
Australasia	276	392	1,044	26.4
North & Central America	979	1,591	7,971	12.3
United States	684	1,187	5,145	13.3
Caribbean	117	188	9,993	1.2
South America	237	321	7,504	3.2
Oceania	421	462	828	50.8
All Areas	37,333	44,073	210,974	17.7

1996

Source	Vancouver Area	Total BC	Canada	Vancouver as a % of Canada
Europe	3,612	5,531	39,253	9.2
Africa	1,118	1,314	14,385	7.8
Asia	35,720	40,529	142,549	25.1
Hong Kong	11,679	12,180	29,802	39.2
India	3,826	6,048	21,059	18.2
Australasia	275	412	1,205	22.8
North & Central America	1,104	1,716	8,955	12.3
United States	732	1,196	5,656	12.9
Caribbean	90	180	8,902	1.0
South America	280	356	5,932	4.7
Oceania	374	435	823	45.4
All Areas	42,573	50,473	222,004	19.2

Source: Unpublished data provided by BC Stats, Ministry of Finance and Corporate Relations, Government of British Columbia, April 1997.

For instance, immigration data for 1992-1996 indicate that BC has received, on average, 54.3 percent of the immigrants in this category during this period.[16] As our analysis will demonstrate, this immigration has had far-reaching economic and socio-cultural consequences.

The impetus behind Vancouver's rapid growth represents an intriguing research question; as suggested above, many of the usual explanations for urban growth do not apply to Vancouver. Unlike Toronto, for example, Vancouver has a relatively underdeveloped manufacturing sector. To a large extent, it has bypassed the classic "industrial city" development phase. With respect to corporate power, Vancouver is by no means a major location for head offices on the scale of Toronto, Montreal or even Calgary. The city not only has a relatively small local market, but its hinterland is thinly populated and in the throes of a serious adjustment process.[17] Unlike Quebec City, Toronto and Victoria, Vancouver is not a provincial capital and therefore lacks the concentration of public-sector decision makers present in capital cities. Unlike Seattle, Vancouver has little in the way of very large, indigenous, propulsive corporations, and unlike Montreal, Ottawa and Seattle, it has at best an incipient high-technology industrial sector.

Overall, Vancouver lacks the large and diversified manufacturing base characteristic of the industrial city and possesses neither the major complex of corporate head offices that (in part) define the services city, nor the world-scale high-technology sector that is associated with the "urban technopoles" of the knowledge or information era.[18] Despite these apparent economic handicaps, Vancouver, almost alone among Canadian CMAs, has achieved sustained growth since the mid-1980s.

Apart from its value as a case study, an examination of Vancouver's distinctive development experience, with appropriate references to other city-regions, contributes to our understanding of contemporary urban growth and restructuring patterns in the following ways:

- as an example of metropolitan transformation among the ascendant city-regions in the Canadian urban system as a whole and a case study of the experience of dynamic, medium-sized cities specifically;
- as a source of insight into the complex interplay of factors influencing urban transformation in the late twentieth century, particularly the strategic interdependencies of culture, technology, environment and economic development;
- as an example of the repositioning of cities within rapidly evolving urban networks, trading systems and ethno-cultural diasporas – a process accelerated by economic globalization, market integration and innovations

in telecommunications and information systems – and, in particular, the key role of city-regions in the Pacific Basin;
- as a reference point for the development of a new conceptual framework for interpreting economic restructuring and the associated processes of metropolitan transformation;
- as a laboratory in which to study fundamental urban change (such as labour force displacement, new land use patterns and the emergence of plural urban societies) as well as innovative planning responses and experiments.

Study Overview

After the context for this study has been established in chapter 1, chapters 2 to 5 will address first the external and then the internal aspects of Vancouver's transformation. Throughout, the analysis and discussion will emphasize what makes Vancouver different, while also referring to commonalities between Vancouver's development path and those of other city-regions in Canada and elsewhere.

Chapter 1 reviews the basic attributes of urban structural change and examines some leading explanations of metropolitan growth and change. A new conceptual framework demonstrating the relationships between economic restructuring and other dimensions of urban transformation will be presented, with specific reference to the Vancouver case.

Chapters 2 and 3 examine the trajectory of Vancouver's external reorientation, including the new (or renegotiated) relationships with other markets, cultures and cities that represent defining features of Vancouver's transformation. Chapter 2 identifies the mix of strategic interdependencies underlying this process of growth and change and compares Vancouver's restructuring trajectory with those of other major CMAs. The city's evolving linkages with the rest of the province – particularly its resource economy – will be described, using five key measures of interdependency. The outline of a new regional milieu for Vancouver, incorporating the Georgia Basin and Cascadia regions, will also be presented.

Chapter 3 explores Vancouver's deepening engagement with the economies, societies and cultures of the Pacific Basin. In this dynamic arena, crucial elements of connectivity are measured not only in terms of traditional indicators such as commodity exports and merchandise trade, but also include trade in services, information flows, air travel and communications, capital flows and immigrant networks. Our thesis here is that not only is Vancouver emerging as an important node of the Pacific Rim urban network, it is quite visibly becoming an Asian-Pacific metropolis as a consequence of inflows of Asian capital and culture.

This discussion sets the stage for chapter 4, which presents examples of metropolitan change to illustrate the character of Vancouver's transformation and evolving identity. It is an overview of the reconfiguration of Vancouver's metropolitan structure, with specific reference to Pacific Place – a mega-project that is redefining the downtown periphery – and the emergence of new production spaces in the inner city. It also outlines the impact of structural change on Vancouver's social morphology and built environment, again underscoring the interdependence of culture, technology, environment and economic development in the emergence of new urban places.

Chapter 5 revisits some of the major themes and issues of the preceding chapters and considers the conditions of urban growth and change on the threshold of the twenty-first century. The chapter describes how certain aspects of urban transformation have led to the emergence of a new economic role for advanced city-regions. Communication, creativity, and innovation as well as the production and diffusion of information, knowledge and technology are paramount in this process. This sets the stage for a critical examination of urban development globally and the competitive advantage of city-regions. The book concludes with a discussion of the need for new policy approaches and tools, given the greatly enhanced economic status of city-regions and the complex problems associated with metropolitan restructuring and transformation.

Notes

1. I.J. Gottmann, "The Metamorphosis of the Modern Metropolis," *Ekistics*, Vol. 292 (1982), pp. 7-11.

2. J. Friedmann and G. Wolff, "World City Formation: An Agenda for Research and Action," *International Journal of Urban and Regional Research*, Vol. 6, no. 3 (1982), pp. 309-44.

3. S. Sassen, *The Global City: New York, London, Tokyo* (Princeton: Princeton University Press, 1991).

4. W. Lever and C. Moore (eds.), *The City in Transition: Policies and Agencies for the Economic Regeneration of Clydeside* (Oxford: Oxford University Press, 1986); S. Cohen and J. Zysman, *Manufacturing Matters: The Myth of the Post-Industrial Economy* (New York: Basic Books, 1987).

5. P. Hall, *Reinventing the City* (Toronto: Centre for Urban and Community Studies, University of Toronto, 1989).

6. P.C. Cheshire and D.G. Hay, *Urban Problems in Western Europe: An Economic Analysis* (London: Unwin Hyman, 1989).

7. W.J. Coffey, *The Evolution of Canada's Metropolitan Economies* (Montreal: Institute for Research on Public Policy, 1994).

8. The classic pattern of the urban space-economy during the industrial city phase featured, at the most basic level, a central core of commercial activity, an inner-city ring of manufacturing, adjacent working-class residential districts and suburban areas dominated by low-density housing and consumer tertiary industries. The advent of the so-called "post-industrial" urban economy has generated major changes in the spatial distribution of services and production industry, as will be shown in chapter 4.

9. T.A. Hutton, "Vancouver: City Profile," *Cities*, Vol. 11, no. 4 (1994), pp. 219-39.

10. P. Rimmer, "The Global Intelligence Corps and World Cities: Engineering Consultancies on the Move," in P.W. Daniels (ed.), *Services and Metropolitan Development: International Perspectives* (London: Routledge, 1991).

11. Calgary's 1991-1996 population growth rate, at nine percent, was more than triple that of Edmonton (2.6 percent), underscoring Calgary's increasing economic dominance within Alberta. Assuming that these growth rates continue in 1996-2001, Calgary's population may exceed that of Edmonton, the provincial capital, by the beginning of the twenty-first century. A measure of Vancouver's dominance within western Canada, however, is the fact that the population of Vancouver CMA exceeds the combined populations of metropolitan Calgary and Edmonton by some 150,000.

12. W.J. Coffey, *Employment Growth and Change in the Canadian Urban System, 1971-94*, Working Paper No. W/02 (Ottawa: Canadian Policy Research Networks, 1996), p. 39.

13. F. Martin and R. Martin, *Harmonization of Canada-United States Metropolitan Area Data with Reference to the Montreal Metropolitan Region* (Montreal: City of Montreal, 1996).

14. This refers to population growth in the Seattle Consolidated Metropolitan Statistical Area (CMSA). In the American system of local areas statistics, CMSAs are metropolis-centred economic regions. Seattle CMSA includes the communities of Bremerton and Tacoma.

15. Statistics Canada, *Daily*, November 4, 1997, Catalogue no. 11-001E, p. 6.

16. On the other hand, BC's share of "social and humanitarian" immigration (i.e., family reunification, refugee and designated), which averaged 15.2 percent over this five-year period, was roughly proportional to its share of the population. These estimates are based on data provided by BC Stats and Citizenship and Immigration Canada in July 1997.

17. T.A. Hutton, "Visions of a 'Post-Staples' Economy: Structural Change and Adjustment Issues in British Columbia," PIPR no. 3 (Vancouver: Centre for Human Settlements, UBC, 1994).

18. These terms describe three principal phases of urban economic development over the past half-century: (1) the high point of Fordist (or mass) production concentrated within the classic "industrial city" during the first two decades after the First World War, (2) the emergence of the post-industrial or service city by the 1960s, manifested in the growth of advanced service industries and the formation of the downtown corporate complex of high-rise office buildings, and (3) the increasing significance of cities as centres of innovation, creativity, information and knowledge, and technology ("urban technopoles"). For a discussion of the latter, see M. Castells and P. Hall, *Technopoles of the World: The Making of 21st Century Industrial Complexes* (London: Routledge, 1994).

1

Vancouver as a Model of Urban Transformation

Over the last several decades, cities in the developed world have been engaged in comprehensive processes of structural or transformational change. This transformation is often manifested largely in economic terms; indeed, economic dynamics, trends and consequences are defining features of contemporary urban change in large and medium-sized city-regions. At the broadest level, economic restructuring has entailed a shift of capital and labour from traditional manufacturing to service industries, and more recently to the production of specialized services and technology-intensive goods.

While the specific nature of urban transformation varies from place to place, some of its most pervasive or generic attributes can be described as follows:

- *Powerful* – Processes of transformational urban change are often driven not only by local influences, but also by external (or exogenous) forces that include the familiar (if imperfectly understood) dynamics of economic globalization, market integration, enhanced capital mobility and technological innovation. Pessimistic observers have concluded that cities – and even nation-states – are almost powerless to respond to these potent, macro-level exogenous forces.
- *Rapid* – With the emergence of global markets, multinational firms and advanced information technologies, cyclical and structural change can be transmitted very rapidly within as well as across national boundaries,

as evidenced by the de-industrialization of large cities among mature economies in the 1970s and the even more abrupt correction that afflicted major financial centres following the boom years of the 1980s.

- *Dynamic* – Although restructuring typically involves the fundamental transformation of urban economies and societies, it cannot be described as an end state. For instance, following several decades of growth in service industries (the "tertiarization" of the urban economy), there is evidence that metropolitan service economies have entered a mature phase. Nevertheless, new divisions of labour within service industries are still discernible and, as new technologies continue to transform service production, further rounds of restructuring can be anticipated.
- *Multifaceted* – While economic factors play a leading role, urban transformation has other dimensions including social structure, cultural mix, built forms and spatial patterns.
- *Interdependent* – The various dimensions of structural change are, to a large extent, interdependent. For example, economic restructuring can strongly influence urban occupational hierarchies and social classes, and factors like culture (values, behaviour and preferences) can in turn influence economic growth and change.
- *Diffusive* – The onset of modern restructuring trends (industrial decline and the rapid growth of services) can be traced to the 1960s in the larger metropolitan areas, but processes of transformational change have now diffused down the urban hierarchy to include medium-sized and even relatively small cities, and, spatially, from "first-world" cities to urban centres in the so-called "newly industrializing" and developing countries.[1]
- *Problematic* – Restructuring and transformational change are by no means outcome-neutral. In many cases, restructuring has involved the massive contraction of industrial capacity, employment, output, incomes and revenues. As a result, certain urban social classes have been eroded and communities displaced and destabilized.[2]

Even in cities that have, on balance, successfully managed the transition to more advanced production modes, restructuring entails planning challenges on many levels, such as adapting land-use policy in the face of changes in the demand for urban infrastructure and services and addressing the need for employment and retraining programmes to meet the new skill requirements of the "information economy."[3]

While restructuring has been devastating and deeply problematic for many cities, it has also, perhaps paradoxically, enhanced the overall status of cities and city-regions in the economic life of advanced nations. Urban societies have borne the brunt of restructuring, but they are also playing a more strategic role as advanced production centres, crucibles of technological and cultural innovation, nodes of the globalized financial system and international gateways. In Canada, cities are increasingly the engines of growth for urban regions and the country as a whole.[4] Globally, they are the gatekeepers of the world's service economy.[5]

Other trends may also be enhancing the position of cities within countries and even modifying power relationships between the city-region and the nation-state. Continuing urbanization trends are concentrating populations, economic activity and, to some extent at least, political influence in metropolitan regions. Moreover, the largest and most powerful business centres are often where corporate head office complexes are located, thus allowing them to project their influence over national and international territories. In Canada, for instance, the ascendancy of Toronto in the 1970s and 1980s raised its status among the world's financial and business centres and established its primacy within the national urban system and the corporate sphere.

Over the past decade or so, the pervasive trend toward market deregulation and integration has also served to modify city-region/nation-state relationships in favour of city-regions. While it is premature to speak of truly borderless economies, it is evident that fewer markets are exclusively subject to national regulation and control. Bilateral and multilateral trade arrangements, such as the North American Free Trade Agreement (NAFTA) and the General Agreement on Tariffs and Trade (GATT), have tended to promote new patterns of trade and investment that are more congruent with circuits of exchange between cities, urban development corridors and other regional economic zones than with those between national entities.

Finally, fundamental changes in national policy may further highlight the role and significance of cities and city-regions. In Canada, the last decade has seen a protracted federal retreat from traditional regional development policies aimed at reducing socio-economic disparities and from major areas of social development policy, such as the nonmarket housing programmes administered by the Canada Mortgage and Housing Corporation (CMHC). Some of these policy spheres and programme responsibilities may be devolved to provincial governments, but it is by no means certain whether the latter have the resources (or the will) to assume them. Indeed, there are indications that provincial authorities may be attempting to further offload these mandates to local governments.[6] The Harris government's recent decision to shift responsibility for social housing to municipalities in Ontario is a good example of this domino effect. It certainly appears that in this new, more fiscally constrained policy environment, higher levels of government will continue to withdraw from major programme and expenditure areas. As a consequence, city-regions will be obliged to be more self-reliant.

The Search for Explanation

The rapid and comprehensive restructuring process that has transformed city-regions over the past few decades has also compromised the integrity of traditional models of urban development. As Simmons and Bourne observed, "each successive census seems to demolish another aspect of our urban and spatial theories."[7] For example, the classical models of urban form and structure, introduced during the first half of this century, were helpful in understanding the spatial form of the industrial city, but they are generally far too rigid and static to apply to metropolitan regions at the turn of the millennium. Economic models advanced by regional scientists and others may provide insights into the organization of urban industries and production systems, but they tend to overlook critical interdependencies between economic change and other important facets of urban transformation. Consequently, over the past 35 years urban studies specialists across a broad range of disciplines have been exploring more robust, integrative and contemporary theories of urban growth and change.

Jean Gottmann's seminal contribution to our enhanced understanding of new urban forms and economic structures includes the concept of the "megalopolis," which originally depicted the metropolitan agglomeration of the US north-eastern seaboard,[8] but now applies to spatially extended, contiguous urban regions in North America, Europe, as well as East and Southeast Asia.[9] Gottmann also identified the special significance of information-based (or quaternary) service industries and occupations, as distinct from the more routine and standardized tertiary industries. In the 35 years since Gottmann first published his book on the megalopolis, information-based services have become dominant in the economies and occupational structures of large and medium-sized cities in the developed world. Gottmann also described the interweaving of higher-order services (in the form of complex backward and forward linkages) within the central business district (CBD) as a defining feature of what he described as the "transactional" city.[10]

About a decade after the publication of Gottmann's *Megalopolis*, the American sociologist Daniel Bell drew our attention to the profound socio-cultural consequences of economic restructuring and the formation of a post-industrial society.[11] Bell's theory of a new society (and social hegemony) characterized by ascendant service-sector occupations and descendant blue-collar or traditional working-class occupations attracted both acclaim and criticism. Its critics included those who disputed the emergence of an autonomous service economy,[12] but Bell's identification of interdependencies between economic restructuring and social class was an original and defining contribution to our appreciation of the nature of contemporary urban change.

Among those who have taken up the challenge of describing the linkages among the various facets of urban transformation, David Ley's depiction of emerging social structures within the context of economic and spatial change is particularly useful. He has written extensively about the influence of gentrification in the reshaping of inner city communities and neighbourhoods in Vancouver and other major Canadian cities.[13] In particular, he wove together elements of economic, spatial and social change in his concept of the "new middle class."[14] This new middle class comprises the well-educated service elite of professionals and managers who tend to work in the CBD and other urban service clusters, and who prefer to live in metropolitan core areas such as gentrified inner city neighbourhoods or in the new high-rise condominiums prevalent in reconstructed downtown districts.

Allen Scott has contributed to our understanding of the form and function of the late twentieth-century metropolis, emphasizing the strategic interdependencies between economic change and other important dimensions of metropolitan transformation. In his work, he stresses the importance of the modern metropolis as "locus of production" and "centre of human settlement" – thus arguing for a more balanced perception of urban development dynamics. Scott has also written extensively about the emergence of "new production spaces."[15] These new production spaces include areas as disparate as office complexes within the metropolitan core, "ensembles" of technology-based production in suburban (and even exurban) environments and the industrial networks of the "third Italy" (for example, in the Emilia-Romagna region). Despite the differences between them, these new production districts have important elements in common, notably their adoption of flexible production techniques (as opposed to Fordist mass production techniques) and their regional cultures of economic cooperation.

An emphasis on the growing importance of specialized information generation and distribution is common to all these models. Manuel Castells took this observation a step further with his notion of the "informational city" as "a new framework for social change."[16] In this interpretation, information is not just another production input or even a defining feature of advanced economic systems, but rather the basis for a comprehensive reorganization of urban society and metropolitan form. The intense interaction among technology, culture and spatial form is the principal dynamic underlying the emergence of the informational city, supplanting the classical mid-twentieth-century "industrial city." Among Castells' valuable insights is his identification of the information economy as a specifically urban manifestation and the enduring importance of urban community and culture in this new economy.

The New Mix of Urban Growth and Change Factors

The search for new models of urban growth and change has stimulated inquiry into the combination of factors that appear to underlie fundamental or transformational change. This inquiry is accompanied by a general appreciation of new factors (or at least a new mix of factors) that are transforming urban society and the attempt to explain the very diverse fortunes of cities over the last years of the twentieth century. Peter Hall, one of the best known commentators on urban development, has addressed the question of what makes cities successful or unsuccessful:

> Cities that put their eggs in one or two baskets, that lived off a basic manufacturing industry or off port activities associated with such a manufacture, faced the most serious problems in the 1970s and 1980s...Cities that were diversified service centres for regions that were themselves diversified generally had no such problems, and readjusted relatively painlessly.[17]

After reviewing the experiences of various cities over the past 20 years, Hall concluded that there are essentially four preconditions for successful urban transformation: (1) an advanced knowledge base, (2) an efficient transportation and communications infrastructure, (3) culture and a high quality of life, and (4) urban mega-projects, which have the potential to dramatically transform and regenerate obsolescent metropolitan districts.[18]

Changes in the mix of factors underlying urban transformation, specifically the shift from the classical industrial city to Castells' informational city or Gottmann's transactional city, are presented in Figure 1.1. Many factors of urban change – such as location, labour, infrastructure and technology – are characteristic of both the industrial city and the contemporary restructured metropolis, but they are now assuming new roles. Thus location is still important, but proximity to natural resources and large consumer markets are less critical than positioning in regional growth corridors and global

figure 1.1

From the Industrial City to the Informational Metropolis: A Comparison of Factors of Urban Growth and Change

Factor	Industrial city	Informational or transactional metropolis
1. Location	Proximity to resource endowments and consumer markets	Positioning relative to regional growth corridors and global networks
2. Capital	Local and domestic capital inputs	Domestic capital, FDI and joint ventures
3. Labour	Semi-skilled labour and operatives; small cadres of managers	Skilled, entrepreneurial and knowledge workers
4. Infrastructure	Seaports, railways, highways	Airports, teleports, communications networks and container ports
5. Technology	Fordist or mass-production technologies	Flexible specialization and information technologies
6. Services	Facilitating or supporting factors	Advanced services as propulsive and strategic factors in flexible production systems
7. Gender	Women as clerical labour and operatives	Importance of women in small business, credentialled professions and management
8. Policy	Emphasis on regulatory instruments (markets, land use)	Emergence of "blended suite" of regulatory, developmental and distributive policies and programmes
9. Immigration	Source of general labour and mercantile activity	Stimulus to entrepreneurship and formation of mobilized diasporas
10. Amenity	Passive or implicit attribute	Key factor in attracting human capital and investment
11. Culture	Elite consumption preference and reflection of hierarchical society	Major shaper/mediator of economic development
12. Community	Expression of industrial class and occupational cohorts	Importance of community and civic institutions in urban resilience and formation of production and information networks

financial, information and cultural networks. Capital is still an important factor in urban growth and change. However, in the context of financial services deregulation and the internationalization of capital flows, capital can be sourced globally, if the returns are attractive enough to investors.[19]

Other important aspects of urban development have assumed much greater significance in the contemporary urban transformation process. For example, although women have been part of the urban labour force for many years, they used to be employed mostly in clerical and assembly functions. They still represent a significant proportion of these occupations, but there are now also many who occupy professional and managerial positions, especially in the so-called "credentialled" occupations such as law, accountancy and planning, but also in small businesses and the public service.

The role of the service sector has undergone a profound transformation over the past several decades. Its growth is, of course, a defining outcome of restructuring, but it is also a major agent of metropolitan transformation. In the 1950s, during the high point of Fordist mass production, services were a relatively small element of industrial activity, fulfilling mainly facilitating functions. With the growth of business services in the 1970s, the tertiary sector was instrumental in enhancing industrial productivity. More recently, with the development of advanced producer services, intermediate banking and finance, information technology and other knowledge industries, the service sector is performing a propulsive, strategic role, especially in advanced, integrated urban production systems. These urban economies are now defined essentially in terms of specialized service production rather than in terms of basic manufacturing; although there is a close services-technology-manufacturing interface.[20]

Other factors such as amenity, culture and community, which in the past were generally regarded as contextual factors, are now increasingly viewed as major influences on urban development and transformation. Moreover, unlike the more pervasive, macro-level forces that are widely recognized as determinants of urban and regional restructuring, these three factors tend to be highly place-specific. As such, they provide further insight into the contrasting aspects of urban transformation and what makes city-regions successful or unsuccessful in an era of rapid and comprehensive urban change.

Amenity was usually subsumed within more general locational attributes during the classic industrial city phase, when proximity to production inputs and markets was of utmost importance. Now, with the mobility of skilled labour and capital, amenity and the quality of life are regarded as important aspects of comparative advantage for cities and city-regions. For instance, it is Webster's view that urban amenity and environmental enhancement should be a priority for both developed and developing city-regions, "not only because there are direct welfare benefits to people inhabiting liveable urban surroundings, but because investors and skilled labour for 'high end' knowledge-based activities are increasingly demanding such urban environments as a prerequisite for location or expansion."[21] This new reality is reflected in the recruitment notices of corporate entities, as well as in the economic development strategies of cities such as Toronto, Ottawa, Calgary and Vancouver. Here, amenity may include the quality of local education and health care, recreational facilities, air and water quality, and the integrity of nearby ecological assets.

Culture is often subsumed within a more generic treatment of amenity. However, Douglass' work identifies culture as a key factor that reasserts the importance of locality in explaining different growth and change experiences. He points to the following aspects of culture as potential elements of transformational change:

- *As a set of national or ethnic characteristics that influences the path of development.* For example, some contend that the "neo-Confucian" qualities of East Asian society are conducive to, and even major factors in, the high growth rates in Hong Kong, Taiwan, Singapore and several of the "open" Chinese coastal cities;
- *As a shaper of labour relations.* For example, exceptionally stable company-employee relationships, characterized by mutual loyalty and benefit, have been observed in Japanese and German corporations;
- *As defined by the coherence of civil organizations that organize themselves for mutual benefit.* Notable examples include strong environmental movements in some regions and the cooperative economic model of the Mondragon (Basque) community of northern Spain. Douglass also refers to the emergence of community consciousness and activism among first nations groups in Canada and the United States.[22]

Clearly, culture can influence development not only as an important part of the local economic base, but also as "a dimension of industrial location and comparative advantage," and as a result of "values, codes and practices that are embedded in relations of power" at the regional and national levels.[23]

Robert Putnam offers a closer examination of the relationship between community, culture and development in his celebrated study of the role of civic traditions in Italy.[24] Putnam tested the thesis that the efficacy of regional governance is closely correlated with wealth indices. Among the attributes he examined are levels of educational attainment and the presence or absence of civil strife. To his surprise, Putnam discovered that the strongest correlation in the Italian example was between the quality of governance and levels of "civic community" in reference to sustained patterns of community tolerance, interaction and vitality. Putnam concluded that contrary to the widely accepted view, "economic development does not explain political development," but rather "long-established patterns of civic community explain both a region's capacity for economic growth and also its capacity for democratic self-government."[25]

Putnam assigned the highest rankings of civic community to the regions of Emilia-Romagna, Umbria and Tuscany, and to the cities of Florence, Bologna and Milan. We should be careful in applying these lessons to other nations and to communities with different political and social cultures, but Putnam's observations provide another valuable lens through which we can interpret urban and regional development and transformation. The adaptability of urban communities should be taken into consideration in assessing the relative resilience of cities and city-regions to the economic stresses and shocks associated with contemporary restructuring, and thus their prospects for urban sustainability.[26]

Immigration is an increasingly significant element of urban transformation. It can contribute directly and indirectly to overall urban growth by increasing population and employment, by expanding local capital pools and by generating more demand for a broad range of consumer goods. In this context, it is important to distinguish between domestic and foreign immigration, as well as the important subgroups of foreign immigrants (including the refugee, family reunification and special business categories). In some Canadian cities, recent immigration trends have quite fundamentally reshaped the social structure, culture, physical landscape, built environment, economy, trade and even local politics.

Toronto and Vancouver are striking examples of cities that have been dramatically transformed by recent immigration trends, especially from overseas. In addition to its *in situ* impacts, immigration can change the nature of a city's external relationships and orientation, not only in terms of trade and investment, but also in the formation and enrichment of socio-cultural networks. This applies particularly to what has been called the "mobilized Diaspora," a term that has been used to describe new immigrant enclaves that maintain active contact, communication and interaction with their homelands and with similar enclaves in other cities.[27] These mobilized diasporas can link cities through extensive cultural networks, act as conduits for capital and entrepreneurship and contribute to globalized urban hierarchies and systems.

The R^5 Framework of Urban Transformation: Five Dimensions of Structural Change

Although there are many scholarly contributions of unquestionable value, it has proven difficult to establish new models of urban development that capture all the major dimensions of structural or transformational change, the underlying dynamics (localized and exogenous, market and policy-directed) and the complex interdependencies among these factors. There are several constraints on the formation of such a model, including the rapid pace of change; problems in measuring such things as service sector output, trade and productivity; the difficulty in distinguishing between structural (permanent) and cyclical (short-term) impacts, especially during deep recessionary periods when both are present; the speed with which external forces transmit change across vast distances; and the complexity of causal and associative relationships among notionally distinct facets of urban transformation.

Figure 1.2 presents a framework of metropolitan transformation, a synthesis of the principal dimensions of structural change with corresponding examples of transitional processes and trends. The "R^5" refers to the five dimensions of change identified in the framework: (1) economic restructuring – the impact on the economy and the labour force, (2) social recomposition – fundamental changes in class and community structures, (3) spatial reconfiguration – changes in the pattern of metropolitan structure, (4) the reconstruction of urban form and the built environment, and (5) the reorientation of city-regions within external networks and systems.

The R^5 framework is inevitably an oversimplification of highly complex processes. However, it illustrates the breadth and depth of metropolitan transformation and the interdependence of the dynamics and trends involved. In this framework, structural change is depicted as interrelated, comprehensive processes that have materially transformed the economy, social structure, built form, spatial patterns and external relations of the late twentieth-century city.

While all five dimensions of metropolitan transformation are significant, economic dynamics and processes are central to the overall experience of structural change, since they directly affect its social, spatial and physical dimensions. To illustrate, economic restructuring has fundamentally reshaped the metropolitan occupational mix and therefore the structure of urban class and community – the city's social morphology. In the most recent phase, economic restructuring has also accelerated the substitution of capital for labour in the production of goods and services, which tends to exacerbate income stratification and social polarization.

Economic processes are also central to important changes in metropolitan structures. The reconfiguration of city-regions includes the increasing importance of administrative and other services in the development of suburban business nodes and regional town centres. In Garreau's "edge city," office complexes are formed within "proto-urban" developments on the metropolitan periphery.[28]

The relation between economic restructuring and the reconstruction of urban form and the built environment may seem more tenuous, but there are quite

figure 1.2
Dimensions of Metropolitan Transformation:
The R^5 Framework of Urban Structural Change

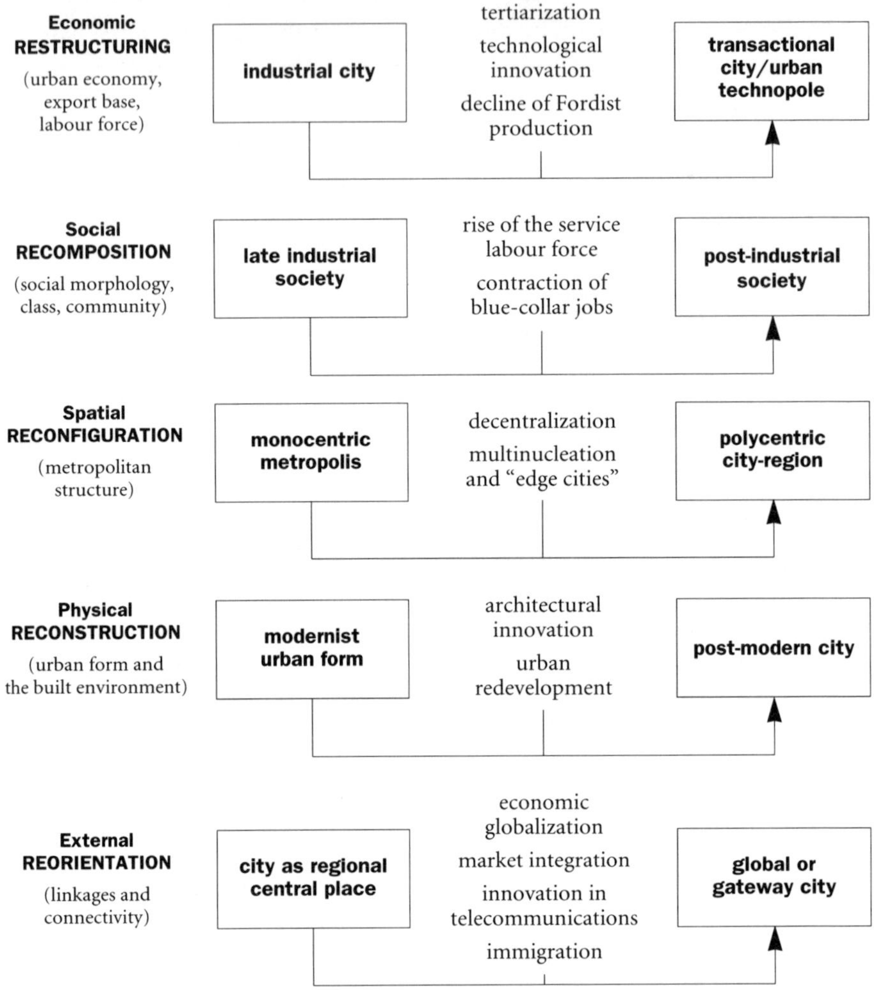

significant links. In addition to the loose association between post-modernism and post-industrialism, the redevelopment of obsolescent industrial districts presents an important connecting point between economic change and shifts in urban form. Moreover, the ornamental post-modern motifs that are appearing in new office, commercial and institutional projects reinforce the relation between economic change and the reconstruction of the built environment. They also represent a departure from the more austere modernist designs that constituted the most prominent architecture influence over the last half-century or so.

Finally, economic dynamics are central to the external reorientation of cities. Economic globalization has pulled cities into the orbit of international markets, foreign investment channels, cultural networks and the new international division of labour. However, the interdependence of urban transformation processes can also operate in the other direction. As was mentioned in the discussion of Douglass' work,[29] urban culture, as defined by behavioural codes, values and priorities, can strongly influence the trajectory of economic development.

Vancouver as a Case Study of Metropolitan Transformation

The Vancouver case features both the general and the more specific aspects of transformational change identified in the R^5 framework. The main elements of structural change in Vancouver are summarized in Figure 1.3. These highlight some of the key aspects of change that define Vancouver's particular transformational experience and that will be explored in more detail in later chapters.

Vancouver exhibits a trajectory of economic restructuring that is characteristic of highly tertiarized metropolitan areas, in particular the rapid growth of its service industries, employment and exports. There has been sustained growth in all the major service industries in Vancouver CMA over the past three decades as measured by changes in the experienced labour force (Table 1.1).[30] This has been accompanied by the distinctly slower growth of the manufacturing sector (Figure 1.4). This pattern was especially evident during the 1980s, when most of the growth was in services.

Business services have experienced the highest growth rates, which is consistent with the experience of other advanced metropolitan economies. In 1991, the business service sector was about three-quarters the size of the manufacturing sector, whereas in 1961 it was only about one-seventh.[31] Since manufacturing in Vancouver has been relatively buoyant (in comparison with many other Canadian cities) over the past three decades, this underscores the vitality and high growth trajectory of its business service sector.

Vancouver's economic restructuring experience is also reflected in occupational trends (Table 1.2 and Figure 1.5). Occupational data are particularly helpful in interpreting trajectories of structural change, because they indicate shifts in the metropolitan division of labour by principal employment function and reveal trends that Standard Industrial Classification statistics tend to mask.[32] Table 1.2 depicts the highly differentiated fortunes of the major labour force categories in Vancouver CMA, with the blue-collar occupations

figure 1.3
Elements of Vancouver's Transformation

Economic RESTRUCTURING	Tertiarization of industrial structure Rapid growth of service occupations (especially professional/managerial groups) Growth of service exports Growth of specialized service institutions and agencies Expansion of technology-intensive production (electronics, telecommunications)
Social RECOMPOSITION	Rise of a "new middle class" (Ley) and a "service elite" Contraction of blue-collar occupations and working class communities in City of Vancouver Increasing ethnic diversity (notably of Asian-Pacific origin) Emergence of new entrepreneurial class (augmenting/ supplanting corporate elite?) Increasing occupational bifurcation → income stratification → social polarization
Spatial RECONFIGURATION	Metropolitan multinucleation – functional specialization of CBD and emergence of suburban regional town centres Growth of various specialized service "clusters" (design districts, medical precinct, tourism and convention area, UBC and SFU, port and airport) Processes of obsolescence, transition and comprehensive redevelopment in inner city Emergence of "new production spaces" in inner city and inner suburbs Growth of metropolitan fringe and exurban areas
Physical RECONSTRUCTION	Role of urban megaprojects in reconstructing metropolitan core The reconstruction of urban frame (e.g., new Georgia/Robson cultural/entertainment axis) Introduction of post-modern influences (e.g., in West Broadway commercial strip) Immigration and the emergence of new cultural landscapes (residential, retail, institutional) Processes of gentrification and densification in the core
External REORIENTATION	Disengagement from national urban systems and markets Redefinition of traditional regional roles and linkages Intensifying connections with the Georgia Basin, Pacific Northwest, and Cascadia Growth of trade (commodities, services, capital) with the Pacific Rim Importance of socio-cultural networks in Vancouver and other Pacific cities and societies

exhibiting relatively modest growth rates compared with most of the service groups. Managerial, administrative and professional occupations in particular enjoyed high levels of growth over the last three decades, which is consistent with the notion of an expanding service sector elite and emphasizes the interdependence between economic restructuring and the recomposition of urban social class.

These occupational trends suggest the emergence of a two-tiered employment structure[33] – also prevalent in other Canadian cities – whose effects

table 1.1

Change in Metropolitan Vancouver's Experienced Labour Force, by Industry and Service Category, 1961 - 1991

	1961	1971	1981	1986	1991
Industry			(000s)		
Agriculture	3.8	5.4	7.7	10.2	11.6
Forestry	2.5	3.4	4.2	3.9	4.1
Fishing & trapping	1.8	1.6	2.3	2.7	2.9
Mining	1.6	3.4	3.3	2.9	2.9
Manufacturing	57.5	78.8	96.3	89.9	98.7
Construction	19.9	32.0	44.6	43.7	64.3
Transportation, communications & utilities	34.9	50.0	69.6	73.8	80.0
Wholesale & retail trade	59.9	85.7	126.5	129.9	162.1
Finance, insurance & real estate (FIRE)	15.9	28.2	47.3	51.9	66.4
Community, business & personal services	70.4	127.8	216.7	265.3	386.5
Business services	7.9	18.2	42.0	50.6	70.1
Education services	12.1	27.5	41.0	41.6	55.3
Health & social services	18.8	30.3	52.3	56.9	76.5
Accommodation, food & beverage	12.9	22.3	42.6	57.0	66.5
Government services	18.0	22.3	37.9	39.5	45.1
Other services	0.7	7.2	0.9	19.7	73.0
Total	268.3	416.2	618.6	673.0	883.1

Source: Statistics Canada, Census of Canada 1961, 1971, 1981 and 1991; mid-term Census 1986.

include social polarization and a disturbing increase in poverty. The growing contingent of urban poor and the emergence of a distinct urban underclass appear in even starker contrast against the highly visible prosperity of much of the city – as evidenced by gleaming commercial buildings, new theatres and other arenas of consumption – and affluent (even opulent) residential neighbourhoods.

But there are other important, even defining, facets of Vancouver's social transformation. Foremost among these is the remarkable increase in ethnic

figure 1.4

Change in Metropolitan Vancouver's Experienced Labour Force, Selected Service Categories and Manufacturing, 1961-1991

(000s)

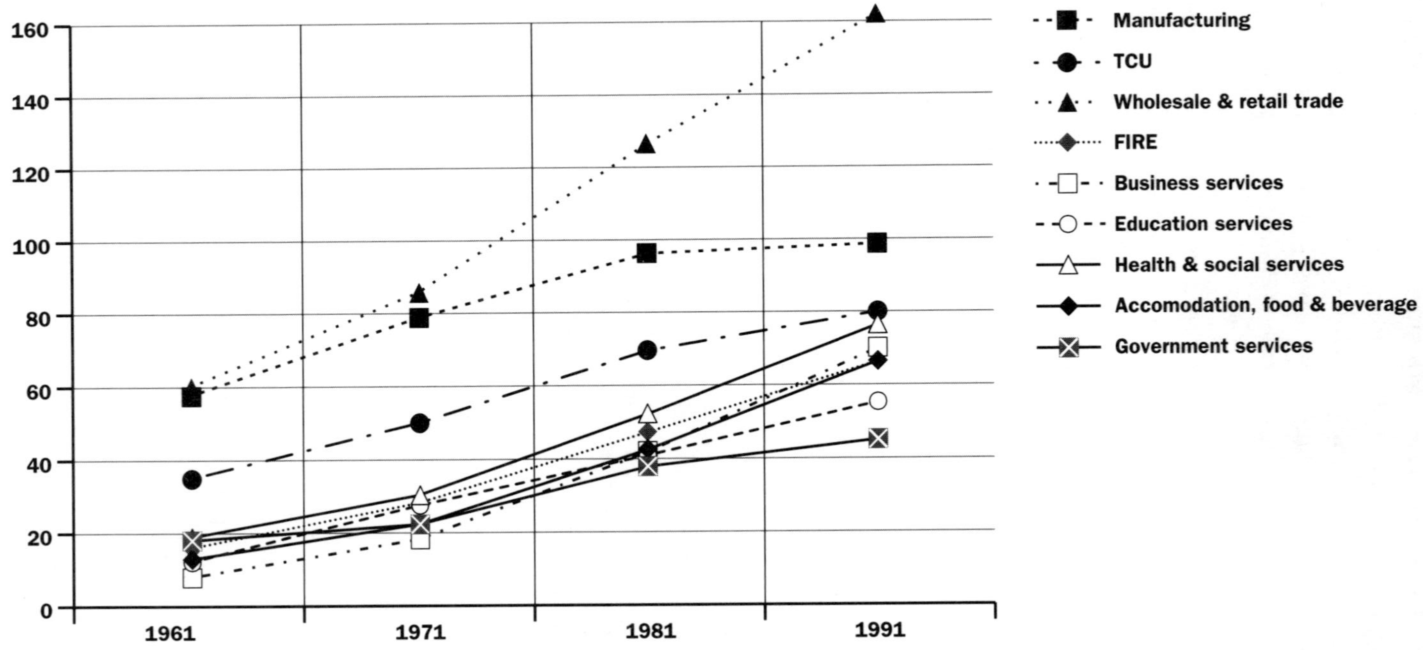

Source: Table 1.1 in this volume.

diversity in the city proper and increasingly in the inner and outer suburbs. While the recent immigrants include people from Latin America, Europe and elsewhere, the preponderance of new citizens are from Asia-Pacific countries and from South Asia. More importantly, many of these new immigrants are highly entrepreneurial; indeed, the emergence of a new entrepreneurial class (which also includes second-generation Vancouver residents) represents a clear departure from the long-established business elite of resource industry executives and managers. At least one observer has recently wondered whether this new entrepreneurial cohort and the older corporate elite can co-exist and enrich one another, or whether the dynamic new entrepreneurs represent a socio-economic hegemony that will, in due course, supersede the traditional elite.[34]

We can identify distinctive physical and spatial aspects of Vancouver's transformation that reflect the new social order and underscore the strong interdependence of specific dimensions of structural change. With respect to

table 1.2
Change in Vancouver CMA's Experienced Labour Force, by Occupation, 1971-1991

	1971	1981	1986	1991
Occupational category		**000s**		
Managerial, administrative	21.0	52.8	85.0	102.3
Nat. sciences, engineering & math.	14.2	25.2	26.2	36.3
Social sciences & related	5.4	12.7	17.5	22.2
Occupations in religion	.8	1.0	1.5	1.7
Teaching & related	16.1	25.3	25.9	35.4
Medical & health	19.5	32.9	38.0	44.5
Artistic, literary & recreational	5.3	10.4	14.8	19.7
Clerical & related	88.7	143.3	146.8	178.8
Sales	55.9	75.3	81.4	101.6
Services	58.7	85.4	108.1	120.7
Farming, horticultural	7.2	9.6	12.3	14.0
Fishing, hunting, trapping	1.8	1.3	2.2	2.5
Forestry & logging	2.4	2.3	2.3	2.3
Mining & quarry	1.1	.9	.8	.7
Processing	18.4	21.4	19.7	21.8
Machining & related	11.8	14.1	11.6	12.3
Product fabricating, assembly	28.9	40.8	40.7	46.4
Construction	32.1	41.7	41.0	52.4
Transport equipment operation	19.2	25.3	27.5	30.7
Material handling & related	15.9	17.3	15.4	17.0
Other crafts/equipment operation	5.7	7.7	5.9	8.9
Total	430.8	646.7	724.5	872.0

Source: Statistics Canada, Census of Canada 1971, 1981 and 1991; mid-term Census 1986.

figure 1.5
Change in Metropolitan Vancouver's Experienced Labour Force, Selected Occupations, 1971-1991
(000s)

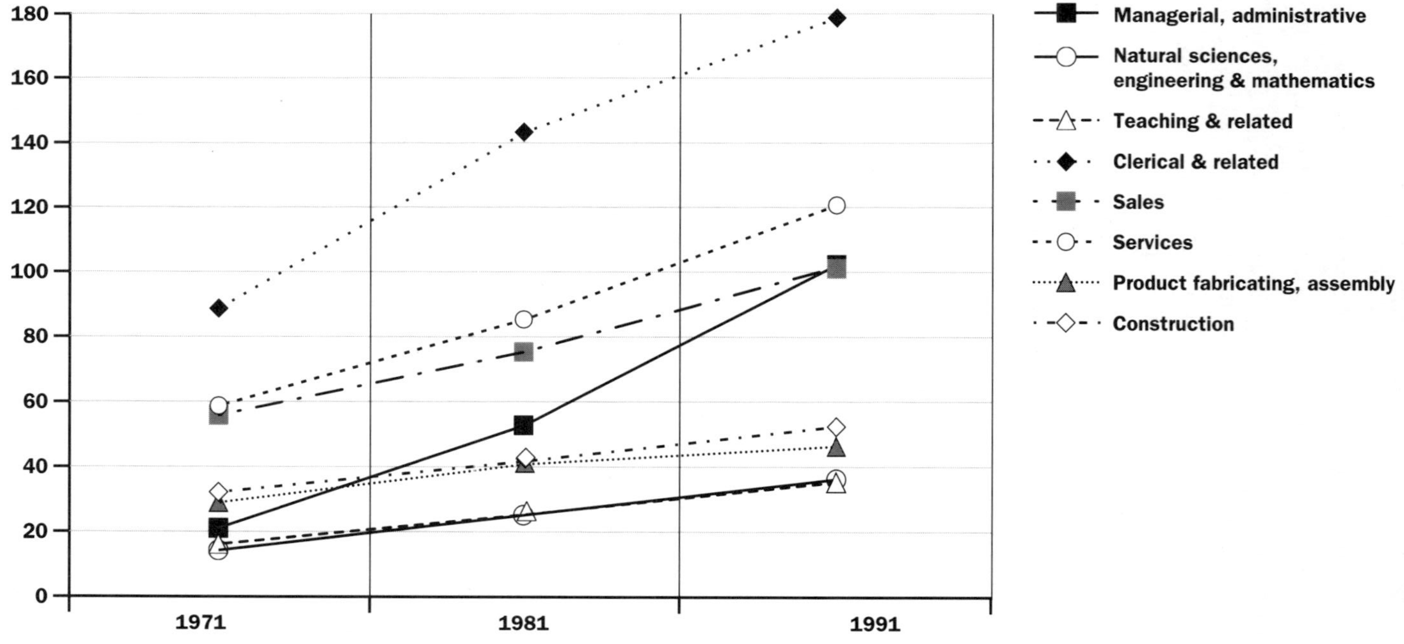

Source: Table 1.2 in this volume.

the reconfiguration of the metropolitan structure, Vancouver's development has included the overlay of a strong CBD and eight policy-designated suburban regional town centres,[35] but also the emergence of interactive, highly specialized service industry clusters that, together with the major commercial nodes, really represent the basic elements of Vancouver's space economy. These service clusters, concentrated largely in the City of Vancouver and the inner suburban municipalities, include the downtown corporate complex; tourism, cultural and entertainment precincts in the central city; concentrations of design-oriented firms and institutions on the downtown fringe and in the inner city; a mid-town medical precinct, one of the largest in North America; the Port of Vancouver and Vancouver International Airport; and the University of British Columbia (UBC), Simon Fraser University (SFU) and several other colleges and educational institutions.

Industrial districts also occupy an important position in metropolitan Vancouver's space economy. They include the belt of resource processing industries along the Fraser River, some consumer product manufacturing and relatively small but dynamic technology-intensive production enclaves in the inner suburbs of Richmond and Burnaby. In confirming the importance of Vancouver's industrial sector, the city council recently adopted (in 1995) an industrial lands strategy whose object is to secure "a place for industry" and to reaffirm the value of a plural urban society and job choice across a range of occupations.[36]

Recent immigrants have played an influential role in the continuing expansion of Vancouver's service economy and its industrial revival. New citizens from the Asia-Pacific are especially prominent in the professions, producer services, small business, trade and finance. But many immigrants have also been involved in industrial development, not only the recent growth of the garment districts of Vancouver's inner city and east end, but also advanced technology industries such as telecommunications. When one considers the entrepreneurship exhibited by new immigrants from the Asia-Pacific countries, Latin America and elsewhere, and their connections with dynamic markets and societies in their former homelands, this recent wave of immigration has contributed significantly to Vancouver's development over the past 10 or 15 years.

Vancouver's recent transformation is also imprinted upon its built environment as more and more districts are redeveloped or reconstructed. Urban megaprojects, such as Concord Pacific's Pacific Place (which encompasses fully one-sixth of the downtown area) and the Marathon project on the central waterfront, are the most significant aspect of this reconstruction process, a pattern that is also observed in other Pacific Rim cities and city-regions. Another important element is the construction of a new cultural and entertainment district along Georgia and Robson streets, extending from the heart of the CBD to the stadium complex (BC Place and the new GM Place, home of the National Hockey League's Vancouver Canucks and the National Basketball Association's Grizzlies) and including a striking new municipal library as well as the Ford Centre for the Performing Arts.

These projects are the centrepieces of Vancouver's redevelopment, but other, more subtle aspects of reconstruction also demonstrate the linkages between socio-economic, cultural and physical transformation. One example is the appearance of new cultural landscapes, such as residential neighbourhoods and retail precincts that reflect the cultures of Vancouver's new citizens. These new cultural landscapes are now increasingly evident in the suburbs as well as in the long-established ethnic districts of the metropolitan core. A similar spatial trend has also been observed in the Greater Toronto Area (e.g., Peel and Markham) and, most notably, in certain suburbs of Los Angeles (e.g., Monterey Park and San Gabriel). At the same time, new immigrant groups such as the Vietnamese and Central Americans are changing the social mix and reshaping the landscape in Vancouver's traditional inner city neighbourhoods.

These internal facets of structural change – the economic, social, spatial and physical changes – and the complex interdependencies among them are the basic parameters of Vancouver's transformation. Changes that are in some respects dramatic and in others more subtle are fundamentally reshaping Vancouver's character, image and identity.

In order to gain insights into the generic and the more distinctive aspects of this transformation, it is important to also examine how Vancouver's external relationships have been and continue to be redefined. Vancouver's trajectory of growth and change is increasingly linked to external markets, societies and urban systems. The development paths of other cities in Canada and elsewhere also provide useful benchmarks against which to compare Vancouver's experience. To this end, the next chapter examines Vancouver's restructuring process in both national and regional contexts. This sets the stage for an exploration of Vancouver's emerging role in the Pacific Basin, which constitutes the most significant catalyst for change.

Notes

1. The term "newly industrializing" as applied to places like Singapore, Hong Kong and Taiwan is clearly anachronistic as these are all advanced industrial economies; the first two in particular are in fact highly tertiarized and can almost be described as post-industrial with respect to their stage of development.

2. Some of the older manufacturing cities (e.g., London, Liverpool, Pittsburgh, Detroit, New York and Montreal) have permanently lost hundreds of thousands of manufacturing jobs over the past two decades or so. In most of these cities, the job losses are usually attributable to outright firm closures rather than to relocations.

3. For analysis and discussion of the changing human capital requirements associated with economic and technological change, see T.S. Alexander, "Human Capital Investment: Building the 'Knowledge Economy,'" *Policy Options*, Vol. 18, no. 6 (1997), pp. 5-8.

4. "The Canadian City: Engine of Growth," *The Globe and Mail*, May 17, 1993.

5. P.W. Daniels, *Service Industries in the World Economy* (Oxford: Blackwell, 1993), p. 113.

6. Provincial governments may argue that local governments are well positioned to undertake housing programmes, in light of (1) the land reserves local authorities may hold, (2) the scope afforded by local authorities to encourage nonmarket housing, and (3) the favourable fiscal position of many local governments compared with higher levels of government.

7. J.W. Simmons and L.S. Bourne, *Urban Growth Trends in Canada, 1981-86: A New Geography of Change*, Major Report no. 25 (Toronto: Centre for Urban and Community Studies, University of Toronto, 1989).

8. I. J. Gottmann, *Megalopolis: The Urbanized Northeastern Seaboard of the United States* (New York: Twentieth Century, 1961).

9. McGee, notably, has acknowledged the value of Gottmann's concept of the "megalopolis" in interpreting the form and configuration of East and Southeast Asian metropolitan regions and mega-cities, while insisting that the appropriate cultural and other localized factors be acknowledged and incorporated. See T.G. McGee, *The Urbanization Process in the Third World: Explorations in Search of a Theory* (London: G. Bell, 1971). For a broader critique of the relevance and limitations of Western urbanization models in the Asian context, see G.C.-S. Lin, "Changing Theoretical Perspectives on Urbanisation in Asian Developing Countries," *Third World Planning Review*, Vol. 16, no. 1 (1994), pp. 1-23.

10. See, for example, I.J. Gottmann, "Urban Centrality and the Interweaving of Quaternary Activities," *Ekistics*, Vol. 29 (1970), pp. 322-31; and "The Dynamics of Large Cities," *Geographical Journal*, Vol. 140 (1974), pp. 254-61.

11. D. Bell, *The Coming of the Post-Industrial Society* (New York: Basic Books, 1974).

12. See, for example, J. Gershuny, *After Industrial Society?* (London: MacMillan, 1978).

13. D.F. Ley, "Gentrification in Recession: Social Change in Six Canadian Inner Cities," *Urban Geography*, Vol. 13, no. 3 (1992), pp. 230-56. Gentrification is a complex socio-spatial process, but it normally involves the introduction of more affluent socio-economic groups into the working-class neighbourhoods of inner city precincts, often displacing long-established residents as the property values are bid up.

14. D.F. Ley, *The New Middle Class and the Remaking of the Central City* (Oxford: Oxford University Press, 1996).

15. A.J. Scott, *Metropolis: From the Division of Labor to Urban Form* (Berkeley: University of California Press, 1988); see also, by the same author, *New Industrial Spaces* (London: Pion, 1988).

16. M. Castells, *The Informational City: Information Technology, Economic Restructuring, and the Urban-Regional Process* (Oxford: Basil Blackwell, 1989).

17. P.G. Hall, *Reinventing the City*, Research Paper no. 179 (Toronto: Centre for Urban and Community Studies, University of Toronto, 1990).

18. Hall, *Reinventing the City*, pp. 4-5.

19. For a comprehensive discussion of this issue, see Daniels, *Service Industries in the World Economy*.

20. See, for example, W.J. Coffey and A.S. Bailly, "Producer Services and Flexible Production: An Exploratory Analysis," *Growth and Change*, Vol. 22 (1991), pp. 95-117; J.N. Marshall, "Linkages between Manufacturing Industry and Business Services," *Environment and Planning A*, Vol. 17 (1985), pp. 1155-67; and S. Illeris and J.P. Philippe, "The Role of Services in Regional Economic Growth," in P. Daniels, S. Illeris, J. Bonamy and J. Philippe (eds.), *The Geography of Services* (London: Frank Cass, 1993), pp. 3-10.

21. D. Webster, "Effective Urban Management: New Challenges, New Responses," *Regional Development Dialogue*, Vol. 15, no. 2 (1994), pp. vii-xvi.

22. M. Douglass, "Bringing Culture In: Locality and Global Capitalism in East Asia," *Third World Planning Review*, Vol. 17, no. 3 (1995), pp. iii-ix.

23. Douglass, "Bringing Culture In."

24. R. Putnam (with R. Leonardi and R. Nanetti), *Making Democracy Work: Civic Traditions in Modern Italy* (Princeton: Princeton University Press, 1992).

25. "Pro Bono Publico," *The Economist*, February 6, 1993, p. 96.

26. T.A. Hutton and H.C. Davis, "Prospects for Vancouver's Sustainable Development: An Economic Perspective," in A.H.J. Dorcey (ed.), *Perspectives on Sustainable Development in Water Management: Towards Agreement in the Fraser River Basin* (Vancouver: Westwater, 1991).

27. Stojanovich defines a mobilized Diaspora as "an ethnoreligious collectivity whose elite members are communication specialists... diasporas engage in international commerce as insurance against the political risks of privilege in a single polity." T. Stojanovich, "Cities, Capital Accumulation and the Ottoman Balkan Command Economy, 1500-1800," in C. Tilly and W.P. Blockmans (eds.), *Cities and the Rise of States in Europe, A.D. 1000 to 1800* (Boulder/San Francisco/Oxford: Westview Press, 1994), p. 80. Stojanovich was writing specifically about the redistribution of Jewish populations after the mid-seventeenth century, which was characterized by information, transaction and production networks and developed into "the foremost mercantile network in the world" (p. 81). The concept of mobilized diasporas as particularly energetic, interactive and enterprising migrant groups is very relevant today, and the role played by overseas Chinese in Pacific Rim urban societies is an especially relevant manifestation of this concept.

28. J. Garreau, *Edge City: Life on the New Frontier* (New York: Doubleday, 1991).

29. Douglass, "Bringing Culture In."

30. The "experienced labour force...refers to persons who, during the week prior to June 4, 1991, were employed or unemployed but who had worked since January 1, 1990. The experienced labour force can be derived by deleting from the total labour force those unemployed persons 15 years of age and over who have never worked or who worked only prior to January 1, 1990." See *1991 Census Dictionary* (Ottawa: Statistics Canada, 1992).

31. T.A. Hutton, "City Profile: Vancouver," *Cities*, Vol. 11, no. 4 (1994), pp. 219-39.

32. For example, much of the growth in the manufacturing sectors in many cities has been in service functions such as managerial and clerical occupations.

33. The two tiers consist of (1) a privileged group of well-educated, numerate and literate professionals and managers who are comfortable with new technologies and business systems and (2) a distinctly marginalized group that includes workers displaced by the contraction of traditional industry, capital substitution, and corporate restructuring or downsizing. See T.J. Noyelle, *New Technologies and Services* (College Park: The University of Maryland Institute for Urban Studies, 1985).

34. R. Ajello, "Bridging Culture's Divide: Can BC's Two Biggest Business Groups Build a Profitable Marriage?", *The Georgia Straight*, August 11-18, 1995, pp. 11-14.

35. These eight regional town centres (RTCs) are the preferred locations for high order commercial activities in metropolitan Vancouver as set out in the regional plan. They will be described in more detail in chapter 4.

36. Minutes of a meeting of the Vancouver City Council, March 14, 1995; *Industrial Lands Strategy* (File no. 5317).

2

Vancouver's Restructuring Trajectory within National and Regional Contexts

Vancouver is an integral part of the Canadian polity and an important node in the national urban network. The city's development is thus influenced by the same forces that are shaping urban structure, social morphology and economic growth and change throughout Canada. These forces include common social values and political traditions, federal programmes, a legacy of urban planning that emphasizes regulation and land use policies but also incorporates significant elements of social planning, and finally a rich urban-hinterland relationship with Canada's vast staple (resource-based) economy.[1]

Historically, economic development in Canada has been resource-based and this has had a profound impact on the nature of urban development. Much of the growth of urban core regions has been determined by the demand for transportation, processing and administration generated by the natural-resource sector. The resource sector has therefore been instrumental in the formation of urban communities in centres like Montreal, Toronto and Vancouver. In these core settlements, cohorts of resource industry managers, production workers and capital holders have constituted important components of urban society.[2] This influence is certainly weakening with the diminishing importance of the primary sector in the Canadian economy as a whole and the corresponding growth of urban manufacturing and service industries with more tenuous connections to the resource economy. Nevertheless, the urban-hinterland connection can still be discerned in major Canadian cities.

Federal government policies and programmes, particularly in the areas of transportation and communications systems, have also shaped urban growth and change in Canada and have imparted a measure of commonality to urban development patterns. Federally supported social programmes, such as unemployment insurance, have helped to maintain an acceptable level of social welfare in Canadian cities, while a number of other national policies have promoted a greater degree of regional equity. Housing programmes initiated over the past several decades by the Canada Mortgage and Housing Corporation (CMHC),[3] as well as other federal infrastructure investments and urban renewal grants have also contributed to similar patterns of urban development across the nation in the post-war period. More recently, however, there has been a pronounced and perhaps irreversible federal retreat from some of these policy areas. Motivated by the need to eliminate the deficit and reduce accumulated debt, and by growing pressure to rebalance inter-governmental powers and responsibilities in the context of ongoing constitutional debates, this retrenchment could accentuate existing patterns of differentiation and divergence and exacerbate disparities among Canadian cities.[4]

In addition to these important domestic trends, a new set of external forces is having a profound impact on the development trajectory of Canadian cities. These pervasive, macro-level dynamics, which include ongoing market integration, economic globalization and the new division of labour within international production systems, have clearly influenced economic restructuring in Canada.[5] The impact of these macro-level forces is, however, mediated and mitigated by national and local factors. Thus, the actual outcomes of restructuring can differ significantly from place to place, particularly in terms of the industry mix and levels of job creation.

As a consequence of these domestic and external influences, Vancouver's development in many ways follows the pattern of urban transformation typical of the Canadian metropolitan network. The common elements observed include: (1) the rapid growth of service industries, employment, output and trade; (2) the relative or absolute decline of heavy or traditional industries; (3) the emergence of a new, more pluralistic social structure dominated by elite service classes but also including a growing underclass; and (4) a reconfigured metropolitan structure.[6]

In other important respects, however, Vancouver's development is demonstrably different and even unique. Its restructuring experience is closely associated with the city's increasingly intimate and complex interface with the societies, cultures and economies of the Pacific Basin – a theme we will explore more fully in later chapters. Examining Vancouver's development path within both national and regional contexts reveals important aspects of Vancouver's distinctive pattern of growth and change.

The key elements of *differentiation* and *divergence* in Vancouver's development include:

- distinctive growth determinants, in particular, a close interdependence between culture, environment and economic development;
- patterns of cyclical and structural change that diverge sharply from those observed in Canada's other large metropolitan areas, reflecting the roller-coaster tendencies of Canadian urban development and restructuring over the past two decades;
- sustained growth in the last decade (after a serious recession in the early 1980s, when unemployment reached 15 percent), which stands in sharp contrast with the fluctuating fortunes of other Canadian cities (e.g., Montreal's steady decline, the resurgence of growth in Calgary in the 1990s and the particularly severe and widespread recession in Toronto during the first half of this decade);
- growth in service industry employment that has been markedly higher than that in Toronto or Montreal in recent years, as well as some growth in manufacturing, compared with the sharp decline in manufacturing employment in both the Montreal and Toronto CMAs;
- shifts in Vancouver's regional context, which is no longer defined primarily by its linkage with the province's resource-based hinterland but increasingly by its position within broader and rapidly evolving urban growth corridors, economic development zones and bioregions (e.g., the Cascadia transborder region).

It can be argued that even the *pace* of urban transformation in Vancouver differs from that experienced in other Canadian cities. A number of factors have accelerated the process of change in the Vancouver case.

- *The openness of Vancouver's economy* – Vancouver is, in many ways, more dependent on international trade, investment and tourism than other large Canadian cities. This dependence, reflected, for example, in the international trade and traffic activities of the Port of Vancouver and Vancouver International Airport (described in chapter 3), makes Vancouver more susceptible to shifts in external demand, commodity-price fluctuations and other rapidly diffused forces of change resulting from increased market integration.
- *High levels of foreign and domestic immigration* – Greater Vancouver has been a net beneficiary of migration flows from all sources since 1978.[7] While both

international and interprovincial migration flows into Greater Vancouver have increased dramatically over the past decade, net international migration has exceeded net interprovincial migration every year since 1981 (Table 2.1). In most recent years, net international immigration has exceeded net interprovincial immigration by a ratio of about 2:1. The size, origin and characteristics of these flows of foreign immigrants have effectively transformed Vancouver's economy, social structure and built environment.

- *New capital formation* – Over the last decade, Vancouver has attracted large flows of capital investment, from domestic and foreign as well as private and public sector sources. Much of this new capital has been directed to infrastructure projects designed to support Vancouver's growth industries and institutions (e.g., new office space, hotels, convention facilities, Vancouver International Airport, a major cruise ship terminal, telecommunications systems, professional sports stadiums, theatres, a civic library and a rapid transit system).

Public sector policies and programmes at all three levels of government have also contributed to Vancouver's transformation over the past decade. In addition to public investments in Vancouver's economic infrastructure, there have been federal initiatives in support of enhanced financial services functions (e.g., legislation establishing international banking centres in Vancouver and Montreal) and official recognition of the city's Pacific role with the establishment of the federal Asia-Pacific Foundation in downtown Vancouver. Notable provincial initiatives include Expo 1986 to commemorate Vancouver's centennial, programmes to stimulate the export of services to Pacific Rim markets and special grants to support academic research and exchange programmes with Asia-Pacific partners. Over the years, the City of Vancouver has also undertaken a number of initiatives both to facilitate economic restructuring and to help realize the city's potential as a Pacific Rim metropolis – although this commitment has weakened discernibly in recent years.

Vancouver's Transformation in the National Context

Canada's economy has undergone a significant structural transformation over the past several decades. This restructuring is characterized by the rapid growth of service industries and the relative decline of manufacturing and resource-based industries. In the period 1961-1991, the service sector's share of national economic output increased from 60.4 percent to 66.4 percent of GDP. Its share of employment has increased from 57.8 percent to 72.7 percent.[8]

table 2.1

Migration in the Greater Vancouver Regional District, 1976-1995

Year	International			Interprovincial			Intraprovincial			Total net migration
	In	Out	Net	In	Out	Net	In	Out	Net	
1976-77	9,523	3,605	5,918	22,677	19,454	3,223	23,373	33,804	-10,431	-1,290
1977-78	7,554	3,263	4,291	24,392	17,177	7,215	22,757	29,448	-6,691	4,815
1978-79	6,836	2,800	4,036	25,556	16,565	8,991	23,448	26,051	-2,603	10,424
1979-80	9,247	2,272	6,975	30,738	12,464	18,274	25,815	28,372	-2,557	22,692
1980-81	13,409	2,086	11,323	27,200	14,533	12,667	22,910	37,033	-14,123	9,867
1981-82	14,954	3,581	11,373	20,033	16,302	3,731	20,350	27,565	-7,215	7,889
1982-83	10,975	4,039	6,936	16,463	14,512	1,951	20,980	23,915	-2,935	5,952
1983-84	9,789	3,786	6,003	17,900	12,409	5,491	22,756	20,882	1,874	13,368
1984-85	8,168	4,204	3,964	16,338	14,353	1,985	23,006	20,753	2,253	8,202
1985-86	8,572	3,384	5,188	17,396	15,824	1,572	26,057	21,808	4,249	11,009
1986-87	11,117	4,307	6,810	22,165	17,026	5,139	30,200	28,252	1,948	13,897
1987-88	15,304	3,453	11,851	25,695	16,594	9,101	32,608	33,674	-1,066	19,886
1988-89	19,715	3,589	16,126	29,383	15,914	13,469	34,313	40,564	-6,251	23,344
1989-90	21,309	3,719	17,590	31,854	16,211	15,643	34,363	51,872	-17,509	15,724
1990-91	25,155	3,847	21,308	27,802	14,266	13,536	30,709	43,820	-13,111	21,733
1991-92	28,569	4,557	24,012	32,421	14,346	18,075	33,946	50,691	-16,745	25,342
1992-93	34,141	4,607	29,534	31,921	13,975	17,946	21,308	40,290	-18,982	28,498
1993-94	41,981	4,818	37,163	33,869	14,911	18,958	20,620	38,284	-17,664	38,457
1994-95	38,354	4,903	33,451	30,719	16,454	14,265	20,000	33,847	-13,847	33,869

Source: Data provided by BC Stats, Ministry of Finance and Corporate Relations, Government of British Columbia, 1997.

Although these figures reflect a national trend, the most crucial arenas for economic restructuring in Canada (as in other OECD countries) are cities, particularly the larger metropolitan areas. The concentration of service sector growth in city-regions is a reflection of the significance of agglomeration and urban economies, among other factors. It is also in the major conurbations that the effects of industrial decline have been most strongly felt. The restructuring process has been pervasive. All major Canadian cities have experienced significant growth in service industries and employment since 1980, while most have also experienced significant losses of manufacturing employment in relative and, in some cases, absolute terms. Within manufacturing industries, blue-collar jobs have declined more rapidly than service occupations, reflecting the continuing division of labour that characterizes modern production systems. The substitution of capital for labour has resulted in the rapid shedding of production workers, while some service occupations, notably in the professional, managerial and knowledge-based categories, remain relatively buoyant. As the recession of the early 1990s demonstrated, however, white-collar employees are by no means immune from corporate downsizing.[9]

Our examination of Vancouver's restructuring in the national context focuses first on the changes observed over two census periods: 1971-1981 and 1981-1991. This allows us to identify and compare broad patterns of transformation among Canada's largest metropolitan areas. A discussion of more recent trends then follows, highlighting the serious effects of the economic recession of the early 1990s and its complex mix of structural and cyclical factors.

Economic Restructuring in Vancouver and other CMAs, 1971-1991

An analysis of employment data (by industry and occupation) for Vancouver and other Canadian CMAs for the 1971-1991 period, supplemented by other empirical studies, reveals some common basic trends in the restructuring experience of Canada's city-regions:

- overall employment expansion between 1971 and 1991, but stronger levels of growth in 1971-1981 than in 1981-1991, due to the recession of the early 1980s and demographic trends;
- a major shift of production and employment toward the service sector in virtually all Canadian metropolitan centres, affecting most of the major service industry groups (business, consumer and public services) as well as the major tertiary occupational categories;
- particularly strong growth of producer or business services in many cities;
- a dramatic expansion of employment in certain higher-level occupational categories (managers, professionals, etc.), which corresponds to

the emergence of the information economy and key knowledge industries;

- the *relative* decline of traditional manufacturing as a result of employment loss and firm closures – some of the largest cities have even experienced net reductions in the level of manufacturing employment in the 1990s;
- the emergence of a new urban social morphology in Canadian cities that is dominated by the service classes, specifically the professional and managerial elites of the information economy.

In 1991, services accounted for between 75 and 85 percent of the total metropolitan labour force in Canada's largest cities, compared to just over 70 percent in Canada as a whole (Table 2.2). Among Canada's three largest metropolitan centres, Vancouver has the highest proportion of its labour force in the service sector – 78.1 percent. While this reflects the advanced stage of tertiarization of Vancouver's economy and employment base, it also points indirectly to the relatively larger manufacturing sectors in Toronto and Montreal. Ottawa also has a very high proportion of its labour force in services, reflecting the preponderance of government and public sector activity in the national capital and recent growth in the business services and knowledge industries.[10]

table 2.2

Employment in Services as a Percentage of the Total Experienced Labour Force in Canada's Largest CMAs, 1971, 1981 and 1991

	1971	1981	1991
CMA		(%)	
Toronto	60.1	69.1	74.3
Montreal	59.2	70.2	74.0
Vancouver	65.8	75.5	78.1
Ottawa	77.4	86.7	86.0
Edmonton	68.6	73.8	78.6
Calgary	65.9	68.7	75.3
Canada	57.2	66.7	71.9

Source: Statistics Canada, Census of Canada, 1971, 1981 and 1991.

The service sector grew at a slower pace between 1981 and 1991 than in the previous decade (Table 2.2). This can be attributed to slower national economic growth and, very likely, to the maturing of Canada's service sector. Other factors such as job losses in the public sector,[11] slackening demand for consumer services (due to demographic factors such as lower birth rates and slower growth in personal and family incomes) and the increasing substitution of

table 2.3

Employment in Business Services as a Percentage of the Total Experienced Labour Force in Canada's Largest CMAs, 1971, 1981 and 1991

	1971	1981	1991
CMA		(%)	
Toronto	4.2	6.7	9.5
Montreal	3.4	5.0	7.3
Vancouver	4.0	6.2	7.9
Ottawa	3.1	5.8	8.9
Edmonton	2.8	5.4	5.8
Calgary	4.6	8.5	9.3
Canada	2.4	4.0	5.6

Source: Statistics Canada, Census of Canada, 1971, 1981 and 1991.

capital for labour in certain service industries may also explain the slower rate of growth in services in the 1980s and 1990s.

In Canada and other OECD countries, business services have grown faster than the tertiary sector as a whole and faster than any other major industrial group, thus steadily increasing their share of total labour force over the past quarter century. The expansion of this service subsector can be attributed in part to the externalization of demand for specialized services, new divisions of labour in advanced production systems and growth in the volume of trade.

Table 2.3 shows employment growth in business services for Canada's six largest cities and the economy as a whole between 1971 and 1991. At the national level, the business service sector more than doubled its share of the total labour force over the 20-year period, from 2.4 percent to 5.6 percent. In all of the CMAs, business services' share of the total labour force exceeded the national average, confirming the strong correlation in advanced economies between intermediate service growth and metropolitan centres. As might be expected, Toronto has the highest proportion of business services jobs; almost one in ten workers (9.5 percent) was employed in business services in 1991. This reflects Toronto's primacy in the national economy, particularly in specialized producer services. However, Calgary was not far behind (9.3 percent), which is consistent with that city's important role as a location for national headquarters and as provider of specialized business services to the petrochemical industry. In both Calgary and Edmonton, however, business services growth slowed appreciably in 1981-1991 compared with the previous census period.

In the case of Vancouver, business services' share of total employment increased from four percent in 1971 to 6.4 percent in 1981 and 7.9 percent in

1991. While these figures are well above the national average, they remain significantly lower than those for the leading cities of Toronto, Calgary and Ottawa. For Vancouver, business services are clearly important. Growth in this sector reflects the city's post-war development as a command and control centre for a vast resource-based hinterland and the more recently developed corporate complex of head offices, financial and business services. What differentiates Vancouver from other Canadian cities is that its economy is not dominated by one specific service industry; rather it is characterized by an ensemble of specialized service activities.[12]

As Coffey reminds us, a comparison of growth rates during the two census periods between 1971 and 1991 provides a better understanding of economic development in Canadian cities. For instance, the fact that during the 1980s, "information and leisure-based activities replaced resource-oriented sectors as engines of growth" in Canada's city-regions, was to the advantage of Ottawa-Hull, Vancouver and Toronto and to the disadvantage of Edmonton and Calgary, two cities that had performed so strongly during the 1970s.[13]

The performance of Canada's largest cities over the two decades is reported in Table 2.4. It shows the urban areas experiencing the highest growth in employment as well as more detailed data for the key manufacturing and business services categories. Employment in Vancouver grew at a faster rate than that in Toronto and in Montreal during both census periods, but lagged well behind Calgary and Edmonton in 1971-1981. In the following decade, Vancouver performed better than Calgary and Edmonton, and was close behind Ottawa-Hull, the growth leader for that period.

In 1981-1991 more jobs were created in Vancouver than in Montreal, Canada's second-ranking metropolis (170,400 new jobs in Vancouver compared to 157,900 in Montreal). Vancouver's employment growth in business services was also strong in both periods, and the city experienced only a small decline in manufacturing during the 1980s, especially in comparison with the large contractions suffered in Montreal and Toronto.

Location quotients, which indicate the relative level of concentration of particular industries in different cities,[14] also illustrate some of the contrasts between Vancouver's economic structure and that of other large metropolitan areas. Table 2.5 shows location quotients by sector and by industry for Canada's six largest CMAs in 1991. Although, as we have seen, Vancouver's manufacturing sector was left relatively unscathed over the 1980s compared to other large Canadian cities, manufacturing is still far more important in Toronto and Montreal than in Vancouver. Vancouver's location quotient for manufacturing employment in 1991 is 0.50, compared to 0.79 for Toronto and 0.84 for

table 2.4

Canadian Urban Areas Experiencing the Highest (Absolute) Employment Growth, by Sector, 1971-1981 and 1981-1991

	Total employment		**Manufacturing**		**Business services**	
	Net Change (000s)	**Rate (%)**	**Net Change (000s)**	**Rate (%)**	**Net Change (000s)**	**Rate (%)**
Urban area	**EMPLOYMENT GROWTH 1971 - 1981**					
Toronto	499.3	44.8	85.2	28.4	42.2	121.2
Montreal	336.3	36.7	44.2	17.4	19.5	77.1
Vancouver	210.4	51.9	17.1	23.7	16.9	124.9
Calgary	188.3	125.8	15.9	93.8	17.4	302.8
Edmonton	177.2	88.9	17.2	70.3	11.4	266.7
Ottawa-Hull	116.1	48.1	4.9	24.0	9.8	185.1
Quebec	83.4	52.5	4.0	18.8	3.2	101.1
Winnipeg	67.2	30.7	5.9	13.9	3.4	83.5
Hamilton	64.3	34.2	12.3	17.7	3.1	101.2
Kitchener	41.5	42.0	10.9	26.7	1.9	167.2
London	41.0	35.5	6.9	25.3	1.9	86.1
Victoria	37.4	52.4	1.1	16.0	2.1	169.5
Halifax	36.6	39.5	1.5	17.3	2.0	113.1
St. Catherines	33.4	29.0	5.1	12.6	1.7	85.8
Saskatoon	33.2	66.9	2.4	46.5	1.9	199.5
	EMPLOYMENT GROWTH 1981 - 1991					
Toronto	333.8	20.7	-46.7	-12.1	64.5	23.8
Vancouver	170.4	27.0	-1.5	-1.6	19.4	63.7
Montreal	157.9	12.6	-42.7	-14.3	32.2	71.8
Ottawa-Hull	116.6	32.6	3.2	12.7	17.4	115.5
Quebec	61.3	25.3	2.0	7.7	6.3	97.7
Calgary	56.9	16.8	-0.2	-0.5	6.6	28.7
Edmonton	45.1	12.0	-4.5	-10.8	2.9	18.7
Kitchener	36.4	25.9	-5.7	-11.1	3.8	122.7
Oshawa	31.3	36.7	-1.2	-3.9	2.9	174.7
Hamilton	31.0	12.3	-19.3	-23.6	5.1	84.4
London	30.8	19.6	-4.4	-13.0	3.0	74.5
Halifax	29.5	22.8	0.9	8.5	2.7	71.0
Winnipeg	27.7	9.7	-7.0	-14.4	2.8	37.4
Victoria	26.0	23.9	-0.8	-10.8	3.3	97.6
Saskatoon	17.7	21.4	0.4	4.9	1.1	38.4

Source: Adapted from W.J. Coffey, *Employment Growth and Change in the Canadian Urban System* (Ottawa: CPRN, 1996), Table 2-6, p. 22.

Montreal. Wood products is the only manufacturing industry in which Vancouver's location quotient exceeds all the others.

As might be expected, the levels of concentration in the service sector are more comparable, although there are some important contrasts in specific service industry groups. For instance, Vancouver's location quotient for employment in finance (1.34) is almost equal to Montreal's (1.41), but much lower than

table 2.5

Sectorial Location Quotients for Canada's Six Largest Metropolitan Areas, 1991

Industry	Cal	Edm	Mon	Ott	Tor	Van
Extractive	**1.55**	**0.81**	**0.14**	**0.22**	**0.17**	**0.44**
Agriculture	0.35	0.62	0.17	0.29	0.20	0.39
Fishing & trapping	0.03	0.06	0.03	0.03	0.03	1.06
Logging & forestry	0.14	0.32	0.10	0.22	0.11	0.68
Mining, quarrying & oil wells	5.99	1.79	0.10	0.22	0.11	0.68
Construction	**1.19**	**1.29**	**0.92**	**0.95**	**1.06**	**1.22**
Manufacturing	**0.37**	**0.39**	**0.84**	**0.27**	**0.79**	**0.50**
Food, beverage & tobacco	0.66	0.71	1.16	0.23	0.93	0.92
Rubber & plastics products	0.44	0.58	1.17	0.11	1.75	0.85
Leather & textiles	0.18	0.27	2.18	0.15	0.95	0.49
Clothing	0.34	0.39	3.90	0.21	1.04	0.79
Wood products	0.38	0.44	0.41	0.18	0.36	1.57
Furniture & fixtures	1.22	0.52	1.42	0.30	1.88	0.95
Paper & allied products	0.20	0.18	0.73	0.78	0.76	0.63
Printing & publishing	1.04	0.87	1.54	1.07	1.89	1.20
Primary metals	0.52	0.57	0.73	0.10	0.66	0.35
Fabricated metal products	0.86	1.13	1.25	0.36	1.55	1.15
Machinery	1.03	1.12	1.14	0.15	1.29	0.89
Transportation equipment	0.19	0.22	1.07	0.13	1.36	0.36
Electrical & electronic products	0.21	0.08	0.42	0.41	0.51	0.20
Non-metallic mineral products	0.88	0.91	1.12	0.47	1.11	0.76
Petroleum & coal	2.27	1.99	1.00	0.22	0.92	1.35
Chemicals	0.59	1.62	1.95	0.45	1.86	0.58
Other manufacturing	0.08	0.07	0.15	0.06	0.19	0.09
Services	**1.15**	**1.20**	**1.14**	**1.32**	**1.14**	**1.20**
Transportation	1.13	1.20	1.27	0.72	0.95	1.45
Storage & warehousing	0.55	0.29	0.29	0.13	0.43	0.65
Communication	1.20	1.41	1.43	1.82	1.32	1.37
Other utilities	1.02	1.22	1.03	0.60	1.13	0.84
Wholesale trade	1.31	1.97	1.39	0.68	1.32	1.53
Retail trade	1.04	1.10	1.10	0.98	1.07	1.10
Finance	1.20	0.86	1.41	0.96	1.88	1.34
Insurance	0.83	1.01	1.37	0.85	1.77	1.16
Real estate & insurance	1.69	1.42	1.08	1.00	1.59	1.87
Business services	1.81	1.12	1.42	1.75	1.85	1.55
Gov. – federal	0.68	0.86	0.59	7.17	0.45	0.73
Gov. – provincial & territorial	0.61	2.05	0.68	0.65	0.86	0.58
Gov. – local & other	0.99	1.07	1.11	1.12	1.10	0.83
Education	1.03	1.21	1.04	1.20	0.99	1.01
Health & social services	1.02	1.21	1.16	1.06	0.89	1.06
Accommodation, food & beverage	1.15	1.18	0.99	0.98	0.91	1.30
Amusement & recreation	1.28	1.18	1.35	0.92	1.32	1.50
Personal & household	1.20	1.08	1.05	0.99	1.06	1.28
Other services	1.84	1.84	1.14	1.14	1.32	1.49

Source: Author's calculations based on Statistics Canada, *Profile of Census Metropolitan Areas and Census Agglomerations - Part A* (Ottawa: Minister of Industry, Science and Technology, October 1992).

Toronto's (1.88). On the other hand, in the accommodation, food and beverage and the amusement and recreation categories, Vancouver has higher location quotients than the other CMAs in the sample, underscoring its status as a tourist destination and convention centre. Vancouver also has the highest location quotient in transportation; storage and warehousing; and wholesale trade. These activities reflect the importance of the city's role as *entrepôt*, gateway city and distribution centre.

While differences in economic structure and industry growth rates reveal important contrasts between Vancouver and other large Canadian cities, the cycles of growth (and recession) also point to divergent patterns of urban and regional development. Table 2.6 shows changes in employment during two four-year periods (1981-1985 and 1989-1993). During each of these periods, all five major regions in Canada were affected by unusually deep and protracted recessions. Yet an examination of the data reveals striking contrasts between the experience of British Columbia and that of the other four regions.

In the period 1981-1985, British Columbia's employment contracted by almost four percent, while Ontario's grew by nearly five percent and the remaining three regions registered modest increases. These figures reflect the effects of the recession, but also a partial recovery in Canada outside BC.[15] Triggered by massive commodity-price shocks, the effects of the recession in BC were initially felt in the hinterland, but in due course were transmitted to the production and service sectors concentrated in the metropolitan areas of southwestern BC, principally in Vancouver.[16] Vancouver's economy remained in recession until the investment boom prior to Expo 86.

The figures for the second period tell quite a different story. Ontario, the best performer during 1981-1985, suffered the largest contraction in employment in the four years between 1989 and 1993. During this period, southern Ontario's automotive production sector underwent severe restructuring, which led to sharply reduced industrial output, employment contractions (in some service industries as well as in manufacturing) and a severely depressed real estate market, especially in the Greater Toronto Area (GTA) and nearby communities.

While Southern Ontario suffered a particularly severe economic contraction in 1989-1993, British Columbia continued to enjoy a sustained growth cycle that started in the mid-1980s. Its overall employment growth reached almost nine percent over the four-year period. However, British Columbia's economic growth also had a strong regional dimension, in that it was mostly concentrated in Vancouver CMA. Further aspects of Vancouver's particular growth trajectory relative to the national context are revealed by comparing employment trends in Canada's largest cities over the most recent period.

table 2.6
Changes in Employment by Region, 1981-1985 and 1989-1993

Region	1981-85 (%)	1989-93 (%)
Atlantic	1.4	-2.7
Quebec	1.7	-2.3
Ontario	4.9	-3.2
Prairies	0.4	1.1
British Columbia	-3.9	8.8

Source: Human Resources Canada and Regional Economic Services Branch, BC-Yukon, *Economic Review*, March 1995.

Vancouver in the National Context in the 1990s: Divergence and Disengagement

The 1970s and 1980s saw a reordering of the Canadian urban hierarchy as a result of highly differentiated economic restructuring trends, and also because the fortunes of individual cities during each of these two decades varied considerably. During the 1990s, Canada's urban transformation and development patterns continued to diverge. Some of the major winners in the 1980s, notably Toronto and to a lesser extent Ottawa, suffered reversals in their fortunes, while Calgary, which had stagnated in the 1980s after its rapid expansion a decade earlier, consolidated its position as a centre of national significance with regard to the location of head offices, senior management and associated business services.

The first half of the 1990s has thus been a continuation of the roller-coaster trend of the previous two decades. In this context, Vancouver's sustained growth performance represents one of the few exceptions (Montreal's protracted decline, now in its third decade, is another). Vancouver is the only major Canadian city to have achieved sustained growth since the mid-1980s, a decade marked by the severe recession of the early 1990s and ongoing economic restructuring. Both these factors have resulted in further major contractions in manufacturing and job losses among lower-skilled occupations (in manufacturing and services) in many Canadian cities.

Although important trends can be discerned in a broader cross-section of Canadian cities, the sharply divergent fortunes of Vancouver and Toronto present the most striking contrasts over the first half of the 1990s.[17] As is well-known, Toronto's economy was hit most severely by the recent recession, and its recovery was protracted and difficult. What is most noteworthy about the Toronto case is the stark contrast between the tremendous boom of the 1980s, during which time the city established its primacy, and the extent of the economic downturn it experienced during the 1990s. Toronto's record during this period has been described as "Canada's economic version of a Roman candle firework – a spectacular 25 percent increase in employment during the 1980s, followed by a fizzling 11 percent slide in the 1990s."[18]

Toronto's deep recession of the early 1990s was caused by both structural and cyclical factors. To some extent, the downturn in Toronto, especially the problems affecting the financial and real estate sectors, can be viewed as a correction following the boom of the 1980s, the "bursting of the bubble" observed in other major financial centres such as London, Tokyo, New York and Los Angeles. But at the same time, the city also experienced a major contraction in the manufacturing sector, as a result of restructuring and outright plant closures. Obsolescence, high operating costs (including taxes)[19] and the North American Free Trade Agreement (NAFTA) are also viewed as contributing factors.[20]

Table 2.7, which shows employment change (by industry) for Toronto, Montreal and Vancouver between 1989 and 1994, illustrates the quite diverse economic performances of Canada's three largest cities over this period. In particular, Vancouver's relative economic buoyancy stands out with employment expanding by 11.7 percent (94,000 new jobs), while employment in Toronto declined by 5.6 percent (122,000 jobs lost) and in Montreal by 2.2 percent (34,000 jobs lost).

More detailed data by industry reveal a substantial loss of manufacturing jobs in Toronto (106,000 jobs) and in Montreal (67,000 jobs), while in Vancouver employment in manufacturing actually expanded by 8.8 percent (approximately 8,000 new jobs). The figures for Toronto reflect the impact of the last recession, while the contraction in Montreal represents a continuation of a long process of industrial decline. However, the large differences in scale among the production sectors in the three cities must be borne in mind: in 1994, the ratio of manufacturing jobs among Toronto, Montreal and Vancouver was about 3.5 : 3 : 1, respectively.

The construction sector data also show important contrasts. From 1989 to 1994, Toronto and Montreal each lost more than one-quarter of their construction employment base (37,000 and 22,000 jobs lost, respectively). At the same time, Vancouver CMA gained 22,000 construction jobs, an increase of almost 40 percent, due to a prolonged construction boom in the metropolitan area which dates back to Expo 86 and continues to this day, largely as a result of rapid population growth and economic expansion in the 1990s. Every year for the past three years, total building permits (for all classes) in metropolitan Vancouver have approached or exceeded $3 billion, about double the levels

table 2.7

Employment Change in Toronto, Montreal and Vancouver CMAs, by Sector, 1989-1994

	1989	1990	1991	1992	1993	1994	1989-1994	1989-1994
	(000s)						(net)	(%)
TORONTO								
All industries	2,165	2,148	2,036	2,021	2,053	2,043	-122	-5.6
Other primary/agriculture	19	14	15	16	15	14	-5	-26.3
Manufacturing	453	429	393	369	366	347	-106	-23.4
Construction	143	134	122	102	101	106	-37	-25.9
Transportation, communications & utilities	169	162	144	152	144	157	-12	-7.1
Trade	351	377	342	345	351	372	21	6
Finance, insurance & real estate	190	205	203	200	201	183	-7	-3.7
Services	737	720	720	734	769	769	32	4.3
Public administration	103	107	96	103	106	96	-7	-6.8
MONTREAL								
All industries	1,557	1,549	1,510	1,493	1,488	1,523	-34	-2.2
Other primary/agriculture	10	11	12	6	8	11	1	10
Manufacturing	357	320	285	281	283	290	-67	-18.8
Construction	82	82	65	70	64	60	-22	-26.9
Transportation, communications & utilities	138	141	125	128	127	123	-15	-10.9
Trade	289	280	278	272	247	271	-18	-6.2
Finance, insurance & real estate	102	98	114	100	106	98	-4	-3.9
Services	504	530	543	551	555	597	93	18.5
Public administration	76	87	88	84	97	74	-2	-2.6
VANCOUVER								
All industries	806	825	840	861	866	900	94	11.7
Other primary/agriculture	15	16	21	14	15	15	0	0
Manufacturing	90	94	96	92	92	98	8	8.8
Construction	56	63	59	60	54	78	22	39.2
Transportation, communications & utilities	71	79	82	82	78	69	-2	-2.8
Trade	167	162	157	177	172	151	-16	-9.6
Finance, insurance & real estate	65	60	58	71	66	74	9	13.8
Services	301	314	328	325	342	368	67	22.3
Public administration	41	37	38	39	47	46	5	12.2

Source: Statistics Canada, *Labour Force Annual Averages 1989-1994* (Ottawa: Minister of Industry, Science and Technology, April 1995).

recorded in the mid-1980s.[21] By 1994, Vancouver's construction sector was appreciably larger than Montreal's, despite the fact that Vancouver CMA's labour force is only about three-fifths the size of Montreal's.

A comparison of trends among the service subsectors indicates important differences and interesting trends. All three cities experienced employment growth in services over the period 1989-1994 (Table 2.7). This demonstrates the relative stability of tertiary employment over the various phases of the business cycle. The growth of service employment over the five-year period was far greater in Vancouver than in Toronto (22.3 percent and 4.3 percent, respectively) but, perhaps more surprisingly, it was not much higher than in Montreal (18.5 percent).[22]

In the key finance, insurance and real estate category, however, employment declined by almost equal proportions in both Montreal and Toronto (3.9 percent and 3.7 percent, respectively), while metropolitan Vancouver experienced significant growth of 13.8 percent (about 9,000 new jobs) over the 1989-1994 period. Again, contrasts in scale should be acknowledged. In 1994, Toronto still had a larger employment base in this category than Montreal and Vancouver combined, underscoring the magnitude of Toronto's leadership in this sector, even after several years of recession. But Vancouver's gains, attributable in part to the city's role in the dynamic Asia-Pacific region, tend to support Simmons' view that Vancouver is "slowly overtaking" Montreal as Canada's second financial centre.[23]

A final set of comparative employment trends is reported in Table 2.8, which shows employment change by occupation in Toronto, Montreal and Vancouver. Despite otherwise divergent experiences, all three CMAs recorded gains in the managerial, administrative and other professional category, indicating the relative dynamism of these occupations at the top of the employment hierarchy. Not all service occupations fared well, however. For instance, in Toronto CMA, 97,000 clerical jobs were lost between 1989 and 1994, a contraction of over 22 percent (Table 2.8). Although this steep contraction of clerical positions may be consistent with a severe recession, it is also a consequence of structural change, notably the substitution of capital and technology for labour in the more routine tertiary occupations. A study conducted by the development office of Metro Toronto revealed that the ratio of secretaries to managers in the city, which was about 90 : 100 in the late 1970s, had dropped to 45 : 100 by 1994.[24]

Market orientation is another factor determining the particular development trajectories of individual Canadian cities, and here again Vancouver's experience sets it apart from other urban centres. In the case of central Canada, there is a substantial volume of trade between Ontario and Quebec and between these two provinces and the American industrial heartland. This long-standing pattern has been reinforced by the US-Canada Auto Pact (and other bilateral arrangements) and, in more recent years, by the Canada-US Free Trade Agreement (FTA) and its successor the NAFTA. On the other hand, British Columbia's (and implicitly Vancouver's) trade is increasingly oriented toward

table 2.8

Employment Change in Toronto, Montreal and Vancouver CMAs, by Major Occupational Category, 1989-1994

	1989	1990	1991	1992	1993	1994	1989-1994	1989-1994
	(000s)						(net)	(%)
TORONTO								
All occupations	2,165	2,148	2,036	2,021	2,053	2,043	-122	-5.6
Managerial, administrative & other professional	735	734	748	744	756	767	32	4.4
Clerical	434	433	391	375	371	337	-97	-22.4
Sales	209	228	191	206	215	232	23	11
Services	227	225	222	241	251	230	3	1.3
Primary occupations	21	16	17	15	21	16	-5	-31.3
Processing, machining, fabricating	276	262	245	226	223	223	-53	-19.2
Construction trades	112	112	88	81	85	83	-29	-25.9
Transport equipment operators	64	62	59	58	57	73	7	10.9
Materials handling & other crafts	86	75	75	75	73	83	-3	-3.5
MONTREAL								
All occupations	1,557	1,549	1,510	1,493	1,488	1,523	-34	-2.2
Managerial, administrative & other professional	475	501	545	530	542	559	84	17.7
Clerical	297	296	291	280	282	265	-32	-10.8
Sales	150	152	148	148	144	146	-4	-2.7
Services	192	187	184	180	182	200	8	4.2
Primary occupations	10	15	14	11	11	11	1	10
Processing, machining, fabricating	242	221	177	190	181	191	-51	-21.1
Construction trades	72	67	56	53	52	50	-22	-30.6
Transport equipment operators	58	53	46	48	45	50	-8	-13.8
Materials handling & other crafts	62	57	50	53	50	51	-11	-17.7
VANCOUVER								
All occupations	806	825	840	861	866	900	94	11.7
Managerial, administrative & other professional	260	279	280	274	305	316	56	21.5
Clerical	145	144	147	159	147	156	11	7.6
Sales	88	92	93	107	103	98	11	12.5
Services	109	104	108	109	116	123	14	12.8
Primary occupations	11	15	18	17	16	15	4	36.4
Processing, machining, fabricating	78	75	77	79	70	71	-7	-9
Construction trades	53	58	50	52	51	64	11	20.8
Transport equipment operators	30	33	39	35	28	26	-4	-13.3
Materials handling & other crafts	31	26	27	28	29	29	-2	-6.5

Source: Statistics Canada, *Labour Force Annual Averages 1989-1994* (Ottawa: Minister of Industry, Science and Technology, April 1995).

the Pacific Basin, notably the Pacific north-west, California and the Asia-Pacific.[25] This external reorientation is a defining feature of Vancouver's transformation, as the next chapter will demonstrate.

While many aspects of structural change, such as the growing importance of the service sector in terms of employment and output, are common to all major Canadian cities, Vancouver's development is clearly distinct when set against the national pattern. Important differences in industrial structure, the growth rates of specific industry groups and occupations, the timing of business cycles and restructuring phases, and market orientation are all indications of Vancouver's gradual disengagement from the rest of the Canadian urban system.

Redefining Vancouver's Regional Milieux

Examining Vancouver's particular development path from a regional perspective is also informative in this context. This regional analysis can be undertaken at different geographical levels. For instance at the continental level, Yeates has described the principal shifts in urban core development in North America as "a gradual contraction in the old US heartland extending from the middle-west to the east coast; an expanding core in the west coast centering around Los Angeles/San Francisco and extending possibly to Seattle/Vancouver; and an incipient core around the Gulf Coast."[26]

At the national level, regional shifts include what Yeates describes as a "refocusing" of core-periphery relations. He argues that the old central Canadian core has contracted and reconsolidated in south and south-western Ontario, "with Toronto serving as the focus of financial, service and industrial development,"[27] and Montreal being relegated to the status of a regional centre. At the same time, a new incipient core has emerged in the Vancouver region that "is in effect part of the Pacific north-west urban agglomeration."[28] This agglomeration is the cornerstone of a redefined regional orientation for Vancouver's development, which involves the decline of certain traditional roles and relationships and the ascendance of others.

A closer examination of Vancouver's evolving relationship with its region provides important insights into the city's external reorientation and its distinctive development trajectory. Regional and provincial linkages that have traditionally been the basis of Vancouver's development and determined the city's primacy over a vast hinterland have effectively been redefined (and in certain respects appreciably diminished) in response to both local and external forces. However, with the emergence of new regional entities, Vancouver is gradually assuming new roles and developing new relationships. These redefined roles and relationships reflect the complex, rich and interdependent regional context in which Vancouver's current transformation is taking place.

Figure 2.1 identifies three important regional milieux in which Vancouver's role is either in relative decline or undergoing fundamental changes. The figure also points to some key trends and dynamics. Given its divergence from the growth patterns and orientations of other Canadian cities and its resulting disengagement from the national urban system, Vancouver cannot be viewed as a generic western Canadian city or even simply as the largest western metropolis. Rather, it must be viewed as a unique case, differentiated by its size, external linkages, industrial structure and socio-cultural composition. To be sure, it shares some of the developmental features of the largest western cities, including traditional linkages with the resource industries, relatively truncated industrial production sectors and rapid tertiarization. But even Calgary, which is perhaps the most comparable western city, differs profoundly from Vancouver in terms of its scale, the diversity of its service sector, its growth trajectory and its socio-ethnic mix. Furthermore, Calgary is not an international gateway. In sum, Vancouver is qualitatively different.[29]

figure 2.1
Elements of Vancouver's Redefined Regional Setting: Declining Regional Relationships

A. As a western Canadian city	Increasing disengagement from the Canadian urban system and domestic markets Divergent growth trajectory *vis-à-vis* other major western Canadian cities Reorientation to transborder/international markets and cultures
B. As urban core to the provincial periphery	Erosion of command and control functions for BC's resource-based economy Contraction of natural resource processing and manufacturing functions Declining influence of the provincial resource-based economy on the city's social structure Growth of urban centres in British Columbia interior
C. As a regional central place	Growth of industries and businesses on the metropolitan fringe and exurban areas Decentralization of public services (e.g., community health) Supplanting of downtown regional service activities by foreign/international businesses and institutions

Perhaps the most decisive element of Vancouver's regional redefinition is the shift in its traditional relationship with the provincial resource economy. For much of the post-war period, Vancouver's development was driven (and its identity largely defined) by its close and complex linkages with a rapidly expanding resource-based economy,[30] which included:

- *Command and control functions: specialized service linkages* – The corporate complex of head office, financial and business services situated in Vancouver's downtown represents the most fundamental element of the core-periphery relationship in British Columbia. The growth of Vancouver's office sector over the period 1960-1980 was largely driven by the expansion of resource-based corporations and ancillary business and financial services, and reflected Vancouver's primacy in the province's staple economy.
- *Transportation linkages: Vancouver as commodity export gateway* – The expansion of the Port of Vancouver, Canada's largest seaport, was driven in large part by the growth of commodity exports (in the range of 60-70 million tons annually) from the provincial hinterland.
- *Production linkages* – Vancouver's industrial development was related to the processing and manufacturing of the province's natural resources (e.g., sawmills and other forest products processing plants, canneries and food processing).
- *Consumption linkages* – The hinterland regions of BC have historically supplied Vancouver's consumer markets (e.g., energy, water and foodstuffs).
- *Socio-cultural linkages* – The growth of British Columbia's natural-resource sector in this century has had a major impact on the formation of particular classes and communities in Vancouver, such as owners of capital and senior executives, who have tended to occupy Vancouver's prestigious residential districts and the North Shore; middle managers, many of whom have favoured the upper-middle-class neighbourhoods of the West Side; blue-collar workers and operatives, who have tended to cluster in the working-class East End and along the Fraser River; and, finally, displaced (or injured) former resource-sector workers, who reside in the Downtown Eastside – one of Canada's poorest communities.[31]

While Vancouver continues to fulfill important functions within British Columbia's resource economy, there is evidence in all the areas cited above that the city's relationship with the periphery is evolving and that this important element of its regional setting is being redefined. First, Vancouver's role as "command and control" centre for the natural-resource sector has been weakened appreciably by a series of corporate mergers, acquisitions and take overs that have increasingly shifted control outside the province.[32] Moreover, many of the business services firms that were initially established to serve the natural-resource sector have recently secured markets offshore,[33] notably in the Pacific Rim (see chapter 3).

Second, many of metropolitan Vancouver's resource processing firms have relocated outside the region or have closed. Over time, this can only weaken the production linkages between the urban core and the provincial hinterland.

Third, the two trends described above, combined with the growth of new industries that are not primarily resource based, have tended to reduce the influence of this sector on Vancouver's community structure and social classes. The resource sector's corporate elites and skilled operatives, who dominated in the post-war period, are being replaced by what Ley calls "a new middle class" of service professionals and managers and new immigrant entrepreneurs.[34]

Finally, the emergence of dynamic urban centres such as Kamloops, Kelowna and Prince George in British Columbia's interior will reduce the traditional dependence of peripheral regions on the province's metropolitan core. These rapidly growing urban centres now have populations of 60,000 or more as well as substantial concentrations of industry, businesses and post-secondary educational institutions, suggesting a progressively diminishing reliance on Vancouver for all but the most specialized goods and services.[35]

There have also been important changes to the city's traditional role as regional central place (Figure 2.1). Historically, the city performed higher order central place functions, providing retail, commercial, financial, administrative and distribution services to its regional market or catchment area. The City of Vancouver, which includes the (CBD) as well as other specialized clusters of service activity, still caters to the immediate regional market in Greater Vancouver and the Lower Fraser Valley. In some respects, this role has even grown recently with the completion of professional sports stadiums (notably GM Place, home of the NHL Canucks and NBA Grizzlies) and theatres (such as the Ford Theatre for the Performing Arts built by Toronto impresario Garth Drabinsky), facilities that attract consumers from all corners of the broadly defined regional market.

In other areas, however, Vancouver's role as regional central place has been transformed substantially. First, over the past decade or so Vancouver, like most large and medium-sized North American cities, has experienced large-scale decentralization, initially of the population, then of industries and consumer services and more recently of business services. The City of Vancouver, long the dominant regional business and employment centre, now represents less than one-third of the population of Vancouver CMA.[36] Suburban development has included the proliferation of retail, personal and business services in new centres such as shopping malls, business parks and regional town centres (RTCs). This has significantly reduced the dependence on Vancouver of those living in its rapidly growing metropolitan periphery. Burnaby – which has attracted four of the largest high-technology companies in BC and whose Metrotown RTC has become an attractive location for head-office operations – is a good example of the process of maturation of the metropolitan economy outside the City of Vancouver.[37]

Second, the last decade has seen the selective deconcentration of important public services to the suburbs. Examples include the establishment of a university and numerous colleges in Vancouver's suburbs and even further up the Fraser Valley, well beyond the metropolitan boundary. Another important policy-propelled process is the shift in health care service delivery away from Vancouver's dense midtown "medical precinct" to a more community-based approach that brings health services closer to the population, and thus to the suburbs.

Finally, changes in Vancouver's traditional role as regional central place include developments in the metropolitan core itself. As in many other cities, suburbanization and decentralization have modified the role of the central city, but this has by no means destroyed the core's vitality and viability. As we shall see in later chapters, there have been massive investments of public and private capital in Vancouver's metropolitan core in the last decade and a half which have generated new retail, commercial, recreational, educational and institutional infrastructure as well as substantial residential development and redevelopment. For the most part, however, this new activity is directed at a quite different market and clientele than in the past.

To a large extent, of course, the central city functions both as employment centre and playground to the "new middle class" of professionals and managers. But Vancouver's core also serves a large and rapidly growing international clientele, a trend that was greatly accelerated by Expo 86 as result of major capital projects and extensive international marketing effort by the provincial government. Vancouver's downtown now features five-star hotels serving tourists and business travellers, speciality shopping precincts, a major cruise ship terminal and other urban amenities that cater in large part to visitors. The metropolitan core therefore increasingly functions as the preserve of the city's new service elite and a large and rapidly growing number of foreign visitors.

Ascendant Roles and Relationships

While several of Vancouver's traditional regional functions are being redefined (and may even be diminishing in the aggregate), Vancouver's linkages with new regional entities are intensifying and contributing to the emergence of a new regional context.

As we have seen, Vancouver's mature roles are largely based on regional administration, production and distribution functions. The more dynamic relationships we are about to describe to some extent incorporate these traditional functions, but they are more clearly associated with Vancouver's evolving regional identity as defined by new developmental interdependencies, common social values, lifestyles (or quality of life) and a regionally shared reorientation toward Pacific Basin markets and cultures.

Although these regional dynamics are incipient rather than fully realized, they provide useful insights into Vancouver's development path. Evidence that Vancouver's development is taking place in a redefined regional milieu is in many respects fragmentary. This is partly due to the fact that the emerging regional entities cut across administrative units as well as national boundaries. Indeed, various attempts to define Vancouver's new regional context reveal considerable differences of opinion. For instance, while *The Economist* (published in London) describes a relatively limited Cascadia that encompasses British Columbia, Washington and Oregon,[38] the *Northwest Journal of Business and Economics* (published at Western Washington University) refers to an extended economic zone that also includes Alberta, Alaska, Idaho and Montana.[39] In ecological terms, Cascadia would comprise the bioregion extending from Cape Mendocino in northern California to Yakutat Bay in the Alaska panhandle and east to the continental divide.[40]

These caveats notwithstanding, we can draw the broad contours of Vancouver's new regional context as well as some of its defining attributes and underlying dynamics. Figure 2.2 describes this new context as it emerges within different geographical entities. At the broadest level, Cascadia represents a unique ecological region, roughly coterminous with Garreau's notion of *Ecotopia* (one of the "nine nations" of North America)[41] and bounded by California to the south, the Great Plains to the east and the sub-Arctic to the north. This bioregion contains vast wilderness areas and other natural assets, the integrity of which must be reconciled with population and economic growth rates well above the North American average. The tension between ecological sensitivity and economic dynamism has given rise to numerous influential environmental movements and agencies in the region – the most prominent of which is Greenpeace, established in Vancouver several decades ago and succeeded by Greenpeace International. In Vancouver as well as in the broader region of

figure 2.2
Elements of Vancouver's Redefined Regional Setting: Ascendant Regional Relationships

A. In the Vancouver–Seattle urban development corridor	As the northern pole of the Vancouver–Seattle metropolitan growth axis Vancouver and Seattle as high-growth cities in a continental context Vancouver and Seattle as major Pacific Gateway cities
B. Vancouver and the Georgia Basin	As the core metropolis of the Georgia Basin extended metropolitan bioregion Growing recreational/leisure linkages with the Georgia Basin's environmental assets Vancouver's development pattern as a growth management priority for the Georgia Basin
C. Vancouver in the Cascadia context	As part of the central metropolitan core of the Cascadia region (Cape Mendocino-Yakutat Bay-continental divide) As centre of innovation for the environmental movement and progressive ecological enhancement programmes Development path influenced by strategic interdependence between environment and culture

Cascadia, deeply entrenched ecological values have spurred the growth of environmental protection industries, technologies and systems, underscoring the interdependency of the environment and progressive development.

Although so vast an area inevitably features many contrasts, Cascadia does present a number of important common elements. In addition to high growth rates and social values and lifestyles that are strongly influenced by environmental concerns, the region's urban centres – including Vancouver – contain many technology-intensive and leading-edge industries in a variety of sectors such as computer software, aerospace, biotechnology and recreational and sporting equipment.

Within Cascadia, the natural-resource sector is still important but has declined both in relative and absolute terms. While overall employment in British Columbia, Washington, Oregon and Idaho has doubled over the past quarter century from 3.5 to 7 million, employment in forestry and mining has declined in the same period from about 300,000 to 260,000.[42] More stringent resource allocation policies, changes in land use and, more important, the continuing substitution of capital for labour have all contributed to the significant losses of employment in this sector.

Cascadia's subregions also share a tendency to look to the Pacific Rim for development opportunities. Not surprisingly, these shared attributes have fostered greater regional consciousness, the most extreme manifestation of which is a vaguely separatist sensibility. This sentiment is enhanced by a collective sense of alienation from eastern power centres in Canada and the US, notably Toronto, Ottawa, New York and Washington. While the realization of Cascadia as a political entity may appear far-fetched, there are certainly many committees, task forces and institutions dedicated to furthering the cause of regional cooperation on a wide range of economic and environmental issues.

An example of economic cooperation in Cascadia is the Pacific Northwest Economic Region (PNWER), a coalition of business interests and political leaders committed to overcoming the barrier of national borders by fostering "a new regionalism designed to give critical mass to economic communities of interest."[43] While there are similar organizations elsewhere along the Canada-US border, PNWER is distinct in its explicit reference to ecological values and environmental priorities and its emphasis on the Pacific Rim as the realm of shared regional destiny.

The Georgia Basin-Puget Sound Metropolitan Bioregion (Figure 2.3) refers to a considerably smaller region than most definitions of Cascadia. This more compact entity allows greater specificity of trends and policy focus. Administratively, the region includes all or part of 13 counties in Washington State as well as nine regional districts in south-western British Columbia.[44] The broadly defined Georgia Basin encompasses Victoria and Olympia, the capital cities of British Columbia and Washington, but the dominant urban core consists of Vancouver and Seattle, the largest cities in the Pacific northwest. Separated by about 200 kilometres of Interstate 5, these two cities are among the most dynamic centres in North America. Over the past decade and a half, they have consistently ranked as the fastest-growing metropolitan areas outside the US sunbelt.[45]

Greater Vancouver (population 1.8 million) and metropolitan Seattle (2.3 million) both perform specialized gateway roles in their respective nations. This similarity of function has led to considerable competition between the two cities, but also to a measure of complementarity based on modal specialization. For example, Vancouver is principally a bulk cargo export centre and has a large, rapidly growing cruise ship sector, while the ports of Seattle (in King County) and Tacoma (in adjacent Pierce County) specialize in container traffic. However, in June 1997, the Port of Vancouver opened the new Deltaport container terminal at Roberts Bank, which represents a significant addition to Vancouver's container traffic capacity and a clear indication that it intends to challenge the Puget Sound ports of Seattle and Tacoma for the lucrative container

figure 2.3

The Georgia Basin-Puget Sound Metropolitan Bioregion[1]

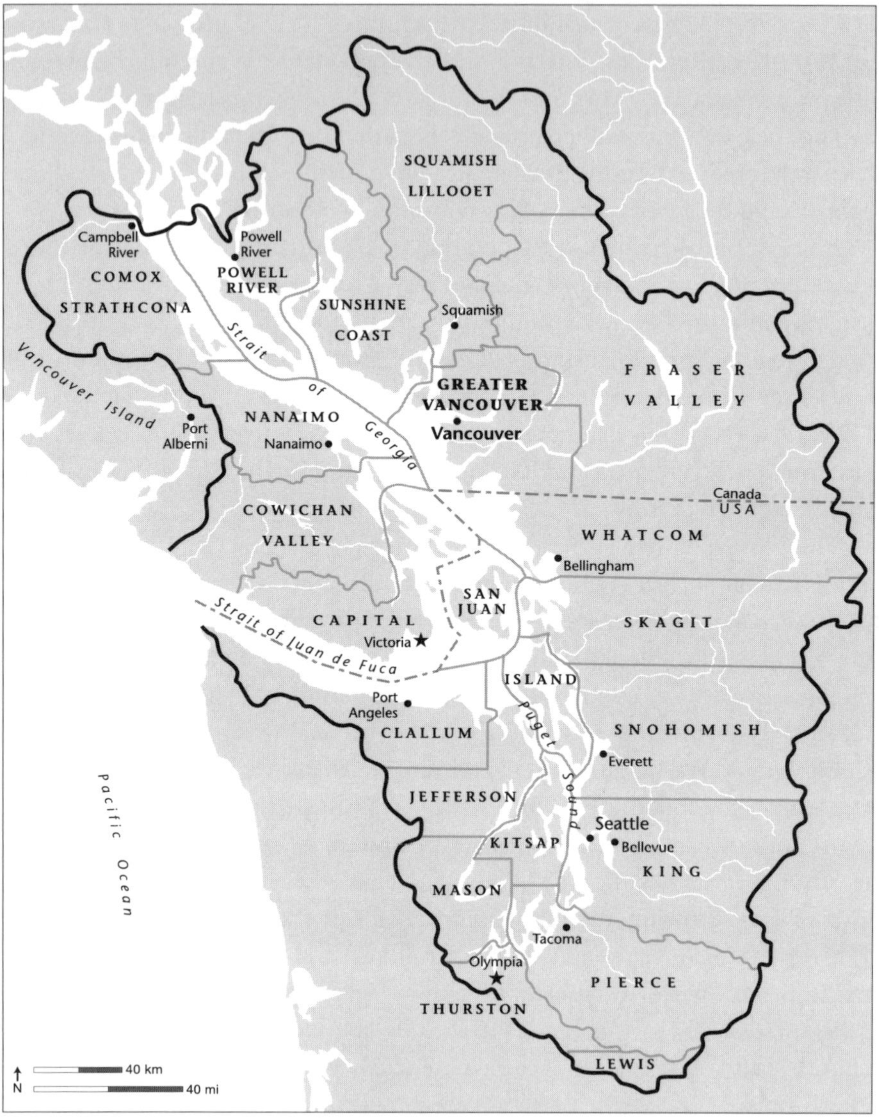

[1] Shows regional districts in British Columbia and counties in Washington State.

trade. Over the next decade, competition among West Coast ports (including Los Angeles-Long Beach and the Bay area ports of San Francisco-Oakland) for Asia-Pacific container trade will intensify, as major shipping lines continue to rationalize and consolidate their Pacific operations.

Important concentrations of advanced-technology industries can be found in both Vancouver and Seattle, although Seattle's high-technology R & D and production sector is orders of magnitude larger than Vancouver's. Much of Seattle's international influence is due to the presence of several mega-corporations, notably Boeing, Microsoft and Weyerhaeuser, for which there are certainly no counterparts in Vancouver (or almost anywhere else). At the same time, Vancouver is generally acknowledged as having richer Asia-Pacific connections, in particular bilateral air services, business links and financial networks. Indeed, a recent study conducted by members of the UBC Faculty of Commerce concluded that Vancouver should be able to build upon its international banking and finance institutions and related expertise to become a key financial relay point between the Asia-Pacific and Cascadia as a whole.[46]

Given their combined economic weight and competitive advantage, Vancouver and Seattle have the potential to play a global role usually reserved for much larger urban agglomerations. The Vancouver-Seattle axis has been identified as a strategic urban development corridor in the Pacific Basin region based on its gateway role, technological development capacity, growth rates and status as a destination choice for immigrants (especially from Asia).[47] The Vancouver-Seattle corridor is much smaller than the other gateway regions (Los Angeles-Long Beach and the San Francisco-Oakland area) on the West Coast, but it has significant advantages such as its greater proximity to Asian markets, quality of life and the entrepreneurial energy of recent Asian immigrants.

There are, of course, significant constraints on the development of the Vancouver-Seattle corridor and the full realization of its gateway role. Washington State has imposed a stringent growth management regime, including the mandatory delineation of urban-rural boundaries, which is likely to prevent the development of a chain of contiguous settlements between Vancouver and Seattle. The competition between Vancouver and Seattle (and indeed between Seattle and Tacoma) for sea-borne trade, aviation traffic and other markets may also be a deterrent. Finally, the Canada-US international border remains a significant barrier, although NAFTA and bilateral province-to-state protocols and arrangements continue to promote and facilitate north-south interaction.

One example of active cooperation is the Georgia Basin Initiative (GBI), which provides a framework for environmental cooperation between the state of Washington and the province of British Columbia.[48] The premier of BC and the governor of Washington have also signed economic partnership agreements, although competition for markets and shared resources places this cooperation under considerable strain, as the so-called "salmon wars" between BC and both Washington and Alaska in 1997 demonstrated.

In this chapter we have examined Vancouver's distinctive development patterns and restructuring path and described its changing role within both a national and a regional context. At the national level, there are still important similarities between Vancouver and other major Canadian city-regions, but the trend is toward divergence and even disengagement. The regional context is still very important, but it is in this area that elements of structural change are discernible. On the one hand, we are witnessing a relative decline in Vancouver's traditional role as provincial core and regional central place. On the other, Vancouver's interactions within the broadly defined Cascadia region and Georgia Basin suggest the emergence of a new regional milieu, based on a new set of development interdependencies defined by shared social values, environmental priorities, culture and technology.

However, as significant as these elements are in assessing Vancouver's development pattern, there is growing evidence that the city's rich and complex associations with the Pacific Basin (and more specifically the Asia-Pacific) have become the determining factors in its transformation. In the next chapter we explore the key aspects of Vancouver's new Pacific destiny.

Notes

1. This was described in Harold Innis' classic work, *Problems of Staple Production in Canada* (Toronto: Ryerson, 1933).

2. T.A. Hutton, "The Innisian Core-Periphery Revisited: Vancouver's Changing Relationships with British Columbia's Staple Economy," *BC Studies*, no. 113 (1997), pp. 69-100.

3. G. Anderson, *Housing Policy in Canada* (Vancouver: UBC Centre for Human Settlements/Canada Mortgage and Housing Corporation, 1992).

4. Another view of these changes is that they will allow provincial governments to "tailor" programmes to suit provincial and local circumstances.

5. D.F. Ley and T.A. Hutton, "The Service Sector and Metropolitan Development in Canada," in P.W. Daniels (ed.), *Services and Metropolitan Development* (London: Routledge, 1991).

6. T.A. Hutton, "City Profile: Vancouver," *Cities*, Vol. 11, no. 4 (1994), pp. 219-39.

7. A large component of the apparent net out-migration from Greater Vancouver to other areas of British Columbia represents in fact an "overspill" of population eastward up the Fraser Valley into adjacent regional districts and should be more properly viewed as an expansion of the Vancouver urban region beyond the GVRD boundary (i.e., much as the movement of population from Metropolitan Toronto to adjoining municipalities has contributed to the formation of a Greater Toronto Area).

8. W.J. Coffey, *The Evolution of Canada's Metropolitan Economies* (Montreal: Institute for Research on Public Policy, 1994).

9. P.W. Daniels, *Services in the World Economy* (Oxford: Blackwell, 1993).

10. W.J. Coffey, "High Order Services in the Ottawa Region: Location Factors and Elements of a Development Strategy," paper presented at the North American meetings of the Regional Science Association, New Orleans, November 8-10, 1991.

11. The large-scale downsizing of the provincial government workforce in British Columbia in 1983 as part of the Social Credit administration's controversial restraint programme was one of the first such initiatives in Canada.

12. T.A. Hutton, "A Profile of Vancouver's Service Sector," paper presented at the Metropolis 90 conference, Plymouth, England, 1989.

13. Coffey, *The Evolution of Canada's Metropolitan Economies.*

14. Location quotients are regarded as *indices of specialization* that compare the level of concentration of a given sector or industry group within a given spatial unit, normally a national or sub-national territory. Calculating location quotients is a relatively simple task. The location quotient for a given sector *i* can be defined as:

$$LQ_i = \frac{R_i/R}{N_i/N}$$

where R_i, N_i are regional and national employment in sector *i*, respectively, and R and N are the regional and national employment totals. If the location quotient for sector or industry *i* exceeds one (1), export employment is presumed to exist in the sector, since the level of concentration of employment in this sector exceeds that for the nation. In these cases, *basic* (or export) employment, E_i, is calculated as:

$$E_i = R_i - R(N_i/N)$$

where $R(N_i/N)$ is an estimate of the amount of regional employment in sector *i* necessary to satisfy local demands, based upon the proportion of national employment allocated to sector *i*. Adapted from H.C. Davis, *Regional Economic Impact Analysis and Project Evaluation* (Vancouver: UBC Press, 1990), p. 16.

15. J. Knauf, "Recessions, Restructuring, and Recoveries," *Economic Review*, Vol. 245 (Vancouver: Regional Economic Services Branch, Human Resources Development Canada, June/July 1994).

16. T.A. Hutton, "Visions of a 'Post-Staples' Economy: Structural Change and Adjustment Issues in British Columbia," *Policy Issues and Planning Responses* (Vancouver: Centre for Human Settlements, 1994), pp. 1-45.

17. Vancouver's average annual net employment growth over the period 1991-1994 (19,900) exceeded the (net) annual average growth levels for Toronto and the next 16 largest Ontario cities combined (19,600) over the same period. (Calculated from Table 2-15 in W.J. Coffey, *Employment*

Growth and Change in the Canadian Urban System, 1971-94, Working Paper No. W/02 [Ottawa: Canadian Policy Research Networks, 1996]).

18. B. Little, "Toronto Struggles to Recover," *The Globe and Mail*, November 14, 1994, pp. B1-B2.

19. M. Gooderham, "Taxes too High, Toronto Warned: Realty Experts Fear Devastated Core," *The Globe and Mail*, August 11, 1995, p. A5.

20. For a discussion of the impacts of economic globalization and market integration on the Toronto region's economy, see E.F. Isin (ed.), *Toronto Region in the World Economy: Proceedings of a Symposium* (Toronto: York University, 1994).

21. The total value of building permits for GVRD municipalities was $1.41 billion in 1984, $1.45 billion in 1985, and $1.57 billion in 1986. Greater Vancouver Regional District, *Economic Bulletin* (Vancouver: GVRD Strategic Planning Department, February 1995); City of Vancouver Permits and Licences Department; Greater Vancouver Regional District Development Services.

22. This may be seen as evidence – as Coffey and Polèse have argued – that Montreal's long decline may have reached its trough. W.J. Coffey and M. Polèse, "Cultural Barriers to the Location of Producer Services: The Montreal-Toronto Rivalry and the Limits of Urban Polarization," *Canadian Journal of Regional Science*, Vol. 14, no. 3 (1991), pp. 433-46.

23. J. Simmons, "Bang Bang Bang – Monitoring the Spatial Distribution of Canada's Financial Sector," in M.J. Bannon and L.S. Bourne (eds.), *Urbanization and Urban Development: Recent Trends in a Global Context* (Dublin: University College, 1991).

24. I. Bromley, quoted in Little, "Toronto Struggles to Recover."

25. D.W. Edgington and M.A. Goldberg, "Vancouver: Canada's Gateway to the Rim," in E.J. Blakely and R.J. Stimson (eds.), *New Cities of the Pacific Rim* (London: Routledge, forthcoming), chap. 5.

26. M. Yeates, *Urban Canada: Changing Core/Periphery Relations*, Kingston, Department of Geography, Queen's University, mimeo, n.d.

27. Yeates, *Urban Canada: Changing Core/ Periphery Relations.*

28. Yeates, *Urban Canada: Changing Core/ Periphery Relations.*

29. We should also note that Vancouver CMA is more than twice as populous as Calgary CMA, has larger and more diversified service and manufacturing sectors, has stronger linkages with the economy and society of the Pacific north-west and is more intimately and comprehensively connected to Asia-Pacific urban networks, markets and cultures.

30. R.N. North and W.G. Hardwick, "Vancouver Since the Second World War," in T. Oke and G. Wynn (eds.), *Vancouver and its Region* (Vancouver: UBC Press, 1992), pp. 200-33

31. Adapted from Hutton, "The Innisian Core-Periphery Revisited."

32. Hutton, "The Innisian Core-Periphery Revisited."

33. The classic case is the complex of corporate, legal and accounting firms established in New York to serve Manhattan's corporate head offices. Even when New York began to lose head offices, many of these business service firms were able to find new markets as distant as Denver by virtue of their highly specialized expertise. See The Conservation of Human Resources, *The Corporate Headquarters Complex in New York City* (New York: Columbia University, 1977). In the Canadian context, some of Montreal's engineering and consulting firms have had impressive success in international markets after an initial period of catering to Quebec's resource economy and hinterland regions.

34. D.F. Ley, *The New Middle Class and the Remaking of the Central City* (Oxford: Oxford University Press, 1996).

35. H.C. Davis and T.A. Hutton, *Structural Change in the British Columbia Economy: Regional Diversification and Metropolitan Transition* (Victoria: British Columbia Round Table on the Environment and the Economy, 1992).

36. Greater Vancouver Regional District, *Livable Region Strategy: Proposals (A Strategy for Environmental Protection and Growth Management)* (Vancouver: GVRD Strategic Planning Department, 1993).

37. Personal communication, City of Burnaby Planning Department, June 1997.

38. "Welcome to Cascadia," *The Economist*, May 21, 1994, p. 52.

39. *Northwest Journal of Business and Economics*, Vol. 1 (Bellingham: Western Washington University, 1993).

40. D. Aberley (ed.), *Envisioning Cascadia: A Bioregional Atlas* (Vancouver: School of Community and Regional Planning, UBC, 1995).

41. J. Garreau, *The Nine Nations of North America* (Boston: Houghton Mifflin, 1981). Garreau's *Ecotopia* (derived from Ernest Callenbach's 1975 novel) consisted of the western littoral of North America, from Point Conception, south of the San Francisco Bay Area region, to Anchorage, Alaska, and bounded by the Coast Mountains and the Sierra Nevada.

42. Data compiled by the Seattle-based Northwest Environment Watch, reported in G. Hamilton, "Land-Based Jobs on Long Decline," *The Vancouver Sun*, December 1, 1994, pp. D1-D2.

43. A. Bluechel, "The Pacific North West Economic Region: A Multi-State, Multi-Province Regional Approach to Economic Development," *Economic Development Review* (winter 1993), pp. 27-29.

44. As of January 1996, the three regional districts of the Lower Fraser region outside the GVRD were amalgamated to form a new Fraser Valley Regional District.

45. Census of Canada; US Bureau of the Census.

46. M.A. Goldberg and M.D. Levi, "The Evolving Experience along the Pacific Northwest Corridor Called Cascadia," *The New Pacific*, no. 7 (1992/93), pp. 28-32.

47. P.J. Rimmer, "Megacities, Multilayered Networks and Development Corridors in the Pacific Economic Zone," in T.A. Hutton and A. McNeil (eds.), *Proceedings of the Third Annual Conference of the Pacific Rim Council on Urban Development* (Vancouver: CHS, 1991).

48. British Columbia Round Table on the Environment and the Economy, *Georgia Basin Initiative: Creating a Sustainable Future* (Victoria, BC: Ministry of the Environment, Parks and Recreation, 1993).

3

Vancouver and the Asia-Pacific

Vancouver (and the region of south-western BC of which Vancouver is a part) has long-established associations with the societies and markets of the Asia-Pacific realm,[1] originating with the migration of aboriginal peoples over the Siberian-Alaska land-bridge some 10,000 years ago. In the modern historical period, initial references to such associations include the Nootka-Canton fur trade and intriguing evidence that the first Chinese settlers arrived over two centuries ago as part of a brief attempt by the British fur-trader, John Meares, to colonize Nootka Sound in 1788, several years before Captain George Vancouver's arrival off what is now Point Grey in 1792.[2]

As is well known, Chinese immigrants played a key role in the development of Vancouver and BC over the second half of the nineteenth century, during the gold rush of 1858 and then in the construction of the BC portion of the Canadian Pacific Railway, which linked Vancouver to other Canadian cities and brought BC into Confederation. The early years of the present century saw the arrival of Chinese, Japanese and East Indian immigrants, population movements that led to the establishment of Vancouver's Chinatown, Japantown and a Japanese fishing community at Steveston, South Richmond.[3] The interwar years also witnessed the expansion of trade and travel between Vancouver and the Asia-Pacific, exemplified by the Canadian Pacific steamship service to Japan and other scheduled sea-borne passenger and cargo services.

These references are an indication of the historical associations between Vancouver and the Asia-Pacific sphere. A more recent development, however, is the extent and complexity of the linkages that characterize the contemporary relationship between Vancouver and the Asia-Pacific, and the transformational impact of these associations on contemporary Vancouver. This chapter examines the city's growing role in the Pacific Basin and describes the strategic aspects of the interdependency between the two regions and its implications for the city's modern development.

As we have already observed, Vancouver's association with the Asia-Pacific has always had an external dimension – expressed in terms of mercantile networks and the movement of peoples since the earliest period of contact – and an internal dimension, represented by new settlement patterns and cultural expressions. Although contemporary relationships are far more complex and extensive, they can also be examined using a similar framework.

The external dimension encompasses Vancouver's deepening engagement with Pacific Basin societies and markets and, more specifically, Asia-Pacific trading systems, financial flows, socio-cultural networks and travel patterns. Cities are playing an increasingly important role in economic development, financial mediation and trade in the Asia-Pacific. Collectively, they form internodal, trans-Pacific urban networks that feature elements of both competition and complementarity[4] as well as close socio-cultural interaction sustained by recent large waves of migration and the formation of mobilized diasporas. Vancouver's role within these networks varies, sometimes acting as a key player and sometimes as a remote outpost.

The internal dimension of Vancouver's emergence as a Pacific Rim city consists of the intra-metropolitan attributes that stem from the city's increasingly intimate association with Pacific markets, societies and city-regions. We refer here to the wide-ranging impacts of Asia-Pacific trade, investment and immigration on metropolitan Vancouver's economy, export base, industrial structure, settlement patterns and built form.

Our analysis is necessarily selective. First, we outline Vancouver's strategic role in the Asia-Pacific, focusing on the gateway functions that define the city as a linchpin between Canada and the Pacific Basin. Second, we examine the services export component of Vancouver's linkages with Pacific markets, which underscores not only changes in market demand, but also larger economic restructuring trends and the increasingly important role of recent immigrants in specialized services production and exchange. Third, we examine recent immigration trends and characteristics, once again highlighting the interdependency between culture, community and urban economic development. The chapter concludes with an examination of the policy responses to Vancouver's engagement with the Asia-Pacific.

Vancouver's Strategic Roles and Gateway Functions in the Asia-Pacific

The contemporary transformation of metropolitan Vancouver reflects a profound and comprehensive economic and socio-cultural reorientation as result of Vancouver assuming more important roles in the markets and urban societies of the Asia-Pacific and the Pacific Basin as a whole. The city's status in the hierarchy of Pacific cities hardly rivals that of Tokyo or Los Angeles, respectively the dominant control centres of the western and eastern Pacific Rim, or even second-order metropolitan regions such as Sydney, Hong Kong, Singapore and Osaka. But Vancouver's diverse and specialized roles in the Asia-Pacific indicate that it has a more strategic niche than its size would suggest.[5]

These elements of functional diversity and specialization are depicted schematically in Figure 3.1, which presents Vancouver's gateway functions, and Figure 3.2, which identifies its complementary educational, political and socio-cultural functions. Vancouver's significance as a Pacific Rim city is conventionally interpreted in terms of its trading and gateway functions, but the activities presented in Figure 3.2 suggest the city has a broader position within the Pacific realm. In fact, it is necessary to look at both sets of functions and their critical interdependencies to obtain a more balanced and comprehensive profile of Vancouver's Pacific reorientation.

Vancouver's secondary and tertiary educational institutions increasingly reflect an Asia-Pacific orientation that is expressed in research, exchange programmes, curricula and the ethnicity of the student body. UBC is probably the leading institution with respect to research and teaching in this area, as articulated in its 1988 mission statement entitled "Toward the Pacific Century." It is also heavily engaged in training programmes for cadres of educators, planners and property managers from many Asian societies. But other institutions are also key players in Vancouver's expanding Pacific role. For example, Capilano College's innovative CANASEAN programme involves exchanges between professionals, educators and business people from Vancouver and Southeast Asian countries. SFU's downtown campus provides an important forum for education, training and professional development programmes pertaining to the Asia-Pacific. SFU and UBC are jointly engaged in a five-year research project (Metropolis-Immigration) that will examine the impact of immigration from the Asia-Pacific (and other regions) on Vancouver. As another measure of Vancouver's expanding educational role in the

figure 3.1
Vancouver's Strategic Asia-Pacific Roles: Gateway Functions

Strategic functions and roles	Facilitating mechanisms and underlying dynamics
I. GATEWAY FUNCTIONS	
A. Trade 1. Natural resource commodities 2. Goods 3. Services	Globalization of commodity markets Growing demand among Pacific Basin markets Externalization of demand for services and Vancouver's competitive advantage in tradeable services
B. Finance and investment 1. Foreign direct investment 2. Joint ventures 3. Private banking	Liberalization of capital markets Role of multinationals Growth of surplus capital accumulation within Pacific region Stability of Canadian political and financial institutions
C. Immigration 1. Business category (entrepreneur/investor) 2. Family reunification and independents 3. Refugees	Concern about political factors overseas Perception of Vancouver as prosperous, multicultural society Canada's immigration policies and programmes Canadian commitment to refugees
D. Travel and tourism 1. Business travel 2. Conventions 3. Tourism (including cruise ships)	Income growth among APEC nations Bilateral air connections to key Asia-Pacific markets Vancouver as tourist destination and gateway to Whistler and wilderness resorts
E. Communications 1. Business/personal	Emergence of information economy and knowledge sector

Pacific realm, the number of Asian students in BC (a large majority of whom are Vancouver residents) tripled between 1985 and 1992, increasing the province's share of the Canadian total from 11 to 17.3 percent.[6]

Vancouver also plays an increasingly important political and administrative role in the Asia-Pacific. There are no fewer than 64 consulates in Vancouver, 18 of which have opened since 1990.[7] In the case of Singapore, an important Asia-Pacific jurisdiction, the Vancouver consulate is its only official government presence in Canada. These consulates facilitate trade between Vancouver, the figure 3.1 (continued)

Key institutions, agencies and programmes	(1) Major markets (2) Urban connecting points
Port of Vancouver Rail and trucking facilities BC Trade Corporation Federal export marketing programmes Vancouver Board of Trade/World Trade Centre	(1) Japan, Hong Kong, China, Russia, South Korea, US, Taiwan, ASEAN nations, Australia (2) Yokohama, Hong Kong, Guangzhou, Vladivostok, Pusan, Los Angeles, Kaohsiung, Singapore, Sydney, Melbourne
Hongkong Bank of Canada (HQ: Vancouver) Other "B" Banks and Canadian "big 6" International Finance Centre, Vancouver Vancouver Stock Exchange	(1) Japan, Hong Kong, China, US, Malaysia, Australia, Taiwan, Singapore (2) Tokyo, Hong Kong, Shanghai, Los Angeles, Kuala Lumpur, Sydney, Taipei, Singapore
Federal immigration and consular services Provincial overseas offices Vancouver-based consulates Community-based immigration service (e.g., SUCCESS, MOSAIC)	(1) China, Hong Kong, India, Pakistan, Vietnam, Philippines (2) Guangzhou, Beijing, Hong Kong, New Delhi, Islamabad, Ho Chi Minh City, Manila
Vancouver International Airport Tourism BC Tourism Vancouver Port of Vancouver cruise ship terminal Vancouver Trade and Convention Centre/BC Place	(1) US, Japan, Australia, New Zealand, Hong Kong, Singapore, Malaysia, Indonesia, Thailand, Mexico, China (2) Honolulu, Seattle, Los Angeles, Tokyo, Osaka-Kyoto, Sydney, Cairns, Auckland, Hong Kong, Singapore, Kuala Lumpur, Jakarta, Denpasar, Bangkok, Mexico City, Beijing, Shanghai
Telecommunications and trans-Pacific fibre optic networks	Links to major Asia-Pacific financial, business and trading centres

Asia-Pacific and other foreign markets. The fact that the city hosted the 1997 Asia-Pacific Economic Cooperation (APEC) summit is also a reflection of its greater political role in the Pacific realm.

Figure 3.1 sets out the basic structure of Vancouver's strategic Asia-Pacific gateway functions (i.e., trade, finance and investment, immigration, travel and tourism, and communications) and identifies the facilitating mechanisms, key institutions and programmes and the major markets and urban connecting points relevant to each. The lists of cities in the last column highlight the significance

figure 3.2

Vancouver's Strategic Asia-Pacific Roles: Educational, Political and Socio-Cultural Functions

Strategic functions and roles	Facilitating mechanisms and underlying dynamics
II. EDUCATION	
A. Universities 1. Teaching 2. Research 3. Training **B. Colleges** **C. Schools and other institutions**	Demand for education and knowledge among Pacific nations Role of R & D and specialized information input in advanced production Human capital formation as priority among Asian societies Openness of Vancouver tertiary educational institutions to overseas students
III. POLITICAL - ADMINISTRATIVE	
A. Government of Canada **B. Pacific Rim nation representatives** **C. Niche-level institutions**	Vancouver's emergence as Canada's Pacific city Vancouver as gateway to Canada Vancouver as specialized service centre within the Pacific Basin
IV. SOCIO-CULTURAL	
A. Vancouver as node of Pacific Basin urban network **B. Vancouver as hosting society for Asian-Pacific culture** **C. Vancouver as Canada's connecting point to Asian culture and society**	High levels of immigration to Vancouver from the Asia-Pacific region Growth of new ethnic communities and neighbourhoods Development of networks among diasporas within Pacific Rim cities

of gateway centres in the burgeoning economies and trading systems of the Pacific Rim, and the different sets of linkages associated with each network. Contact, interaction and exchange between and among these gateway cities is facilitated by what Peter Rimmer has termed "multi-layered urban networks" of sea-borne trade, air connections and telecommunications (including fibre optics and satellite links).[8]

While these facets of Vancouver's gateway role are to some extent interdependent, each has its own set of dynamics. With respect to the city's crucial role as an export centre for bulk commodities and resources, the dominant influences on the supply side are clearly BC's massive reserves of staples such as forest products, coal and other minerals, and grains from Alberta and Saskatchewan. On figure 3.2 (continued)

Key institutions, agencies and programmes	**Examples of important groups and constituencies**
UBC's mission statement: *Toward the Pacific Century* (1988) UBC's strategic research programmes and training UBC Asian Centre SFU-UBC Metropolis-Immigration project Capilano College's CANASEAN programme Commonwealth Distance Learning Centre	Overseas students Overseas faculty Domestic students Various businesses and industries
Federal foreign affairs office in Vancouver Consulates of Asia-Pacific nations International Centre for Commercial Arbitration; International Maritime Centre; Centre for the Reform of Criminal Law	Expatriate business interests Local/domestic businesses and industries Recent immigrants and prospective citizens Client groups in the commercial sector
Federal multicultural policies Asia-Pacific Foundation of Canada (HQ: Vancouver) Ethno-cultural associations and bilateral business groups	Expatriate citizens New and expanding cultural groups General population in Vancouver Interested parties elsewhere in Canada

the demand side, there are the large industrial and consumer markets of East and Southeast Asia and the United States. In the smaller (but growing) area of service exports and trade (discussed in detail below), the externalization of specialized services (i.e., contracting out to other businesses and industries) is prominent on the demand side, while Vancouver's competitive advantage in specialized services production is the most important factor on the supply side. Macro-level forces include the globalization of commodity markets, which has stimulated the export of natural resources from Vancouver and increased capital accumulation among East Asian societies. Some of this capital has been directed to Vancouver in the form of investments and has facilitated the growth of tourism in the Asia-Pacific to the benefit of Vancouver and BC as a whole.

table 3.1

Principal Destinations of Exports from the Port of Vancouver, 1990 - 1994 (millions of metric tonnes)

	1994	Rank	1993	Rank	1992	Rank	1991	Rank	1990	Rank
Japan	21.0	1	20.6	1	20.6	1	23.7	1	23.6	1
South Korea	8.6	2	8.6	2	6.6	2	9.2	2	6.6	2
China	4.5	3	3.0	3	4.3	3	4.6	3	3.8	3
Brazil	2.6	4	1.9	4	1.9	4	1.5	7	1.5	7
Taiwan	2.0	5	1.7	5	1.7	6	2.0	4	1.9	4
US	1.6	6	1.3	6	1.7	5	1.7	6	1.4	8
Mexico	1.6	7	1.0	8	-	-	-	-	-	-
UK	1.4	8	-	-	1.3	7	1.4	8	1.6	6
Indonesia	1.1	9	1.2	7	1.2	9	-	-	-	-
Australia	1.0	10	.9	10	-	-	-	-	1.2	9
Total foreign cargo exports	57.3		50.3		53.5		60.7		55.7	

Source: Vancouver Port Corporation, Port of Vancouver, Corporate Communication.

Some Measures of Vancouver's Gateway Functions

The significance of Vancouver's strategic gateway functions, specifically the increasing orientation toward Asia-Pacific markets, can be illustrated with recent trade and travel statistics. The natural starting point is the Port of Vancouver, by far Canada's largest port and a major Pacific Rim deep sea port. It exports 60-70 million tons of commodities annually, mostly to the Pacific Rim and more specifically to Asia-Pacific ports and markets. In fact, the increase in commodity exports to Japan and other Pacific markets "was a decisive factor in the growth of the Port of Vancouver to the status of the largest in Canada, as well as the largest on the Pacific coast of North America by tonnage."[9] Typically, the top three destinations for Port of Vancouver shipments are Japan, South Korea and China (Table 3.1).

The Port of Vancouver also handles a substantial volume of imports. Although these are considerably less important than its exports in terms of tonnage, they typically consist of high value-added consumer items such as automobiles, electronics and apparel. Vancouver is thus tightly integrated in a network of major Pacific gateway ports such as Tokyo-Yokohama, Hong Kong, Pusan, Vladivostok and Singapore.

Over the longer term, the Port of Vancouver faces increasing competition from the other major West Coast ports of Seattle-Tacoma, San Francisco-Oakland and Los Angeles-Long Beach. As in other transportation and distribution sectors, the major carriers are consolidating their routings and destinations, and it is possible that one or two of the leading West Coast ports could experience substantial decreases in volume over the next decade or so. However, the Port of Vancouver has an aggressive long-range capital investment and marketing programme designed to enhance its competitive advantage, and it has also achieved a measure of diversification. As evidence of Vancouver's competitive position, South Korea's Hanjin Line, a major container line, recently commenced service to the Port of Vancouver.[10] A new container facility commenced operation during the summer of 1997 at Roberts Bank, complementing the major coal port facility and adding significantly to the Port of Vancouver's container throughput capacity. In addition, the Alaska cruise business has experienced throughput increases in each of the past 10 years, and now stands at 240 sailings and over 0.5 million passengers a year.[11]

As important as the port is to Vancouver's economy, its gateway role and its position in Pacific Rim trade networks, air travel is the most dynamic component of metropolitan Vancouver's gateway functions. Indeed, the quality and frequency of direct flights to major business centres is commonly seen as a crucial measure of a city's connectivity in international markets and its global status.[12]

Over the past decade, Vancouver International Airport has emerged as one of the leading aviation gateways in Canada and on the west coast of North America, ranking second to Toronto in Canada and Los Angeles on the West Coast. Vancouver International Airport handles about twice as much international traffic as Seattle's SeaTac Airport, a considerably larger facility.[13] The airport's business in the Asia-Pacific has more than doubled over the 1990s, again highlighting Vancouver's Pacific gateway role (Table 3.2).

There are a number of demand-related factors associated with the rapid expansion of Vancouver International Airport's Asia-Pacific traffic, including increases in business and tourist travel, high levels of immigration to Vancouver from Asian nations and other travel (for personal and family reasons) associated with this immigration. On the supply side a number of factors can be listed, including recent improvements to the airport (e.g., the current $500 million capital plan, which includes a second parallel runway and a new international terminal); the city's tourism and convention infrastructure (hotels and convention facilities), which has been considerably expanded; and the city's proximity to international tourist destinations such as the Whistler-Blackcomb resort – now rated the top ski resort in North America.[14]

The increased capacity of Pacific flights is another important supply-side factor that has contributed to the expansion of air passenger traffic between Vancouver and other Pacific Rim gateway cities. Table 3.3 shows the number of weekly flights between Vancouver and 11 major Asia-Pacific metropolitan centres offered by various carriers. Together, the 10 carriers offer 94 flights a week to these important destinations. Vancouver's Pacific Rim air network is

table 3.2

Increase in Total Passenger and Asia-Pacific Passenger Traffic at Vancouver International Airport, 1990-1996[1]

	Total passengers	Increase	Asia-Pacific passengers	Increase
	(000s)	(%)	(000s)	(%)
1990	9,911		790	
1991	9,388	-5.2	950	20.2
1992	9,935	5.8	1,095	15.3
1993	10,235	3.0	1,233	12.6
1994	10,830	5.8	1,407	14.1
1995	12,006	10.9	1,605	14.1
1996	14,037	16.9	1,848	15.1
1990-1996	4,126	41.6	1,058	133.9

[1] Enplaned and deplaned passengers

Source: Vancouver International Airport Authority, Vancouver International Airport Strategic Services.

also supplemented by numerous daily flights to Los Angeles and San Francisco, Sydney and Melbourne, and Auckland and Nadi.

There are, of course, direct and indirect economic benefits arising from the increasing volume of Pacific air traffic (e.g., fees, salaries and concessions), but the pattern of air connections shown in Table 3.3 also emphasizes the extent of Vancouver's contact with Asia-Pacific's principal business centres, notably Tokyo, Hong Kong, Seoul, Sydney and Singapore, and with emerging centres such as Kuala Lumpur and Shanghai. The 26 (soon to be 29) weekly direct, non-stop flights from Vancouver to Hong Kong are indicative of the particular importance of Vancouver's linkages with this strategic Asia-Pacific gateway centre.

Vancouver also has direct air connections with major European financial and business centres such as London, Paris and Milan. These intercontinental connections, coupled with a time zone location that enables overlapping contact with global financial centres in London, New York and Tokyo, represent an element of comparative advantage in banking and finance. Vancouver has been relatively underdeveloped as a financial centre, reflecting the primacy of Montreal and Toronto in this sector, and it still lacks the concentration of indigenous financial institutions typical of major regional financial centres. However, it has made significant gains as a financial intermediary centre. Its finance, banking and investment institutions include the Vancouver Stock Exchange, one of North America's principal exchanges for venture capital in the resource sector; major regional offices of Canada's "big six" chartered banks; about 20 foreign (or class B) banks; and VanCity Savings, one of Canada's largest financial co-ops.

table 3.3
Scheduled Direct Air Services Between Vancouver International Airport and Major Asia-Pacific and South-Pacific Centres, 1995 and 1996

		Summer 1995		**Summer 1996**	
Destination	**Airline**	**Flights per week**	**Aircraft**	**Flights per week**	**Aircraft**
Asia Pacific					
Beijing	Canadian Airlines	3	DC10	4	B767
Bangkok	Canadian Airlines	No service		6	B747/DC10
Hong Kong	Air Canada	No service		4	B747
	Canadian Airlines	12	B747/DC10	9	B747/DC10
	Cathay Pacific	8	B747	13	B747
Kuala Lumpur	Malaysia Airlines	No service		2	B747
Nagoya	Canadian Airlines	2	B747/DC10	5	B747/DC10
Osaka	Air Canada	7	A340	7	A340
Seoul	Air Canada	3	747	3	A340
	Korean Air	3	B747	3	B747
	Singapore Airlines	2	B747	2	B747
Manila	Philippine Airlines	No service		3	B747
Shanghai	Air China	1	B747	1	B747
Tokyo	Canadian Airlines	9	B747/DC10	9	B747/DC10
	Japan Airlines	12	B747	12	B747
Taipei	Canadian Airlines	4	B747/DC10	6	B747
	Mandarin Airlines	4	B747	5	B747
South Pacific					
Auckland	Canadian Airlines & Air New Zealand	4	DC10/B767	4	DC10/B767
Nadi	Canadian Airlines & Air New Zealand	1	DC10/B767	1	DC10/B767
Sydney	Canadian Airlines & Quantas	7	B747/DC10 B767	7	B747/DC10 B767

Source: Vancouver International Airport Authority, Sabre Reservations System.

Other Vancouver-based institutions are engaged in Asia-Pacific merchant banking and/or trade financing. Here the Japanese connection is quite significant: of the 12 major Japanese trading companies (or *sogo shosha)* that were established in Canada after the Second World War, no fewer than seven selected Vancouver as their local headquarters (the other five are located in Montreal or Toronto). This is consistent with the strong Japanese orientation of BC's trade; Japan represented less than five percent of Canada's exports in 1994, but accounted for fully 24.8 percent of BC's exports in that year.[15]

Perhaps the single most influential financial institution underpinning Vancouver's recent transformation as a Pacific Rim city and gateway centre is the Hongkong Bank of Canada (HKBC). In less than two decades, HKBC has become Canada's seventh largest bank. Technically a foreign banking subsidiary of the London-based Hong Kong and Shanghai Banking Corporation, HKCB stands out from other class B or foreign banks domiciled in Canada by virtue of its size, asset base, links to the Asian market, retail network and association with BC business people, especially, but by no means exclusively, those of Chinese ethnicity. Headquartered in Vancouver, HKBC gives the city a measure of strength in the Canadian financial system and provides important links to Asia-Pacific markets. With assets of $17.6 billion and over 100 branches across Canada, HKBC is the only foreign bank rated by the Dominion Bond Rating Service without reference to its parent company.[16]

The growth of HKBC's operations in Vancouver outside the CBD reflects the strength of the bank in retail markets as well as the recent dispersion of the Chinese community and its commercial operations, which has led to the expansion of the Chinatown, South Granville and Richmond branches. For instance, the Chinatown branch of HKBC serves over 20,000 clients, more than 1000 of whom are reported to have millionaire status.[17] According to the branch manager, 70 percent of the city's developers are Chinese, and the HKBC "is financing 70 percent of them."[18] Even allowing for some degree of overstatement, these estimates underscore the status of HKBC in Vancouver's burgeoning financial sector and its role as capital provider for local development and key institutional connecting point between Vancouver and the Asia-Pacific.

Other, smaller niche-level institutions also perform strategic service functions (Figure 3.2: III). They tend to be cooperative ventures between business interests and the public sector. Vancouver's International Financial Centre (IFC Vancouver) is one example. Created simultaneously with a similar agency in Montreal, it involved federal and provincial legislative initiatives to allow international transactions to be undertaken without Canadian tax implications.[19] Another example is the BC International Maritime Centre, which was established in 1991 with a view to encouraging and assisting foreign shipping line owners to transfer their head operations to Vancouver by providing them with the opportunity to establish domicile in a politically stable jurisdiction while exempting them from Canadian taxes on profits earned from international operations.[20] At least six Hong Kong shipping line owners have applied to do so.

Vancouver's Service Exports and Pacific Rim Markets

Consistent with the development of an advanced, highly tertiarized urban economy is the expansion of the service sector's role in the metropolitan export base. In many cities, the loss of manufacturing export capacity associated with the decline of traditional industrial production has been partially offset by the growth of service exports. These exports occur in a variety of forms including direct sales of specialized services to clients outside the producing region;[21] services embodied in goods and commodities (e.g., the knowledge or informational component of computer software); capital (e.g., fees, investments, commissions), banking and financial services; and services consumed in the producing region by non-residents (e.g., tourist facilities, convention services and education of foreign students in local colleges and universities).

Service exports are particularly important for global gateways such as London and New York that have experienced massive contractions in their traditional manufacturing and port functions but continue to have the largest concentrations of head office, banking and financial activities.[22] However, they are also increasingly important to dynamic, medium-sized metropolitan regions. For example, in a large sample study of the Seattle-Central Puget Sound region conducted in the mid-1980s, Beyers discovered that more workers depended on the export of services than of manufactured goods, despite the presence of industrial mega-firms such as Boeing and Weyerhaeuser.[23]

In the case of Vancouver, the growth of service exports not only reflects an advanced stage of metropolitan tertiarization and the growing tendency of firms to contract out specialized services like accounting and legal services, it also illustrates (1) the city's comparative advantage in specialized services production, (2) the complementarity between its producer services and gateway functions, (3) its accelerating orientation toward the Asia-Pacific markets, and (4) the key role of immigrants in this context.

As observed in the previous chapter, many of the service firms active in export markets initially catered only to local or domestic markets. In many cases, Vancouver business service firms (e.g., consulting engineers, management consultants and geological firms) were established specifically to provide services to corporations associated with the expansion of BC's resource sector. Other firms, notably accounting and legal firms, established locations in the downtown core in order to provide specialized services to the head offices of major resource corporations. At the same time, property developers in the industrial, commercial and investment (ICI) sector catered to the needs of firms wishing to locate in Vancouver, either with purpose-built or "spec-built" premises. Over the past two decades, many of these service firms have developed substantial export capacity.

The increasing export orientation of specialized service firms, and in particular their gradual penetration of markets in the Asia-Pacific region, can be illustrated with reference to five empirical studies undertaken since the early

1970s. The results of these survey-based studies point to several distinct stages in the development of export activity by Vancouver service firms.

First, a major input-output (I-O) study by Davis in 1971, which examined firms representing one-quarter of metropolitan Vancouver's total employment, revealed that the vast majority of services (about 88 percent) were destined for the local and provincial markets (in almost equal proportions).[24] These findings reflect the main economic role of Vancouver at the time as a regional service point and control centre for the province's resource economy with relatively little presence in international markets (or even domestic markets outside BC).

The second survey, conducted by Hutton and Ley in the mid-1980s, showed that there had been considerable growth in Vancouver's export of services to other provinces and to foreign markets. In particular, 11 percent of the firms surveyed reported sales to the Asia-Pacific.[25] This trend was also identified in a survey by Barnes and Hayter.[26] Both these studies found a push-pull dynamic motivating service exports: the push factors involved concerns about the future of the BC economy – particularly the prospect of a contracting resource sector – following the severe downturn of the early 1980s, while the pull factors centered on the dynamism of new markets in the Asia-Pacific.[27]

Davis and Hutton's 1990 survey of 251 business service firms (supplemented by some 30 structured interviews) confirmed the powerful attraction of Asia-Pacific markets for Vancouver companies. Of 251 firms surveyed, no fewer than 64 reported sales in the Asia-Pacific, including several engineering, management consulting and computer service firms.[28] Similarly, an earlier survey of 133 environmental industry firms in BC "overwhelmingly indicated that the markets that provide the greatest export opportunity are in the Asia-Pacific region."[29]

This last survey underscores the strong interdependency of the environment and economic development in the Vancouver case. Many of the firms that were initially established to provide environmental enhancement systems and programmes in this locality – known for its concern for ecological integrity – have subsequently looked to the Asia-Pacific as a particularly promising market. These environmental service firms now provide environmental impact analysis for projects in places like China and Indonesia and constitute an important element of Vancouver's competitive advantage in specialized service production and trade, both regionally and internationally.

Kilborn Engineering (Pacific Division) is an example of a Vancouver company engaged in this type of activity in the Asia-Pacific. The company is involved in several major projects (in the $100-500 million range) in Russia, China, Indonesia, Vietnam and Thailand. Prior to its export success, the firm had been working on important domestic projects, including the Quintette Mine in northern BC.[30] In a similar vein, long-established Vancouver architect Bing Thom is currently engaged in major projects in China, notably a new port community for Dalian.

In addition to private sector marketing efforts, public sector trade promotion policies have also contributed to the growing presence of Vancouver service companies in the Asia-Pacific region. About one-third of the firms in the 1990 Davis-Hutton study confirmed that government trade promotion efforts were significant in the initiation of export marketing in the Asia-Pacific realm.[31] More recently, the BC Trade Development Corporation, a provincial agency, has collaborated with the Consulting Engineers of BC to form the Asia Marketing Group. This approach draws on the European example of small and medium-sized service firms forming flexible networks of complementary establishments to market themselves more effectively internationally.[32] By "pooling their expertise and resources and maximising their financial investment, companies can get benefits that may have been previously denied to them by virtue of their size or other limitations."[33] The successful export marketing of services depends, therefore, on realizing economies of scope as well as economies of scale.

The Role of Immigrants in Service Exports

High levels of immigration from the Asia-Pacific nations over the past 15-20 years have also played a significant role in the growth of Vancouver's service exports.[34] These immigrants have contributed in a variety of ways by establishing new businesses engaged wholly or partially in export trade; enhancing the expertise and exportable specializations of existing firms; generally increasing the entrepreneurial quality of metropolitan Vancouver's human capital base; and enriching the commercial networks between Vancouver and their countries of origin.[35]

First, many immigrants to Vancouver have established new businesses with (initial or developed) trade potential. Compared with other Canadian cities, Vancouver's immigrant population includes larger proportions of individuals in the "investor" or "entrepreneur" category (see the introduction to this volume), as well as large contingents with strong entrepreneurial skills and trading traditions (for example, Cantonese and Punjabis).

Second, immigrants have significantly augmented the expertise of existing firms and have stimulated their export efforts. These include immigrants employed in export-active professions and trading companies. Many of Vancouver's accounting, legal and management consulting firms, for example, have designated Asian practice units, frequently staffed with immigrant professionals.[36] A recent Australian study of the contribution of Asian immigrants to the export of services found a similar pattern. It estimated that Australian firms active in Asia-Pacific markets have on average 3.5 times as many employees of Asian ethnicity as those not active in those markets.[37]

Third, a somewhat less direct contribution of immigrants to the export of services relates to their overall enhancement of entrepreneurship in metropolitan Vancouver's human capital base. The suggestion here is that with the increasing multiculturalism of urban societies comes an increase in productive diversity.[38] The export skills and trading propensities of new immigrant groups can, in essence, spill over to the general business population. This form of spillover is facilitated by partnerships, informal meetings, the media, bilateral and other business associations and "social learning" over time.

The transmission of entrepreneurship and incentives to trade are also enhanced by the operation of complex networks (family, cultural and commercial) among immigrants and their societies of origin. These networks usually take the form of active production, exchange and distribution systems, but also include incidental flows of market intelligence of many kinds. Given the nature of new and emerging Asian enclaves and groups in metropolitan Vancouver, these networking effects are important. However, immigration patterns are having an even broader impact on the trajectory of Vancouver's growth and change.

The Role of Asia-Pacific Immigration in Vancouver's Transformation

The migration of peoples over vast distances has been a recurrent feature of human development since prehistoric times, including, as we have already observed, the settlement of aboriginal peoples (or First Nations) in BC. Migration has been a central force in the formation of Canada, from the establishment of New France to the massive inflows following the two world wars and the current wave of new immigrants.

Over the past five centuries, international migration has been a crucial element in the most important periods of history, including colonialism, industrialization, the rise of nation states and the emergence of global capitalism.[39] However, the extent of current population movements across national boundaries is so significant that the last decade of the present century and at least the first decade of the new millennium are being referred to as "the age of international migration."[40]

Although levels of immigration in Canada as a whole have been high for much of the twentieth century, we can identify three principal factors that differentiate the current phase of immigration from other phases in this century:

- *Urban focus and degree of concentration.* A significant proportion of immigrants to Canada in the earlier part of this century settled in agricultural regions and small communities, reflecting the country's agrarian character. This is no longer the case; immigrants now settle mainly in urban areas. Toronto and Vancouver, with about 20 percent of the national population, have accommodated 50 percent or more of Canada's immigrants in recent years.[41]

- *Origin of recent immigrants.* The highly Eurocentric character of immigration in earlier migration periods has given way to a much more diverse pattern since the early 1980s, with the increase in visible minority groups being particularly noteworthy. It has been estimated that the share of visible minorities in the Toronto and Vancouver CMAs will at least double between 1986 and 2001, attaining levels of 45 percent and 39 percent, respectively.
- *Socio-economic status.* Earlier waves of immigrants to Canada were, for the most part, drawn from the less well off and even impoverished segments of originating societies. While recent cohorts of immigrants still include poor people as well as refugees, they also include much wealthier individuals, some of whom have entered under various business categories (investor and entrepreneurial immigrants).[42]

The Pattern of Asian Immigration to Vancouver

An important feature of current international immigration to Canada is the differences in ethnic origin among groups of immigrants destined for various regions of the country and their impact on the ethnic profile of the particular cities and city-regions where they choose to settle. With respect to the two leading metropolitan receiving areas, for example, Toronto's immigrants include large numbers of individuals from the Caribbean and Latin America, as well as Asia, while the ethnic profile of Vancouver's recent immigrants is predominantly Asian.

The impact of these different immigration profiles is clearly reflected in Table 3.4, which depicts Asian ethnicity (both in absolute numbers and as a proportion of total population) in five major Canadian CMAs: Vancouver, Toronto, Montreal, Edmonton and Calgary in 1991. The proportion of residents of Asian ethnicity ranges from less than four percent in Montreal to close to 21 percent in Vancouver. The proportion of Vancouver residents reporting Asian ethnicity in the 1991 census (including single and multiple ethnicity responses) exceeds that of Toronto residents by five percent, again confirming Vancouver's status as a leading host society for Asian immigrants in Canada. More recent data based on the 1996 mid-census results indicate that more than one-third (35 percent) of Vancouver's population is foreign-born. Of the 633,745 immigrant residents in Vancouver CMA, the largest proportion is

table 3.4

Asian Ethnicity in Selected Canadian Metropolitan Areas, 1991[1]

	Calgary	Edmonton	Montreal	Toronto	Vancouver
Ethnic origin (Asian)	(000s)				
Punjabi	1.2	1.5	1.0	7.6	7.6
East Indian	17.0	17.6	20.1	166.7	72.5
Pakistani	2.5	2.3	4.7	20.7	3.2
Sri Lankan	0.5	0.5	4.1	22.5	0.8
Chinese	36.1	36.3	38.4	252.4	178.8
Filipino	8.7	7.9	11.0	72.4	28.4
Cambodian	0.9	1.1	7.2	1.9	1.1
Laotian	0.4	0.4	3.6	3.0	0.7
Vietnamese	7.3	6.8	19.3	24.6	10.1
Japanese	2.9	1.8	2.4	17.1	19.8
Korean	1.4	2.3	2.6	22.2	8.8
Total population of Asian ethnic origin	78.9	78.5	114.1	611.1	331.9
Total population	754.0	839.9	3,127.2	3,893.0	1,602.0
Population of Asian ethnic origin as % of total population	10.5%	9.3%	3.7%	15.7%	20.7%

[1] Single and multiple ethnicity responses

Source: Data provided by the Asia Pacific Foundation of Canada based on the 1991 Census of Canada.

from Hong Kong (86,215, or 13.6 percent), followed by the United Kingdom (76,145, or 11.9 percent), China (72,910, or 11.5 percent), and India (53,475, or 8.4 percent).[43]

Although Vancouver has been a destination choice for immigrants from Asia-Pacific nations since its inception, there has been a pronounced acceleration of this trend since the 1960s. Table 3.5 shows the top 10 source countries of immigrants to BC in 1994, and the annual rankings of these countries in 1980 and since 1990.[44] In 1980, Vietnam was the leading source country, with India ranking second and England, the dominant source country for most of Vancouver's early years, third.[45]

Since 1990, Hong Kong has been the most important source of foreign immigrants to BC, with twice and in some years even three times the number of immigrants from the second leading source country (China in 1991, Taiwan in 1992, and India in 1993 and 1994). In 1994, Hong Kong immigrants (16,159) accounted for about one-third of BC's total immigration (48,529). The dramatic increase in international immigration to the province over the past decade and a half – it has almost doubled since 1980 – has contributed significantly to its overall population growth.

table 3.5

The Ten Principal Source Countries of Immigrants to British Columbia, 1980 and 1990-1994

Country of origin	1994	Rank	1993	Rank	1992	Rank	1991	Rank	1990	Rank	1980	Rank
	(000s)											
Hong Kong	16.2	1	11.3	1	10.1	1	6.3	1	7.7	1	1.7	6
India	5.5	2	6.0	2	3.2	8	3.5	3	2.9	2	3.1	2
Taiwan	4.8	3	5.9	3	4.1	2	2.6	4	1.7	4	0.2	-
Philippines	3.8	4	3.7	4	2.5	4	2.0	5	1.9	3	1.0	7
China	3.0	5	2.2	5	2.2	5	3.5	2	1.4	7	2.2	4
England	1.4	6	-	-	-	-	-	-	-	-	2.6	3
US	1.4	7	1.7	7	1.5	7	1.3	7	1.3	6	2.1	5
South Africa	1.3	8	-	-	-	-	-	-	-	-	-	-
South Korea	0.9	9	0.8	10	-	-	-	-	-	-	-	-
Vietnam	0.8	10	0.9	9	0.9	9	1.0	9	0.9	8	4.0	1

Source: BC Stats, *Immigration Highlights* (Victoria: Ministry of Government Services, Government of British Columbia, April 1995).

The large and growing contingent of Hong Kong citizens in Vancouver and BC generally is to a great extent linked to concerns about political, economic and social stability in the Crown Colony following its reversion to Chinese control in 1997. Since the signing of the Sino-British accord in 1984, which confirmed and set the terms for China's reassertion of control over Hong Kong, almost half a million of Hong Kong's six million inhabitants have applied for passports from offshore jurisdictions, principally Canada, the United States, Australia, New Zealand and Britain. Of the 430,000 Hong Kong residents who have obtained passports and visas from other countries since 1987, about 67,700 (or almost one-sixth) have arrived in BC, with the vast majority settling in Vancouver.[46] Vancouver is clearly one of the preferred destinations of Hong Kong citizens, a preference that has far-reaching and multi-faceted implications.[47]

There has also been a large increase in Taiwanese immigration over the past 15 years (see Table 3.5). In 1980, only 230 Taiwanese settled in Vancouver, but by 1993 the annual total had increased to almost 6,000 – more than a twenty-fold increase – and by 1996 it had reached 9,000. This growing influx of Taiwanese citizens, along with ethnic Chinese from the Philippines, Malaysia and elsewhere, adds to the overall growth of residents of Chinese ethnicity in Vancouver (although there are, of course, significant socio-cultural differences between the largely Cantonese Hong Kong immigrants and the other groups). Some estimates place the Taiwanese expatriate population in Vancouver at about 40,000.[48] This figure is certainly large enough to provide a certain "critical mass" for a strong, vibrant and distinctive Taiwanese community as expressed in business and social organizations and other reflections of collective identity.

As important as the ethnic Chinese are to the formation of Vancouver's new social profile, the role and presence of other Asian groups should also be acknowledged. The South Asian population of Vancouver (over 75,000), including Indians, Pakistanis, Bangladeshis and Sri Lankans, has made a distinctive impact on metropolitan Vancouver's social morphology, economic base and cultural landscape. South Asians are less well represented in Vancouver's metropolitan core than the Chinese, but are prominent in communities south and southeast of Vancouver, in Richmond and Surrey, and in the central Fraser Valley, just outside the GVRD. Many South Asians are engaged in professional, commercial and industrial endeavours, while a substantial number of Punjabis are agricultural workers, representing continuity with their occupations in their original homeland in northern India.

Impacts of Asian Immigration on Vancouver's Transformation

The dramatic expansion of immigration from the Asia-Pacific region, especially over the past 15 to 20 years, has provided a major growth impulse for metropolitan Vancouver in terms of population, employment, income, demand for housing and public services, production and exports.

Foreign immigration has also been an important agent of transformational change. For instance, Sassen has found a strong link between immigration, economic restructuring and the emergence of the post-industrial city. While some immigrants enter professional and managerial occupations, which are characteristic of the upper echelons of the urban service labour force in advanced service economies, many others perform the low-skilled, low-wage functions that are also concomitant features of post-industrial societies. Because of their responsiveness to opportunity and demand, immigrants "are almost akin to a rapid deployment force" in the restructured, post-industrial urban economy.[49]

To identify the complex and multi-faceted relationships between immigration and Vancouver's contemporary transformation, we refer to the R^5 framework of metropolitan change introduced in chapter 1. Figure 3.3, which provides a summary of the impacts of immigration and foreign investment on Vancouver, underscores the crucial interdependencies between immigration and each of the five principal dimensions of structural change relevant to the Vancouver case.

It is important to distinguish between the effects of immigration and investment. By no means are all immigrants wealthy,[50] and a considerable portion of

figure 3.3
Asia-Pacific Investment and Immigration and the Transformation of Metropolitan Vancouver

	Immigration	**Investment**
Economic RESTRUCTURING (urban economy, export base, labour force)	Growth of human capital Enhancement of entrepreneurship in production, trade and small business Increase in market intelligence, economic responsiveness and resilience	New capital formation – production and infrastructure Stimulus to growth in banking and finance Stimulus to growth in business and other intermediate services
Social RECOMPOSITION (social morphology, class, community)	Greater ethnic diversity and cultural enrichment Introduction of new values, preferences Emergence of new cultural groups, social institutions, business networks	New contingent of capital owners Displacement effects among more vulnerable classes and communities Rise of new socio-economic hegemony?
Spatial RECONFIGURATION (metropolitan structure)	New ethnic enclaves and neighbourhoods Impetus to suburban growth (selective) New *consumption landscapes* in metro core and suburbs	Internationalization of the CBD Megaprojects and transformation of the inner city New production spaces (e.g., inner city garment district)
Physical RECONSTRUCTION (urban form and the built environment)	Reconstruction of residential landscapes New cultural landmarks and institutions Metropolitan *densification* or intensification	Transformative impact of large capital investments Ethnic retail centres and markets (e.g., Cantonese, Punjabi, Filipino) Introduction of new architectural motifs
External REORIENTATION (linkages and connectivity)	Growth of *mobilized diasporas* Expansion of linkages between Vancouver and originating societies, cultures, communities Vancouver as a key node in international network of diasporas	Vancouver's development as gateway centre Acceleration of Vancouver's integration within Pacific Rim capital markets and investment flows Vancouver as *relay* or *transmission* point in Asia-Pacific urban system and information networks

the capital flows that are transforming Vancouver are in the form of foreign direct investment (FDI) from offshore corporations. There are, nevertheless, significant connections between foreign immigration and investment. With respect to economic development, for example, DeVoretz found that each investor-class immigrant to BC brought in an average of $2.1 million.[51] Over the recent period, this combination of immigration and capital inflow has contributed over $4 billion in new income to the BC economy (mostly in Vancouver), "an investment pool that helped BC escape the recession [of the early 1990s]."[52] Although much of this investment is channelled into residential development rather than business or industry, it nonetheless represents a significant expansion of Vancouver's capital base.

These large capital inflows from the Asia-Pacific – in the form of FDI from corporations and investor-class immigrants and financial assets brought in by numerous independent-class immigrants – are also linked to another important facet of economic restructuring. They create demand for the mediation and management of financial assets on a very large scale, which in turn stimulates growth in Vancouver's financial and producer services. In a recent review of the "invisible empire of the overseas Chinese," Seagrave predicted that the build-up of Vancouver's capital base derived from FDI and immigrants and the associated institutional impacts "will soon transform Vancouver into a leading world financial centre, as the Overseas Chinese have done for Hong Kong and Singapore."[53] This prediction may be overstated, but it illustrates the correlation between foreign investment from the Asia-Pacific and the expansion of Vancouver's (hitherto underdeveloped) status as a banking and financial centre.

There are other less well known but nevertheless important implications of Asian immigration for Vancouver's economic restructuring that should be mentioned. Over the past decade or so, there has been some diversification of immigrant investments and FDI into industrial development. The role of Asian immigrants in the revival and growth of Vancouver's garment district (concentrated in the inner city and east end) is well known, but there are also examples in more advanced production industries. For instance, immigrants from Hong Kong and Taiwan (and to a somewhat lesser extent Singapore and Malaysia) are currently engaged in several manufacturing industries, especially in the inner suburban municipality of Richmond. Examples include a television assembly plant built on Annacis Island by Hong Kong's Great Wall Electronics that will employ 250 workers; MTC Electronic Technologies in Richmond, which manufactures fax machines; and Qualidux Industrial, a plastics plant in the inner suburban municipality of North Vancouver controlled by the Ting family of Hong Kong.[54]

As significant as these economic impacts clearly are, arguably the most consequential implications of immigration for Vancouver's transformation are social and cultural. The scale and pace of immigration from the Asia-Pacific nations have effectively restructured metropolitan Vancouver's social morphology, especially in terms of ethnic diversity. This social recomposition is more than a statistical observation, it has enormous transformational implications.

The socio-cultural effects of foreign immigration on Vancouver result from differences between immigrants and the host society in terms of behaviour, values, tastes and preferences, social organization (at the level of communities, extended families and households), occupational choices, religion and beliefs. It is exceedingly difficult to generalize about the impacts of immigration on Vancouver, given the important cultural contrasts among, as well as within, different ethnic groups (e.g., class, occupation and other attributes); the "blurring" of inter-cultural distinctions because of assimilation and integration; and the importance of individual characteristics.

While it is beyond the scope of this study to provide a detailed analysis of the impact of immigration on Vancouver's socio-cultural milieu, we can identify some of the principal implications for Vancouver's social composition.

- *Diversity.* The nature and scale of immigration to Vancouver has significantly enhanced the ethnic diversity of the city and the metropolitan region as a whole. Vancouver is not only part of the trading systems and urban networks of the Pacific Basin, it is swiftly and visibly becoming an Asian city.
- *Class.* While the impact of immigration upon Vancouver's social structure is highly complex, worth highlighting is the contribution of Asian immigrants to the rise of a new entrepreneurial class. This new entrepreneurial cohort differs markedly from the long-established business elite composed mainly of resource corporation executives (Figure 3.3) and owners of capital.
- *Culture.* The impact of Asian immigration on Vancouver's culture has been profound. It is manifested not only in important institutional symbols (e.g, the Suzhou classical Chinese garden downtown, the Sikh temple on Marine Drive in South-East Vancouver and the Nitobe Japanese Garden at UBC), but also in popular culture (e.g., the "Cantopop" vocalists favoured by Vancouver's Chinese population that feature star performers from Hong Kong and the Pearl Delta Region).[55]
- *Organization.* The large-scale Asian immigration of the past two decades has stimulated new institutional and organizational responses among the individual ethno-cultural groups. These include (1) agencies designed to facilitate the adaptation of new immigrants to the host society, such as SUCCESS and MOSAIC;[56] (2) social clubs that allow members to maintain cultural contact and to develop networks; (3) religious institutions which, in addition to enabling the expression of faith and observance of

collective ritual, are crucial to the maintenance of ethno-cultural identity; and (4) business organizations, including bilateral business and professional associations that constitute important networking institutions.

- *Connectivity.* Immigration also helps establish and enhance socio-cultural networks between the host city and the immigrants' societies of origin. Thus, in addition to transforming the city's internal social composition, immigration can considerably reinforce the external reorientation process.

The growth of new immigrant enclaves and communities in suburban municipalities represents another important facet of Vancouver's reconfiguration. The increase in the number of immigrants of Chinese ethnicity is a defining feature of Richmond's social morphology, culture and economy, whereas South Asians (and to a lesser extent Chinese) immigrants are central to the development of the outer suburban municipality of Surrey. As a result, business and social networks linking Vancouver's Asian communities with other ethnic enclaves (as well as to their original homelands in East, Southeast and South Asia) have been further enhanced, thus adding another element of connectivity between Vancouver and the Asia-Pacific and contributing significantly to the city's spatial reconfiguration (see chapter 4), economic restructuring and social recomposition. This (relatively) new suburban phase of immigrant settlement is evident in a few other North American cities, notably Toronto and Los Angeles. In Los Angeles, Chinese immigrants have formed a new "transnational business enclave" in the San Gabriel Valley, which has been described as an important node in the international Chinese economy "linking Vancouver, Sydney, Singapore, Kuala Lumpur, Bangkok and Manila."[57]

The pace, scale and complexity of change associated with Vancouver's engagement with the Asia-Pacific suggest the emergence of a new urban identity. At the moment, Vancouver exhibits a kind of socio-cultural dualism, with a dynamic, highly entrepreneurial Asia-Pacific society (or set of societies, each distinct in many ways) superimposed upon the established European base. However, significant integration (and some degree of assimilation) will likely occur over time.

Public Policy Responses

We have described the increasing importance of Vancouver's role as a Pacific Rim gateway, its deepening engagement with Pacific markets, cultures and urban networks and its socio-cultural transformation. Another important element to consider is the role of public policy in this process. Indeed, it can be argued that federal and provincial legislation, programmes and policy initiatives are leading factors in Vancouver's emergence as a Pacific city. At the federal level, we can cite relatively open foreign immigration policies, external market development and export trade support programmes and investments in infrastructure (e.g., the City's trade and convention centre) as influential policies and interventions. Bilateral air travel agreements between the federal government and Asia-Pacific nations have also favoured Vancouver's gateway role in recent years.

The BC government has also actively supported Vancouver's roles as a Pacific gateway city and node of the Pacific urban system. During the 1960s and 1970s, provincial governments encouraged large infrastructure projects in the province's interior (including highways, rail connections, hydroelectric projects) in an effort to open up the vast, resource-rich hinterland, but the 1980s saw a significant shift in focus toward Vancouver and the metropolitan southwest of the province. Here, important provincial government initiatives included funding for Expo 86, the development of a 22-kilometre fixed-rail rapid transit system, a 60,000 seat stadium and exhibition centre and a series of promotional policies undertaken (in conjunction with the federal government and local authorities) under the rubric of the Asia-Pacific Initiative.

While the higher levels of government wield the big "policy levers" in support of Vancouver's Asia-Pacific roles and activities, various local governments in the metropolitan region have also been active. The GVRD has for the most part focused on growth management, strategic land use, transportation, environmental enhancement and shaping the regional structure. It has also played a modest role in informational services and liaison among municipalities in Pacific Rim marketing.

A number of municipalities, notably the inner suburbs of Richmond and Burnaby, have also been active in promoting Pacific Rim trade and Asia-Pacific cultural events. The policies of the City of Vancouver, however, offer the most instructive case study. The City's policy approach toward the development of Vancouver's role and opportunities in the Asia-Pacific over the past decade and a half can be described in terms of three more or less distinct periods.

In the first phase, prior to 1980, the City was generally content to have the provincial and federal governments act on its behalf in the area of Asia-Pacific investments and initiatives – with the exception of a sister city relationship with Yokohama, characterized largely by routine ceremonial events and exchanges. For instance, the initial mandate of the Economic Development Office (EDO), established in 1978, was not to pursue opportunities in foreign markets, much less to promote Vancouver's Pacific Rim involvement, but rather to stem the (perceived, rather than actual) flight of industry to the suburbs.

The second phase began with the election of Michael Harcourt as mayor in 1980. This is when the City of Vancouver actively started to explore opportunities in the Pacific realm. A municipal economic strategy, among the first in Canada, was approved by Vancouver City Council in 1983. It emphasized the benefits to be derived from supporting Vancouver's Pacific gateway functions (port, airport, finance, education and communications), promoting the export of services as well as resource commodities and establishing new relationships with other urban centres of the Pacific Basin. The latter objective was realized in part by forming sister relationships with Los Angeles and Guangzhou, and by designating other Pacific cities, such as Hong Kong, Singapore and Kuala Lumpur, as "strategic" to Vancouver's interests. During the early 1980s, the City sponsored or participated in a succession of business, trade and investment missions to these cities in cooperation with higher levels of government, the private sector and the community as a whole.

Reflecting Harcourt's personal view of Vancouver's potential in the Pacific realm, the City also engaged in what Patrick Smith has termed "para-diplomacy."[58] Mayor Harcourt and senior City officials, in partnership with the Montreal Urban Community, successfully lobbied higher levels of government to enact legislation creating international banking centres (against Toronto's strenuous objections). The City also actively encouraged the negotiation of bilateral air agreements between Canada and Asia-Pacific nations, with a view to expanding the roster of Pacific cities with which Vancouver enjoyed direct air connections. For instance, Harcourt met with senior officials of Singapore Airlines and the Canadian High Commissioner in Singapore in 1986 to help press the case for a direct link between Vancouver and this key Southeast Asian business and financial centre.

Following Harcourt's departure into provincial politics after the municipal elections of 1986, the City, under Mayor Gordon Campbell, began to articulate a new policy approach toward the Asia-Pacific – the third phase. Under the Campbell administration, the City continued to support trade, investment and cultural relationships with Asia, but with sharply reduced budgets and discernibly less conviction. The City was generally content to leave the more strategic elements of Vancouver-Asia-Pacific relations to higher levels of government and business and began to shift its attention to the accommodation of the new immigrant populations from Asia and elsewhere. In particular, the City was increasingly concerned about its capacity to integrate the large inflows of foreign and domestic immigrants (as were the suburban municipalities, notably Richmond). It began to explore models of social interaction in the context of an increasingly multicultural and, more specifically, Asian society.

This new policy direction was influenced by the view that external trade development is the responsibility of federal and provincial governments. There was also a growing sense of confidence among city councillors and in the community at large that following a decade of substantial growth in Asia-Pacific trade, investment and immigration, Vancouver had achieved sufficient critical mass in terms of connectivity and status in the dynamic Pacific realm. It was argued that the growth of infrastructural, financial and human capital resulting from the immigration and investment flows of the 1980s and early 1990s had given Vancouver a considerable competitive advantage and a strategic niche in the Pacific urban hierarchy. Vancouver was now considered an "active participant" among Pacific markets and societies, rather than merely a "facilitator."[59]

The City gradually directed its policy attention toward the management of internal issues, focusing on the problems commonly associated with rapid urban growth and change as well as the particular pressures resulting from the *in situ* impacts of Asia-Pacific trade, immigration and investment. This involved reallocating resources to social planning, adopting regulatory rather than developmental policy approaches and giving less priority to economic policies and programmes.

Notes

1. With respect to terminology in this chapter, the Pacific Rim (or Pacific Basin) is a geographical term (with somewhat weaker applications as an economic or trading entity) that encompasses the nations of the western and eastern Pacific, i.e., North and Central America, the Pacific South American nations, Northeast Asia (Russian Far East, Japan, North Korea and South Korea), the Peoples' Republic of China, Taiwan, Hong Kong, Southeast Asia and Australasia. The Asia-Pacific realm includes the nations of Northeast and Southeast Asia, as well as southern Asia (principally India, Pakistan, Bangladesh, Sri Lanka and the smaller Himalayan states).

2. K. Bolan, "Chinese First Settled in B.C. 200 Years Ago, Exhibit Shows," *The Vancouver Sun*, September 27, 1995, p. B6.

3. See S. MacLeod, D.W. Edgington and T.G. McGee, "Vancouver on the Edge: Vancouver and the Outside World," in T.G. McGee (ed.), *Vancouver and Yokohama, Emerging Cities in the Pacific Rim* (Vancouver: UBC / Yokohama: Yokohama City University, 1993).

4. M. Douglass, "The Future of Cities on the Pacific Rim," in M.P. Smith (ed.), *Pacific Rim Cities in the World Economy: Comparative Urban and Community Research*, Vol. 2 (New Brunswick, NJ: Transaction Publishers, 1989), pp. 9-67.

5. T.R. Puri, "Urban Development: New Towns Around the Pacific Rim," paper presented at the Fifth Annual Conference of the Pacific Rim Council on Urban Development, San Francisco, October 1993.

6. D.W. Edgington and M.A. Goldberg, "Vancouver: Canada's Gateway to the Rim," in E.J. Blakely and R.J. Stimson (eds.), *New Cities of the Pacific Rim* (London: Routledge, forthcoming), chap. 5.

7. G. Will, "Consular Corps Find Province a Busy Place," *The Vancouver Sun*, June 6, 1995.

8. P.J. Rimmer, "Megacities, Multi-layered Networks and Development Corridors in the Pacific Economic Zone," *Proceedings of the Third Annual Conference of the Pacific Rim Council on Urban Development* (Vancouver: CHS, 1991).

9. Edgington and Goldberg, "Vancouver: Canada's Gateway to the Rim."

10. A. Daniels, "Port Acquires New Asia Link," *The Vancouver Sun*, January 3, 1996, p. A1.

11. Vancouver Port Corporation, *2010 Port Land Use Management Plan* (Vancouver: VPC, January 1994).

12. S. Sassen, *The Global City* (Princeton, NJ: Princeton University Press, 1991).

13. Edgington and Goldberg, "Vancouver: Canada's Gateway to the Rim."

14. This includes rankings by the leading American magazine *Skiworld* and Japanese tour operators.

15. Edgington and Goldberg, "Vancouver: Canada's Gateway to the Rim."

16. "DBRS rates Hongkong Bank of Canada," *The Globe and Mail*, Report on Business, November 14, 1995, p. 3.

17. "Hongkong Bank Eyes Taiwanese Cash in B.C. with New Branches," *Pacific Business* (October/November 1995), p. 14.

18. "Hongkong Bank Eyes Taiwanese Cash."

19. M.A. Goldberg, R. Helsley and M. Levi, *Factors Influencing the Development of Financial Centres* (Vancouver: Faculty of Commerce and Business Administration, University of BC, 1988). The City of Toronto vigorously opposed the federal government's IFC legislation on the grounds that it discriminated against Toronto, Canada's principal banking and financial centre. Part of the government's rationale for the legislation was the notion that Vancouver would offer a special window for Canada on the Asia-Pacific, while Montreal could perform an analogous role in the French-speaking nations of *la Francophonie*.

20. A. Daniels, "Tide Turns in Favour of Shipowners: Hong Kong Firms Closer to Moving Staff, Jobs Here," *The Vancouver Sun*, March 12, 1993, p. D1.

21. These flows consist of transactions between firms or agencies, but a substantial volume of specialized informational inputs is also transmitted between units of the same firm located in different centres.

22. See, for example, P.W. Daniels, "Foreign Banks and Metropolitan Development: A Comparison of London and New York," *Tijdschrift voor Economische en Sociale Geografie*, Vol. 78

(1987), pp. 269-87; and M.P. Drennan, "Gateway Cities: The Metropolitan Source of US Producer Service Exports," *Urban Studies*, Vol. 29 (1992), pp. 217-35.

23. W.B. Beyers, *The Service Economy: Export of Services in the Central Puget Sound Region* (Seattle: Central Puget Sound Economic Development Department, 1985).

24. H.C. Davis, *An Interindustry Study of the Metropolitan Vancouver Economy*, Urban Land Economics Report No. 6 (Vancouver: Faculty of Commerce and Business Administration, University of BC, 1976).

25. D.F. Ley and T.A. Hutton, "Vancouver's Corporate Complex and Producer Service Sector: Linkages and Divergence in a Provincial Staple Economy," *Regional Studies*, Vol. 21 (1987), pp. 413-24.

26. R. Hayter and T. Barnes, "Innis' Staple Theory, Exports, and Recession: B.C., 1981-86," *Economic Geography*, Vol. 66 (1990), pp. 156-73.

27. As Peter Daniels has recently observed, the dramatic growth of manufacturing output and trade among Asia-Pacific nations has not, in most cases, been matched by similar growth in the advanced business service industries, thus providing opportunities for export-capable service firms based in other jurisdictions such as Vancouver. (At the same time, it must be acknowledged that many large integrated East Asian corporations, notably in Japan [Keiretsu] and South Korea [Chaebol], internalize demand for specialized services rather than contracting out, as is the case with many North American and European corporations.) P.W. Daniels, "Producer Services and the APEC Region in a Global Context," *Working Papers on Producer Services*, No. 40, University of Bristol and Service Sector Research Unit, University of Birmingham, May 1997.

28. H.C. Davis and T.A. Hutton, "An Empirical Analysis of Producer Service Exports from the Vancouver Metropolitan Region," *Canadian Journal of Regional Science*, Vol. 14 (1991), pp. 375-94.

29. Price Waterhouse, *Export Market Capabilities of the B.C. Environmental Industry* (Vancouver: Asia Pacific Initiative, 1988).

30. W. Chow, "Engineering Firm Finding Asia Market its Goldmine," *The Vancouver Sun*, June 21, 1995, pp. D1, D4.

31. H.C. Davis and T.A. Hutton, "Marketing Vancouver's Services to the Asia Pacific," *The Canadian Geographer*, Vol. 38 (1994), pp. 18-28.

32. As we saw in chapter 1, a culture of co-operation can lead to gains in regional economic competitiveness by, for example, providing a supporting context for interfirm collaboration in export marketing. For a discussion of the role of interfirm networks in the development of advanced service industries, see A. Mayère and F. Vinot, "Firm Structures and Production Networks in Intellectual Services," in P.W. Daniels, S. Illeris, J. Bonamy and J. Philippe (eds.), *The Geography of Services* (London: Frank Cass, 1993).

33. O. Exell, "B.C. Businesses Flex Muscle in Asia," *Pacific Business* (October/November 1995), p. 5.

34. For a more detailed discussion of the city's comparative advantage in export-oriented service industries, see H.C. Davis and M.A. Goldberg, "An Empirical Estimation of Vancouver's Comparative Economic Advantages," Paper No. 16 (Vancouver: School of Community and Regional Planning, University of BC, 1988).

35. For a discussion of the role of networks in the operation of overseas Chinese businesses, see K. Olds and H. W.-C. Yeung, "The Changing Structure of Overseas Chinese Business Activity in a Globalizing Era" (Singapore: Department of Geography, National University of Singapore, 1997).

36. For example, the Vancouver office of Price Waterhouse has a Chinese Practice Group, with five professionals of Chinese ethnicity, which networks "with local offices in Hong Kong, Taiwan and other countries in Asia" (Price Waterhouse Chinese Practice Group brochure, undated).

37. P. Dawkins, S. Kemp and H. Cabalu, *Trade and Investment with East Asia in Selected Service Industries: The Role of Immigrants* (Canberra, Australia: Bureau of Immigration, Multicultural and Population Research, 1995).

38. C. Aislabee, J. Lee and J. Stanton, *Australian Cultural Diversity and Export Growth* (Canberra, Australia: Office of Multicultural Affairs, 1994).

39. S. Castles and M.J. Miller, "The Age of International Migration," *The Urban Age*, no. 3 (1994), pp. 1, 4-5

40. Castles and Miller, "The Age of International Migration."

41. The concentration of recent immigrants in Canada's largest cities is reflected in the proportion of "foreign-born" populations: Toronto, with 11.5 percent of Canada's population, has 44.8 percent of Canada's total foreign-born population, while Vancouver, with 5.9 percent of Canada's population, has 13.2 percent, and Montreal, with 11.5 percent of Canada's population, has 13.8 percent. (Calculations provided by Professor D. DeVoretz, Co-Director, Vancouver Centre of Excellence for the Study of Immigration and Integration, Simon Fraser University.)

42. D. Hiebert, D.F. Ley and D. DeVoretz, "The Metropolis Project: Immigration and Integration in Vancouver" (Annex D, "Introduction: Immigration and the Metropolis") (Vancouver: University of BC and Simon Fraser University, 1995).

43. Statistics Canada, *Daily*, catalogue 11-001E, p.6.

44. Although we cannot be precise about the exact destination of immigrants into BC, the vast majority certainly settle in metropolitan Vancouver, with smaller but significant numbers locating in the central and eastern Fraser Valley, Victoria and major inland urban centres such as Prince George, Kamloops and Kelowna.

45. The Netherlands was the 10th leading source country of BC immigrants in 1980, but no European country has approached top 10 status since, with the exception of Yugoslavia in 1993. This anomaly appears to be associated with the war in Bosnia, reinforcing the notion that immigration has different motivations for different groups.

46. Department of Citizenship and Immigration Canada, as quoted in B. Yaffe, "As '97 Approaches, We Must Let China Know We're Watching," *The Vancouver Sun*, July 22, 1995, p. B3.

47. Immigration to BC from Hong Kong declined to 12,000 both in 1995 and 1996, but there has been a corresponding increase in immigration from China in the most recent period. Canadian consular officials in Beijing report that there is a very substantial number of approved (or pending) applications from the People's Republic of China, and a large proportion of these applicants have indicated they intend to resettle in Vancouver. The motivations of these prospective Chinese immigrants to Vancouver vary, but include employment, education and family reunification. Zeng Yi and Zhang Qinwu, "Conditions in China Influencing Outmigration to Other Countries" (Beijing: Institute of Population Research, Peking University, 1997).

48. D. Bramham, "Taiwan Cash Pouring into Vancouver," *The Vancouver Sun*, March 14, 1996, pp. D1, D4.

49. S. Sassen, "International Migration and the Post-Industrial City," *The Urban Age*, no. 3 (1994), p. 3.

50. To illustrate, the incomes of foreign-born residents of the Vancouver CMA were only 82 percent of those of Canadian-born Vancouver citizens in 1991 (Hiebert *et al.*, "The Metropolis Project").

51. D. DeVoretz, *Diminishing Returns: Immigration Policy in the 1990s* (Ottawa: C.D. Howe Institute, 1995).

52. R. Mason Lee, "One Bad Apple in Toronto Costs the West Millions in Investment," *The Globe and Mail*, October 27, 1995, p. D4.

53. S. Seagrave, *Lords of the Rim: The Invisible Empire of the Overseas Chinese* (New York: G.P. Putnam's Sons, 1995).

54. G. Lamphier, "Vancouver's New Power Elite," *Financial Times of Canada*, June 1, 1992, p. 10.

55. M. Cernetig and Williamson, "Vancouver Feels Impact of Rising Asian Influence." A recent "Cantopop" concert in Vancouver raised over $1 million for charities.

56. SUCCESS (the United Chinese Community Enrichment Services Society) and MOSAIC (Multilingual Orientation Services Association Immigrant Communities) are important NGOs in the field of immigrant services, significantly supplementing the work of the three levels of government in Greater Vancouver engaged in facilitating the settlement of recent immigrants.

57. Y.-F. Tseng, "Chinese Ethnic Economy: San Gabriel Valley, Los Angeles County," *Journal of Urban Affairs*, Vol. 16, no. 2 (1994), pp. 169-89. Tseng observes that Monterey Park, east of Los Angeles City, has emerged as "the nation's first suburban Chinatown"

(p. 172), with 37 percent of its population of Chinese ethnicity. Spillover population from Monterey Park has contributed to the growth of a new Chinese enclave in the nearby San Gabriel Valley.

58. P.J. Smith, "The Making of a Global City: Fifty Years of Constituent Diplomacy: The Case of Vancouver," *Canadian Journal of Urban Research*, Vol. 1, no. 1 (1992), pp. 90-112.

59. T. Barnes, D.W. Edgington and K.G. Denike, "Vancouver, the Province, and the Pacific Rim," in T. Oke and G. Wynn (eds.), *Vancouver and its Region* (Vancouver: UBC Press, 1992), chap. 6.

4

Vancouver's Internal Transformation

So far we have examined Vancouver's restructuring trajectory in international, national and regional settings in order to identify macro-level influences on the city's development. We have seen that these external influences are having a profound impact on Vancouver's economic base, industrial mix, social structure and cultural diversity. As a result of these changes, the city and the metropolitan region as a whole are undergoing a fundamental socio-economic transformation.

Vancouver's transformational change is also expressed in spatial and physical terms. *Spatial* change involves the reconfiguration of basic patterns of settlement and economic activity. For instance, in many city-regions the following trends can be observed: (1) the functional specialization of the CBD favouring higher-order services, (2) transition and redevelopment in the inner city, and (3) the emergence of multiple employment nodes or nuclei in suburban areas. These processes cumulatively alter the city-region's basic distribution of economic activity, or the metropolitan space-economy. At the same time, the occupational changes associated with these economic processes, together with demographic factors, patterns of migration, ethno-cultural attributes, planning policies and regulations, and trends in the supply of housing gradually reshape the geography of human settlements, or the urban social morphology.

Metropolitan transformation also involves the *physical* reconstruction of the urban form and built environment in response to architectural innovation, local and more universal cultural influences, public policy initiatives and large-scale urban redevelopment schemes or mega-projects. Together, these physical and spatial processes comprehensively transform the internal structure and built environment of the contemporary metropolis.

Vancouver exhibits many of the characteristic features of spatial reconfiguration and physical reconstruction described earlier (see Figures 1.2 and 1.3 in chapter 1). Examples of the former include the emergence of a *multinucleated* regional structure (i.e., the development of suburban commercial nodes in addition to the established CBD); displacement, transition and comprehensive redevelopment in the inner city districts; and the increasing importance of specialized service industry clusters such as the port and airport, universities and colleges. The physical reconstruction of Vancouver's built form includes the introduction of postmodern influences in commercial districts, the transformation of Vancouver's *urban frame* on the CBD fringe, the gentrification of inner city residential landscapes and the introduction of *densification* initiatives designed to increase intensity of land use.

However, there are also quite distinctive aspects to Vancouver's spatial and physical transformation over the past two decades, which can be ascribed to a number of factors:

1. *Rapid pace of growth and change* – The rapid pace of economic restructuring combined with high population and employment growth rates have accelerated spatial and physical change (e.g., the expansion of service industry clusters and the growth of new suburban communities).
2. *High levels of capital investment* – Starting from the mid-1980s, when the pre-Expo building boom generated building permits averaging $1.5 billion annually, up to the present – $3.5 billion worth of construction permits have been issued annually for the past three years – metropolitan Vancouver has benefited from high levels of capital investment (public and private; foreign and domestic) that have profoundly affected both the pattern and the form of development.
3. *Immigration and culture* – Large-scale immigration over the past decade or so, especially from the Asia-Pacific, has found expression in new cultural landscapes, such as retail centres, religious and social institutions and housing styles.
4. *Architecture and local design influences* – Local design has had a considerable impact on the reconstruction of Vancouver's urban form. Influences include important Vancouver architects like Erickson, Merrick and Pratt; a

distinctive West Coast residential style (favouring the use of cedar and other native softwoods); and First Nations designs and motifs.

5. *Public policy and planning guidelines* – A wide range of policy interventions are influencing the reconfiguration of Vancouver's metropolitan structure and the reshaping of its urban form. They include municipal planning strategies and official community plans (OCPs), special district plans, neighbourhood design guidelines, heritage policies and negotiated (or discretionary) arrangements.

This chapter examines Vancouver's internal transformation as well as the role of these five local factors in this context. Following a discussion of overall changes in metropolitan structure and urban form, we present specific examples of physical reconstruction in order to identify the mix of factors reshaping urban spaces; illustrate processes of transition, conversion and redevelopment in the Vancouver case; and introduce comparisons with the processes of urban transformation in other dynamic post-industrial and post-modern city-regions.[1]

The Reconfiguration of Vancouver's Metropolitan Structure

Over much of the period since the Second World War, Vancouver's basic spatial configuration has, with some important qualifications,[2] been consistent with classical models of urban and regional structure, in particular with regard to the following elements: (1) a central city area containing dense concentrations of commercial activity, including a large corporate complex of high-rise offices as well as retail operations; (2) an inner-city ring incorporating industrial and quasi-industrial activities (manufacturing, warehousing and distribution); (3) working-class neighbourhoods outside the industrial ring; (4) secondary, mid-town commercial strips; and (5) suburban areas characterized by residential districts (with mostly single-family dwellings), industrial precincts and a limited amount of commercial activity.

Against the backdrop of this simplified spatial model, we can identify some important benchmarks that have influenced the reconfiguration of Vancouver's metropolitan structure in the postwar period. For instance, in the mid-1950s Park Royal, which was the first suburban retail centre in the region (and indeed in Canada as a whole), was built in West Vancouver. In the following decade, zoning changes facilitated the development of a new high-rise residential district in the West End, in the western portion of the downtown peninsula (Figure 4.1, sub-area 21). This area now houses some 40,000 people.

figure 4.1

Planning Sub-Areas in Vancouver's Metropolitan Core

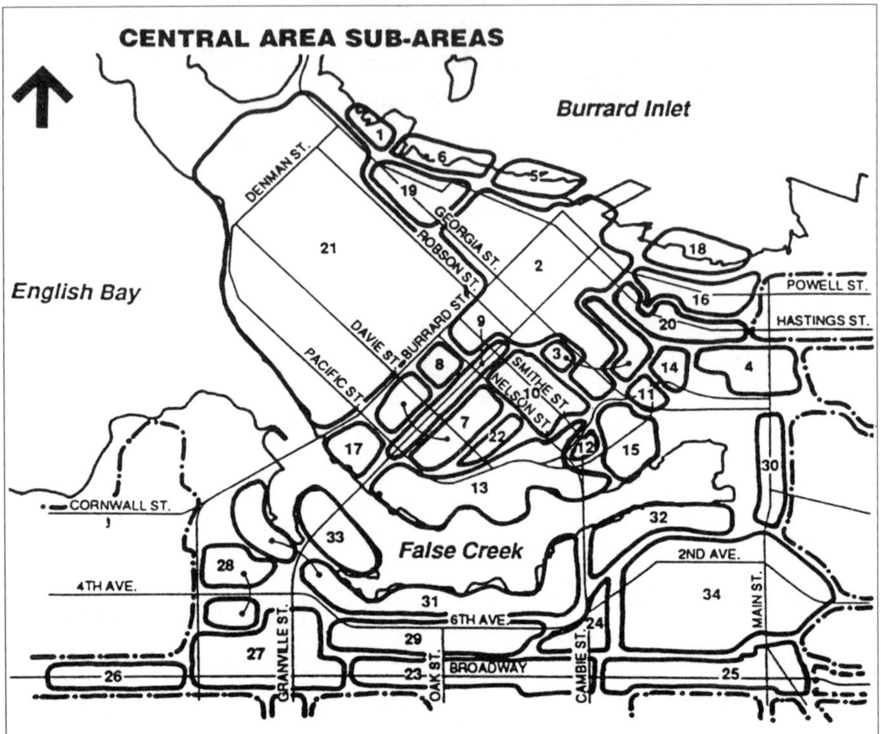

DOWNTOWN PENINSULA

1. Bayshore
2. Established (CBD)
3. (CBD): Fringe
4. Chinatown
5. Coal Harbour East
6. Coal Harbour West
7. Downtown South
8. Downtown South: Burrard-Granville
9. Downtown South: Granville Street
10. Downtown South: Northeast Quadrant
11. False Creek North: Apex
12. False Creek North: Cambie Bridge
13. False Creek North: Granville-Cambie
14. False Creek North: International Village
15. False Creek North: Stadium
16. Gastown
17. Granville Slopes
18. Port Lands
19. Triangle West
20. Victory Square
21. West End
22. Yaletown

OUTSIDE DOWNTOWN PENINSULA

23. Broadway: Centre
24. Broadway: Cambie Bridge South
25. Broadway: East
26. Broadway: West
27. Burrard Slopes: Broadway-Burrard-Granville(C-3A)
28. Burrard Slopes: South of Granville Island
29. Fairview Slopes
30. False Creek East
31. False Creek South
32. False Creek Southeast
33. Granville Island
34. Mt. Pleasant Industrial

Source: City of Vancouver, Planning Department, Central Area Division.

In addition to the substantial growth in Greater Vancouver in the 1970s, there were other developments that had significant implications for the city's metropolitan structure. First, there was a sustained office-space construction boom in the CBD (Figure 4.1, sub-area 2), in large part as a result of growth in head office, financial and producer services linked to British Columbia's expanding resource economy. The hitherto modest commercial core was thus transformed into a true corporate complex.[3] This corporate growth gave rise to Vancouver's high level of control over the province's resource sector and contributed to the definition of its most strategic economic role during this period.

Second, the rezoning of industrial lands on the south shore of False Creek accelerated the closure or relocation of long-established heavy industries (including forest products industries and steel fabrication) and enabled the development of a new, medium- to high-density residential community. Although many of the former industries were clearly obsolescent, the establishment of this new inner-city residential community can be seen as an important public policy initiative. Indeed, the City initiated the rezoning, owned most of the land on the site and established the development guidelines, which included a significant social housing component. False Creek South (Figure 4.1, sub-area 31) has been interpreted as a municipal affirmation of Vancouver's emergence as a post-industrial city.[4]

The 1970s saw other important trends in Vancouver's metropolitan core, not the least of which was a significant increase in gentrification, notably in the Fairview Slopes district (Figure 4.1, sub-area 29), adjacent to the False Creek South project. In terms of metropolitan structure, the expansion of the CBD, the continuing growth of high-rise apartments in the West End and the False Creek South development constitute the defining events. The rapid growth of a high-rise corporate complex within the CBD, the development of new medium- to high-density residential districts facilitated by zoning and other municipal initiatives, and the concentration of control functions, employment and retail services enhanced the core's dominance within the growing Vancouver metropolitan region.

Vancouver's suburbs also experienced substantial (but dispersed) growth during this decade. The growing dominance of the Vancouver core and concerns over the environmental costs of suburban sprawl led to the adoption of a new regional plan, *The Livable Region 1976-1986*, by the GVRD following an extensive process of public consultation. Its central element was the idea of introducing four new metropolitan nodes or *regional town centres* (RTCs), two in the inner suburbs (Burnaby-Metrotown and New Westminster) and two in the outer suburbs (Whalley-Guildford in Surrey and Coquitlam Town Centre). The intention was to provide a focus for suburban development and a counterweight to the growing power of the core. The RTCs, which were to attract at least one million square feet of office space as well as significant retail and residential development, were also expected to provide further definition to Greater Vancouver's metropolitan structure.

Over the life of the 1976-1986 regional plan, progress on the development of the four designated RTCs was disappointing. The realization of the RTC concept (i.e., a more multinucleated metropolitan structure) proved difficult for a number of reasons:

1. *Behaviour of the office market* – Those who produced the regional plan had apparently underestimated the agglomerative tendencies of office activities, especially for contact-intensive service industries, which require proximity to the dense clusters of suppliers, clients, capital and market intelligence present in the metropolitan core.
2. *Failure to designate locational priorities* – Rather than attempting to simultaneously promote four RTCs in a relatively small market, a more effective strategy might have been to designate one (or possibly two) suburban centres and concentrate resources and policy efforts on them.
3. *Ineffective local policy approaches* – The municipalities in which the RTCs were to be located failed to establish vigorous implementation strategies (e.g., with respect to land use and zoning, public investments and information services) to support them; in some cases (for example, in Surrey) they even encouraged the development of multiple smaller centres in the interest of providing consumer services over a large municipal area, rather than promoting the designated RTCs.
4. *Competition from existing centres* – The RTCs failed to attract large shares of new office development and activity. Even within the suburban markets, development remained quite dispersed, while a significant share of new office activity located in existing suburban business centres such as Richmond and North Vancouver, which are close to the CBD and metropolitan core but were not among the areas designated in the metropolitan plan.
5. *Inadequate central city/RTC connections* – Unlike more successful European models that included rapid, fixed-rail transit service between suburban office nodes and the central city, the four Greater Vancouver RTCs were not well connected to the downtown, which contributed to a perception of market isolation.[5]

Other events served to undermine the RTC programme and the regional plan generally. In the early 1980s, a province-wide economic downturn severely impacted Vancouver's development and diminished the prospects for new employment centres, including the four RTCs. In 1983, the province removed statutory authority for land-use planning from the GVRD (and other BC regional districts). This measure, which was undertaken "by a Social Credit provincial government anxious to promote development rather than regulate it,"[6] further diluted the power of the GVRD to foster the RTC programme.

Over the last decade conditions have been more favourable to the development of the RTCs and thus to the emergence of a more polycentric metropolitan structure. First, a sustained period of high growth (population, employment and investment) since the mid-1980s has provided considerable momentum to development in the region as a whole.

Second, the completion in 1985 of a fixed-rail transit system linking the two inner suburban RTCs of Burnaby-Metrotown and New Westminster to the CBD, coupled with high growth in the service industries, have encouraged further development of the GVRD's multinucleation strategy. In addition to the original four RTCs, two more inner suburban centres, Richmond Centre and North Vancouver-Lonsdale, were added. Richmond Centre had already experienced considerable growth as a result of its proximity to the CBD and to Vancouver International Airport, while North Vancouver had attracted provincial crown corporations as well as private firms.

Third, the region's industrial buoyancy found expression in the emergence of "new production spaces" in the city and suburbs and in the maturation or renewal of some existing manufacturing districts. It is perhaps ironic that while Vancouver never achieved the status of a major industrial city during the high point of the classical Fordist era, manufacturing growth is a significant factor in the region's contemporary development.

The Structure of Vancouver's Space-Economy

The basic structure of Vancouver's reconfigured space-economy is depicted in Figure 4.2. It consists of three principal layers of economic activity, each comprising related sets of production and labour. First, we can identify an industrial base of manufacturing, processing, warehousing and distribution. As Figure 4.3 shows, this industrial base presents a relatively dispersed pattern of production-related districts throughout the metropolitan region, including (1) residual resource-processing operations concentrated in strips along the Fraser River; (2) industrial parks, prevalent in the inner and outer suburbs; (3) relatively small but dynamic advanced-technology production enclaves in Richmond and Burnaby, specializing in electronics, communications, marine and aerospace industries; (4) city-serving industries such as printing, publishing and food

figure 4.2

Basic Structure of Metropolitan Vancouver's Space-Economy

I. Industrial base	Residual heavy industry and resource processing Industrial parks Advanced technology enclaves in inner suburbs (Richmond, Burnaby) City-serving production Wholesaling, warehousing and distribution
II. Overlay of principal commercial nodes and axes	(CBD) West Broadway Commercial Axis Inner suburban regional town centres (Richmond Centre, Burnaby, Metrotown, North Vancouver-Lonsdale) Outer suburban Regional Town Centres (incipient "edge city" of Surrey City Centre, Coquitlam) District-level centres (Tsawwassen, Newton)
III. Specialized service industry clusters – city and inner suburbs	Port of Vancouver Vancouver International Airport University of British Columbia Simon Fraser University Community colleges Vancouver's midtown medical precinct Tourism district-metropolitan core New cultural and entertainment district in central city Applied design districts in the downtown fringe Local government operations

production, concentrated in the City of Vancouver; and (5) wholesaling, warehousing and distribution, located on the city's central waterfront and on major suburban transportation arterials.

The largest of Vancouver's industrial districts is Crestwood/Bridgeport in Richmond (Figure 4.3), on the south bank of the Fraser River's northern arm across from the City of Vancouver. With over 10 million square feet of floor space, Crestwood/Bridgeport is almost twice as large as the second-ranking industrial precinct in the metropolitan region (Port Kells in North Langley) and comprises almost one-tenth of the total Greater Vancouver inventory of 115 million square feet.[7] Although the maturing of the region's production economy has resulted in an increasingly suburban development pattern, the City of Vancouver still accounts for almost one-third of Greater Vancouver's industrial floor space and employment, affirming the overall strength of the metropolitan core and the city generally.[8]

figure 4.3

Industrial Districts in Greater Vancouver

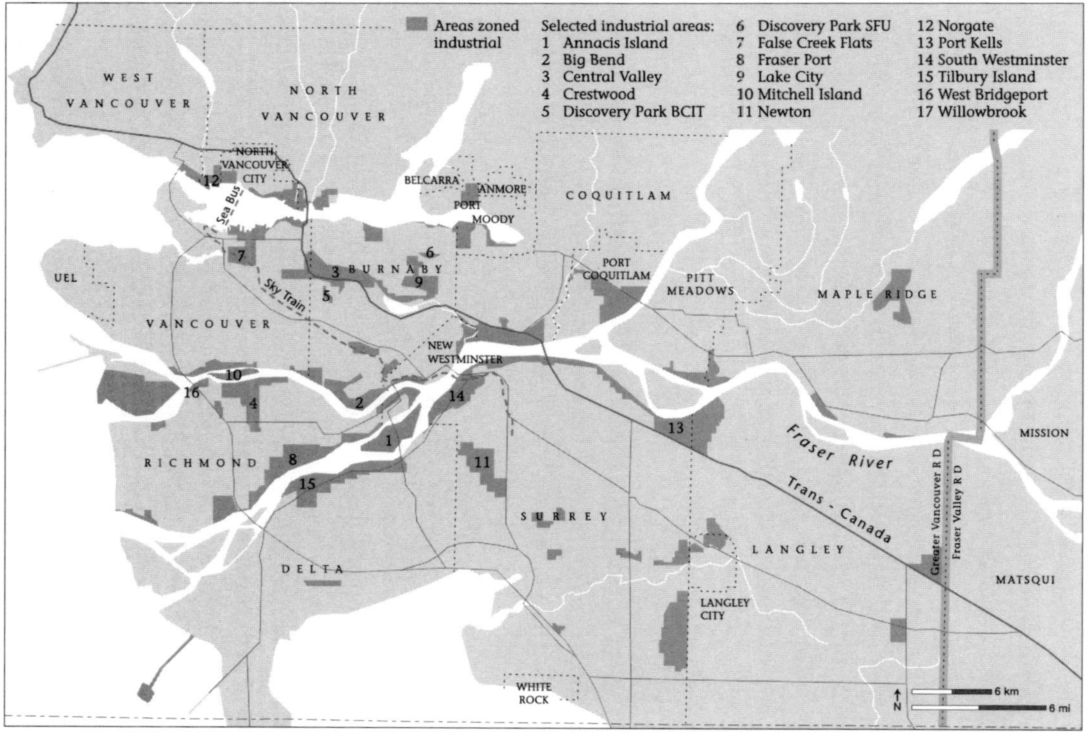

Source: Greater Vancouver Regional District.

The second layer of metropolitan Vancouver's space-economy takes the form of an overlay of essentially nodal commercial centres. The pattern of the principal commercial nodes in the GVRD (and the adjacent Lower Fraser Regional Districts) is presented in Figure 4.4. We can identify an hierarchical framework of centres, including (1) the metropolitan core, which includes both the City of Vancouver's CBD and the West Broadway commercial axis, (2) the six policy-designated RTCs (the original four plus Richmond Centre and North Vancouver-Lonsdale), and (3) two new centres, located in Langley and Haney.

These centres are at quite different stages of development, but the pattern of commercial nodes depicted in Figure 4.4 suggests a more polycentric metropolitan structure than was evident at the end of the 1976-1986 planning period. At the same time, the metropolitan core remains the dominant office-commercial centre in the region. In 1991, the CBD had 43 percent of the total regional inventory of office space, while the West Broadway commercial axis had more than double the amount of office space in the largest of the suburban RTCs.[9]

The third principal layer of metropolitan Vancouver's space-economy is a series of large, interactive and functionally specialized service industry/institution *clusters*. These include Vancouver's main transportation facilities (the Port of Vancouver and Vancouver International Airport), tertiary educational complexes, the city's midtown medical precinct, local government, and the tourism, entertainment and cultural districts.

Taken as a whole, these specialized service clusters, together with the region's principal commercial nodes, confirm Vancouver's status as an advanced post-industrial urban economy. Significantly, most of them are situated in the city proper or the inner suburbs, in contrast with the industrial districts and retail nodes which are dispersed throughout the region. In general, Vancouver's specialized service clusters tend to be located in the central metropolitan area because of their need to access markets, information and highly skilled labour.[10]

We can identify the principal service industry clusters at two spatial levels. First, at the metropolitan level, the important clusters (Figure 4.4) include the Port of Vancouver (including the Central Waterfront or CWF, Roberts Bank and Lynnterm), Vancouver International Airport (YVR), UBC, SFU, the British Columbia Institute of Technology (BCIT) and Discovery Park in Burnaby, and Vancouver's midtown medical precinct (one of the largest concentrations of health-related institutions and facilities in North America).

The second group of specialized service industry clusters is concentrated in the metropolitan core (Figure 4.5), an indication of both the vitality and functional evolution of Vancouver's Central Area. To be sure, the CBD proper, with its concentration of high-rise offices and business-class hotels, continues to

figure 4.4

Major Commercial Nodes and Specialized Service Clusters in Metropolitan Vancouver

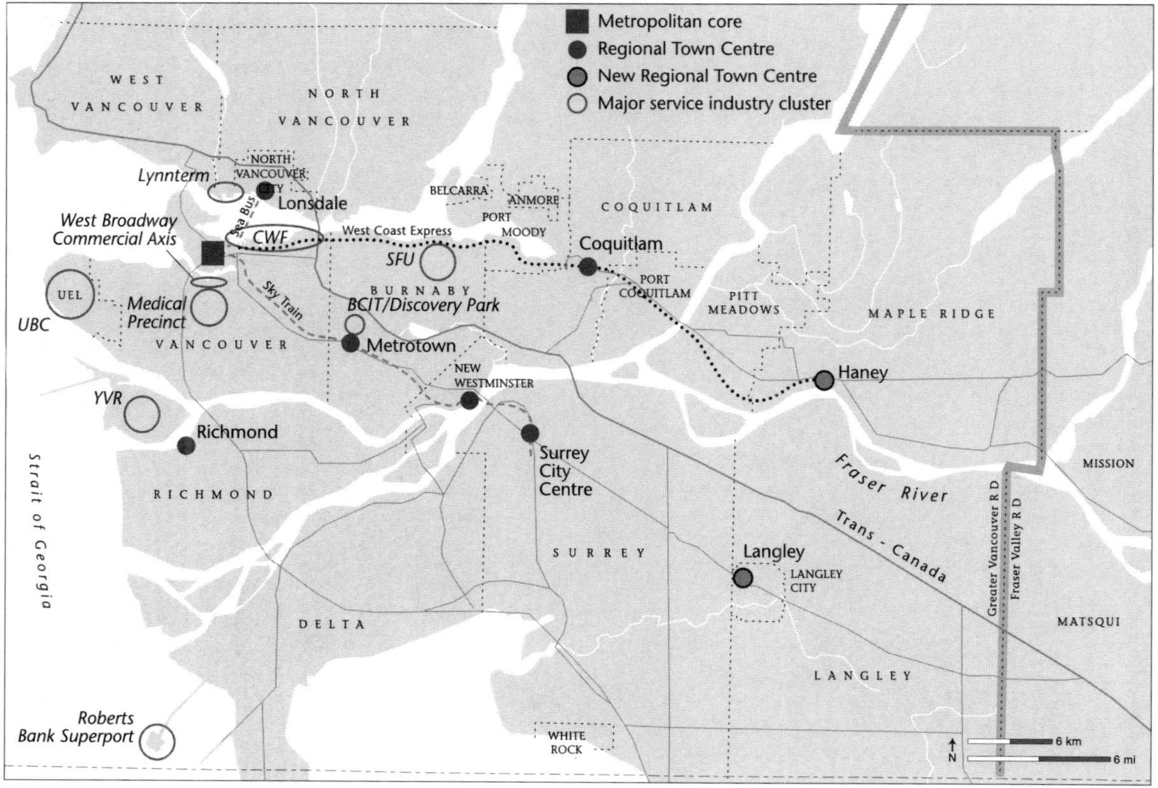

figure 4.5
Service Industry Clusters and Major Redevelopment Projects in Vancouver's Metropolitan Core

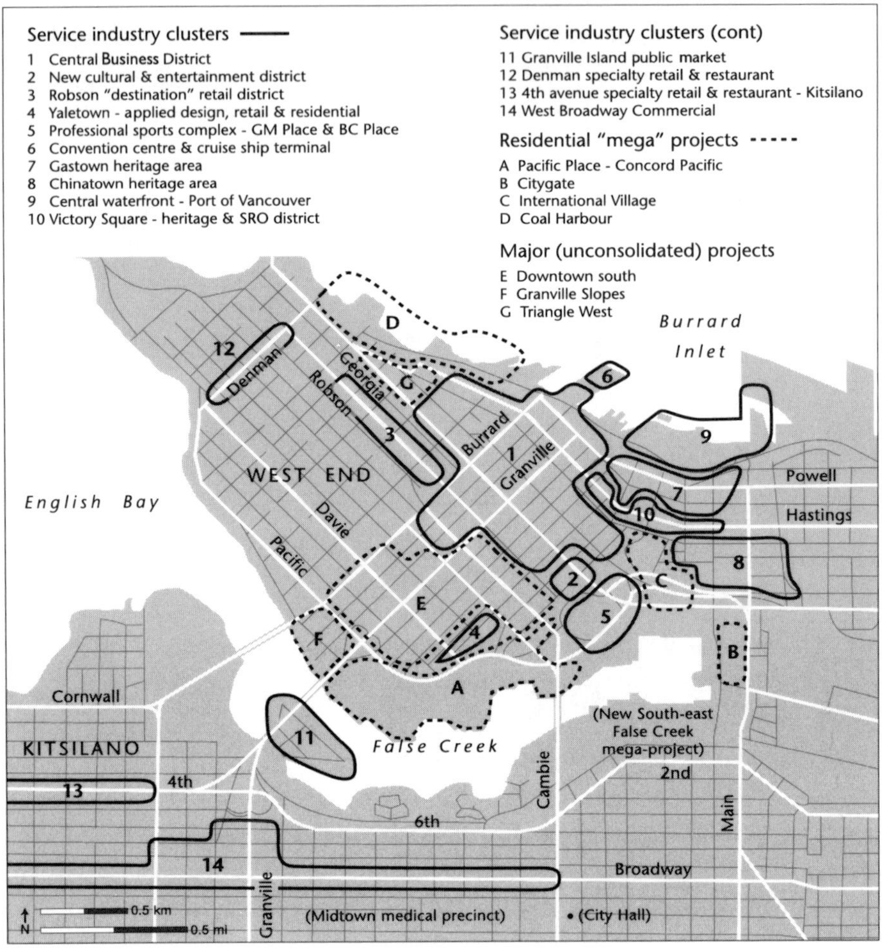

exhibit considerable vitality, but the emergence of new retail, tourist, cultural, creative and institutional districts in the downtown peninsula and inner city can be seen as the onset of a process of *specialized diversification* in the metropolitan core, reflecting new patterns of economic demand, socio-cultural factors and policy initiatives.

Some of these clusters represent very large concentrations of employment and production. The port accounts for about 10 percent of the regional GDP (and 10,800 jobs), while the airport accounts for approximately six percent of GDP.[11] UBC has about 7000 faculty and staff, while the hospitals, chronic care institutions and associated retail operations in the medical precinct (bounded by Broadway, Oak, Cambie and 37th Avenue) include over 15,000 workers. The City of Vancouver employs about 5000.

Other clusters have emerged more recently and reflect aspects of the city's social, economic and cultural transformation. They include the cultural and entertainment district, extending eastward from the CBD along Georgia and Robson streets; applied design services (e.g., architecture, graphics, fashion and industrial design), concentrated in Yaletown and Gastown; and the expanding international tourism and convention clusters around Canada Place and Robson Street. These clusters indicate the recent functional diversification of the metropolitan core (outside the CBD) as new investment and redevelopment occur in the Central Area but outside the corporate office complex. The emergence of the cultural, entertainment and tourist districts also reflects the growing demand for more public use of the core and for activities that contribute to the central city's vitality and amenity. These preferences were acknowledged with the City Council's approval of the 1991 *Central Area Plan*, which consolidated and delimited the central office district.[12]

A review of recent capital investment and public policy decisions offers some insight into the continuing reconfiguration of Vancouver's metropolitan structure. It confirms the recent trend toward a more nodal, multinucleated pattern of settlement and economic development as well as higher density development in the city and the inner suburbs, in contrast with the more dispersed growth of the 1970s and early 1980s.

Unlike the experiences of many other North American cities, however, Vancouver's emerging structure will certainly include major new capital investment and development in the metropolitan core. Although the pace of office development in the CBD in the 1970s and 1980s has not been sustained, a series of urban mega-projects and redevelopment plans will enable the core to escape the disinvestment and decline documented in some Canadian cities, notably Montreal, and in many American cities. The hallmark project in the core is unquestionably Concord Pacific's Pacific Place, which will encompass about one-sixth of the entire downtown peninsula and include 40 buildings and 8500 residential units over a 10- to 15-year period (Figure 4.5, district A). Other major capital projects in the core include the Coal Harbour development on the Central Waterfront (Figure 4.5, district D), which is projected to include 2250 residential units and a new $100 million convention centre that is expected to attract major international conventions and conferences. In addition to these large-scale projects, there is also substantial new high-rise residential development in the Granville Slopes (Figure 4.5, district F) and Downtown South (Figure 4.5, district E), and preliminary planning is currently underway for South-east False Creek (Figure 4.5).

Outside the core, a series of new and impending projects will maintain the recent trend toward nodal, rather than dispersed, suburban development in Greater Vancouver. In the inner suburban municipalities, new high-rise office and residential development projects will redefine the regional town centres of Burnaby-Metrotown and Richmond Centre. Richmond Council has approved plans to create a new commercial core, reversing previous tendencies toward strip development and extensive retail malls to include medium- to high-density accommodation for 40,000 residents.[13] The more mature RTC of Burnaby-Metrotown will be enhanced by the construction of three new high-rise office towers and two combined office-residential towers.[14] However, in Vancouver's outer suburbs, development is still largely characterized by low density, dispersion and sprawl. In some municipalities, there is only weak adherence (or even opposition) to the regional strategy. These include Langley, where a pro-business council has expressed impatience with the constraining effects of planning on development, and Surrey, where the current Council has effectively reversed its predecessor's strong support for a major new metropolitan commercial node in Surrey City Centre, in favour of promoting numerous smaller centres.

Vancouver's Transformation at the Community Level: The Reconstruction of Urban Space

The preceding discussion addressed important features of spatial change in Greater Vancouver at the macro level and examined the reconfiguration of its metropolitan structure, with reference to the region's space-economy, specialized service nodes and clusters and new production zones. These structural changes in the pattern of settlement and economic development are clearly very important for planning policy at the metropolitan level as they have strategic implications for land use, transportation, environmental management and public finance.[15]

To bring the more specific aspects of Vancouver's physical transformation into sharper focus, however, we must also examine change at more local levels, that is, at the district, community[16] and even neighbourhood levels. The processes and outcomes of transformational change at the local level may vary for several reasons:

1. *Specific community impacts of structural change* – Although restructuring is often analysed at the metropolitan level, it is experienced very differently at the district and community levels; for example, the CBD, low-income

inner city neighbourhoods and more affluent communities differ in their capacity to absorb and respond to change. They are therefore likely to be affected in quite different ways.

2. *Fragmentation of urban spatial structure* – The process of structural change tends to accentuate contrasts in industrial structure, income levels, social morphology, urban form, built environments and community identity and image.[17]
3. *Determinants of change* – Processes of metropolitan transformation are associated with a new (or reordered) set of determinants, including culture, amenity, information technology and immigration (see chapter 1). These factors may be present within the metropolitan region as a whole, but may vary considerably from one area to another.
4. *Local policy issues and priorities* – The reconstruction of urban form and the built environment generates significant tensions and conflicts among various interest groups and communities. These tensions may be masked at the broader metropolitan level, but are brought into sharper relief at the district and neighbourhood levels.
5. *Community planning approaches* – The specificity of local issues is reflected (and even legitimized) in the increased tendency to initiate separate planning efforts for relatively small local districts, particularly in dealing with issues relating to the re-development or "reconstruction" of urban sub-areas and districts. The community "empowerment" movement, in which the special interests and needs of particular districts are validated by area-specific planning initiatives, is an example of this. These community planning efforts may encompass a broad range of issues, but focus mostly on the form of development and re-development.

Dynamics of Change in Vancouver's Urban Form and Built Environment

There are many complex influences on the reconstruction of Vancouver's districts and communities and some interaction among them. Generally, three major sets of factors can be identified at the community level: (1) market forces such as foreign direct investment (FDI) and domestic capital, technological innovation, obsolescence and succession in land use and building types, and agglomeration economies; (2) social and cultural influences such as occupation, class, ethnicity, social values and aesthetic trends; and (3) public policy initiatives and planning interventions.

The determinants of change within each of these categories are listed in Figure 4.6 with some examples of the reconstruction of Vancouver's urban form. Although this selective sample can only hint at the extent of change in

figure 4.6

Vancouver's Transformation at the Micro-Level: Influences on the Reconstruction of Urban Districts and Communities

PRINCIPAL DYNAMICS	EXAMPLES
Market forces	
Foreign direct investment	Concord Pacific's Pacific Place
Industries with new locational preferences	Garment district within inner city/east end
Development of agglomeration economies in new locations	Development of suburban commercial nodes
Local investment and renewal	Metamorphosis of Yaletown
Response to changing consumer demands	Growth of multiple-unit dwellings and high-rise condominium districts
Social and cultural influences	
Emergence of service elite or new middle class	Gentrified neighbourhoods in the urban core
Preferences of artists and designers	Growth of live/work studios in Gastown, selected industrial areas.
Immigration from the Asia-Pacific societies	Suzhou Classical Chinese garden in Chinatown; Asia West retail complex in Richmond
Environmental values and sensibilities	Proliferation of recreational outlets and environmental agencies in the Kitsilano district
Influence of leading Vancouver architects and designers	Legacy of major Vancouver buildings
Influence of postmodernism	Postmodern motifs in West Broadway commercial area and CBD
Public policy and planning	
Strategic municipal land-use policies and programmes	False Creek South, Champlain Heights
Suburban regional town centre policies	Growth of Burnaby-Metrotown
Municipal heritage designation and policies	Vancouver's Chinatown, Gastown districts
Specific local authority investments	New civic library in Vancouver's emerging cultural district
High-level government initiatives	Granville Island public market (CMHC)

metropolitan Vancouver's district and community-level urban form, it does illustrate the breadth of both dynamics and outcomes.

Within each category, we can identify the impact of transformational change at the district, community and neighbourhood levels. The impact of market forces ranges from the 80 hectare Pacific Place project to the more localized reconstruction of the Yaletown historic district on the southern fringe of the downtown area and even to individual sites. As an example of the latter, the old American Can building on the east side, near the Central Waterfront, was reconstructed as a centre of design and related production activity specializing in fashion. This transformation illustrates the shift from Fordist (or mass) manufacturing to more flexible or custom-run production as well as the significance of design inputs to value-added production (Figure 4.7). The recent development of agglomeration economies and critical mass in the large RTCs, which has facilitated new office development and service industries – notably in Burnaby-Metrotown RTC – is another example of the influence of the market on the reconstruction of urban form.

The impact of social and cultural influences on metropolitan Vancouver's built environment is perhaps more subtle, but nonetheless important. They reflect tensions between local and international culture and the expression of competing dynamics at the district and community levels. To some extent, these influences and trends are pervasive. For example, the postmodernist building styles in commercial districts and the gentrification in and around the metropolitan core can be found in many of Canada's other large cities.[18] But in the Vancouver case, gentrification is a particularly powerful agent of neighbourhood change, owing to the size, growth rate and residential preferences of the city's new middle class of professionals and information industry workers. These individuals are strongly drawn to inner city neighbourhoods by the presence of new theatres, stadiums, restaurants and cultural amenities. To them, the metropolitan core offers not only better employment opportunities, but also a unique urban lifestyle.

As observed in the previous chapter, immigration from Asia-Pacific societies has left its imprint on Vancouver's urban form and built environment. Important examples include the classical Chinese garden situated in Vancouver's Chinatown (constructed by skilled artisans from Suzhou) and the large Sikh temple in South East Vancouver. These (and other) institutions are not only important cultural symbols of their respective ethnic groups, they also offer a visual testament to Vancouver's social transformation.

Vancouver architects, many of whom have won important commissions internationally, have also contributed significantly to the reconstruction of Vancouver's built environment. Prominent among them is Arthur Erickson, whose distinguished buildings in Vancouver include the downtown courthouse complex and the striking Museum of Anthropology at UBC in Point Grey. Ned Pratt's 1960s design for the BC Electric building was a distinctive interpretation of the New International style.[19] Indeed, Vancouver became an important Canadian centre for the modernist architectural style, a development depicted in a recent exhibition in Montreal curated by UBC professor

figure 4.7
Design Centre (Former American Can Building),
Inner City/Central Waterfront Area

Rhodri Windsor-Liscombe.[20] Frank Musson is largely responsible for the comprehensive reconstruction of the corporate complex on Burrard Street between Hastings and Georgia, including the landmark Bentall Centre project. James Cheng is an example of the younger architects who are influencing Vancouver's new built form.

Public agencies play an important and even leading role in the transformation of *cityscapes* at local levels (Figure 4.6). The City of Vancouver, for example, has directly and indirectly reshaped Vancouver's urban form over the last several decades with projects like False Creek South and the Champlain Heights housing development in South East Vancouver. In both cases, the City provided land below market price on a leasehold basis, thereby retaining public ownership of the land and options for new uses beyond the lease period.

Municipal authorities can also reshape urban form at the local level by investing directly in important buildings. In Vancouver's case, the recent opening of a new public library designed by Montreal architect Moshe Safdie has generated some controversy with its striking neo-Roman design (Figure 4.8). The new library anchors the city's emerging cultural and entertainment district (Figure 4.5, district 2), situated on Robson and Georgia streets and extending from Richards Street to BC Place Stadium and the new GM Place at the Georgia Viaduct.

This new cultural and entertainment district, which also includes the long-established Queen Elizabeth Theatre and the CBC Building, represents an important facet of the Central Area's reconstruction, encompassing physical and design aspects in addition to its implications for the city's cultural life. As in other cities where new cultural landmarks have generated substantial public interest and controversy (I.M. Pei's pyramid for the Louvre entrance precinct in Paris comes to mind), opinions have been mixed about the merits of the process employed to select an architect for the library, and more specifically about the design of the building. To devotees of the modernist school such as Bruno Zevi, student of Bauhaus founder Walter Gropius, Vancouver's new library, with its echoes of the Roman Colosseum, "seems to be a parody of even the best of classical eclecticism – and an act of abdication by a former protagonist of the avant-garde."[21] At the same time, the general public in Vancouver seems more favourably disposed to and even thrilled with the new municipal library. What is indisputable is Safdie's influence on the reshaping of Vancouver's cultural precinct. In addition to the new library, Safdie designed the Ford Theatre for the Performing Arts (Figure 4.9) directly across from the new library on Homer Street.

Other significant public initiatives in the city include the heritage designations for the Chinatown and Gastown historic districts. In each case, the City

figure 4.8
Vancouver's Public Library in the New Cultural and Entertainment Precinct

is concerned with encouraging preservation while at the same time allowing a measure of physical renewal and reconstruction, a delicate balance. Certain projects by other levels of government are also influential: the Granville Island public market – a successful venture that is managed by CMHC and attracts local people and tourists in large numbers – is a case in point.

figure 4.9

Ford Theatre for the Performing Arts in the New Cultural and Entertainment Precinct

A final example of public authorities' role in the transformation of the built environment is Burnaby Council's sustained support for the Burnaby-Metrotown Regional Town Centre. The success of this major inner-suburb RTC is due in part to the achievement of agglomeration effects conducive to contact-intensive commercial uses, but it is also attributable in no small measure to the commitment of Burnaby Council to facilitating development in the designated area. In particular, it has steadfastly discouraged developers who have applied to undertake large projects in potentially competing areas in the municipality outside Metrotown.

Although the principal influences on the reconstruction of urban spaces can be identified, the physical transformation of a city is normally the consequence of a complex combination of factors and decisions taken by various actors or agents. In Vancouver as elsewhere, elected officials, planners, senior city staff managers, design professionals, active community groups (and individuals), powerful domestic and foreign business interests, and other stakeholders all have an influential role in urban development.

The interaction of these groups and the tensions and conflicts arising from competing interests and values are especially evident in Vancouver's broadly

figure 4.10
Consolidation of Vancouver's Central Business District

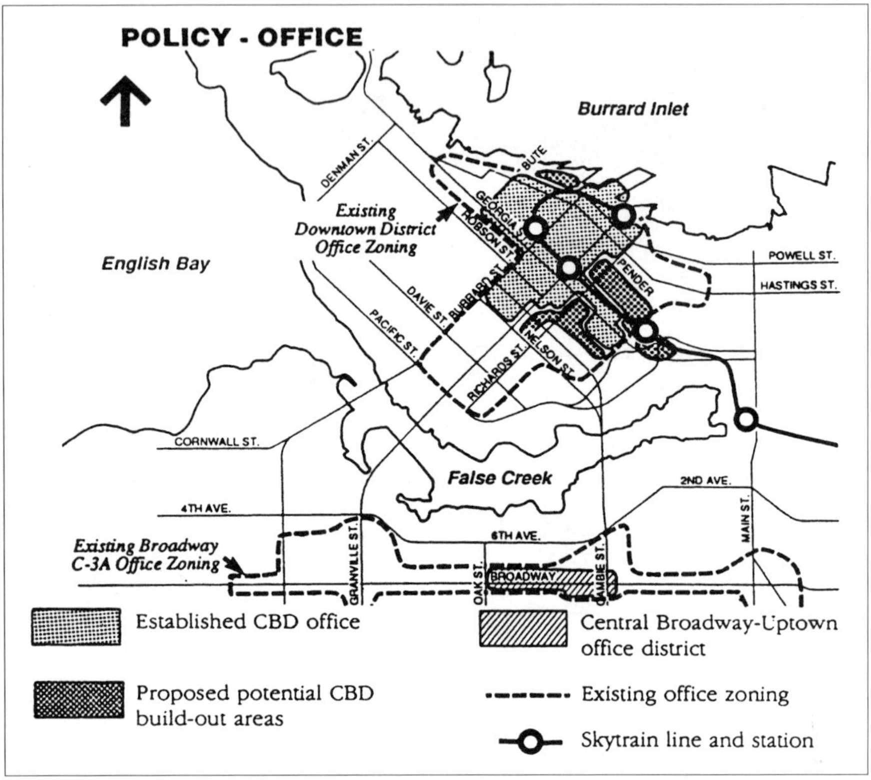

Source: City of Vancouver, *Central Area Plan* (Vancouver: Planning Department, 1991).

defined metropolitan core. This area features the highest land values in the metropolis, the largest concentrations of capital and labour, the region's information nexus, a significant presence by all three levels of government, major commercial institutions and organizations, the largest concentration of foreign and international concerns and the most complex (and polarized) social structure. Consequently, it is in this "contested space" of Vancouver's metropolitan core that we observe the most instructive examples of contemporary urban reconstruction.

The Planning Policy Context for Vancouver's Central Area

The metropolitan core's economic importance, sustained development pressures, competing interests and diverse landscapes and societies all contribute to the scope and complexity of planning for Vancouver's Central Area. Over the past decade and a half, we can trace a progression of strategic planning initiatives undertaken by the City, directed wholly or principally toward the core.

In the early 1980s, the Planning Department undertook the preparation of *CorePlan*,[22] an ambitious growth management strategy intended to establish constraints on the expanding urban core, in particular, the commercial office sector. Although this plan was not sufficiently flexible to withstand the changes in priorities brought about by an unusually deep and protracted recession, it did bequeath an important legacy of planning concepts, including a useful critique of eight growth management options. The most enduring idea, however, was that of a conceptual and empirical relationship between office development, demand for housing and transportation and environmental capacity.

These concepts provided the valuable cornerstone for the successful 1991 *Central Area Plan*. This plan combined the fundamental idea of linkages between downtown commercial development and residential and transportation requirements with excellent process management. It established a land use strategy for the Central Area that acknowledged both the crucial and unique economic functions of the CBD (understated in *CorePlan*) and the potential for residential and public uses outside the corporate complex. Unlike Seattle and San Francisco, where concerns about the effects of unrestrained CBD commercial expansion were addressed by imposing annual development quotas, Vancouver's *Central Area Plan* linked the optimal long-term office capacity of the core to projected residential and transit capacity. The two principal policy directions enunciated in this plan are (1) reconsolidation of the CBD, delimiting the corporate complex but allowing the office market to operate relatively freely within this zone (Figure 4.10); and (2) a preference for residential and public uses outside the newly demarcated CBD (Figure 4.11).

Examples of Vancouver's Physical Reconstruction

With the approval of the *Central Area Plan* in 1991, the Planning Department's work programme has focused on detailed planning for 34 sub-areas and districts of the Central Area (see Figure 4.1).[23] This detailed articulation of Central Area sub-areas represents a major refinement of the classic model of urban structure, which essentially identifies a CBD and inner city zone in the urban core. The Planning Department is also involved in planning exercises for the Coal Harbour project (Figure 4.5, district D); Downtown South (district E), where housing is the preferred use; Granville Slopes (district F), where high-rise residential towers have recently been constructed; and Victory Square (district 10).

The *Victory Square Concept Plan* illustrates some of the tensions and conflicts associated with the reconstruction of urban space in the core and the need to

figure 4.11

Designation of Residential Districts in Vancouver's Metropolitan Core

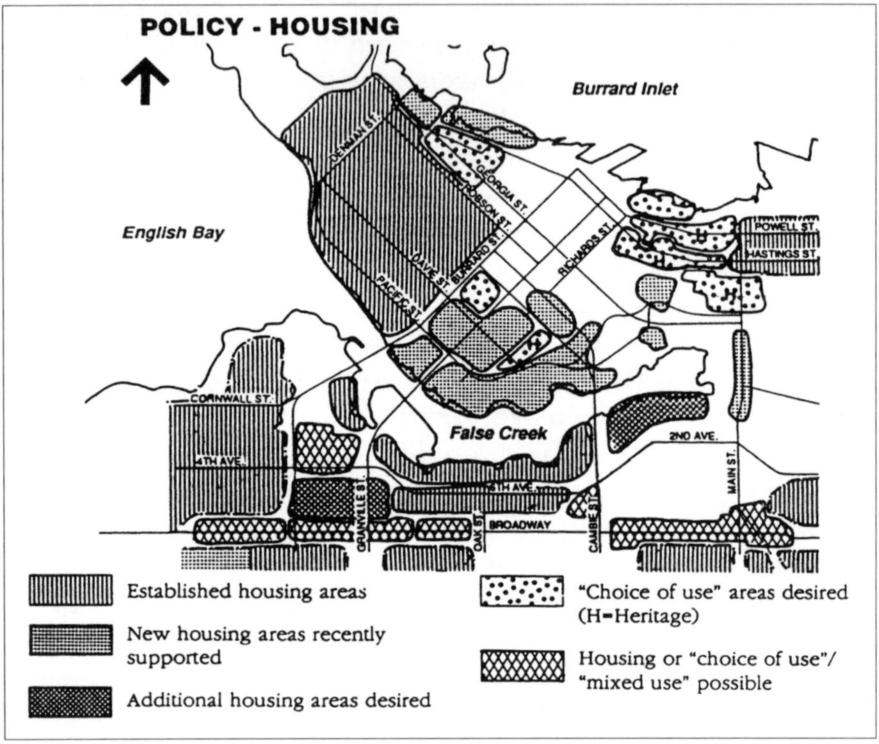

Source: City of Vancouver, *Central Area Plan* (Vancouver: Planning Department, 1991).

balance reinvestment and redevelopment with the interests of more vulnerable communities.[24] Although it is an area that has been in economic decline for more than a decade, it adjoins Central Area districts characterized by high development pressures – notably the CBD, Chinatown and the International Village – making it a likely prospect for redevelopment. At the same time, however, Victory Square is home to over 1000 people, most of whom live in modest single-room occupancy hotels (SROs), and it contains many heritage buildings of various grades. In the words of the concept plan, "[b]alancing the wide range of competing interests has not been an easy or simple task."[25] This assessment also applies to other districts in the Central Area.

Ongoing *adaptive re-use* projects involving the conversion of older office buildings on the CBD fringe to residential uses are another important example of reconstruction in Vancouver's Central Area. This follows a trend observed in other cities such as Toronto, where at least six such office-residential conversions are under way, and Chicago, the birthplace of the modern high-rise office building (or skyscraper).[26] The leading example in Vancouver is the old BC Electric building on Burrard Street. Other adaptive re-use projects in the Central Area include the development of the downtown campus of SFU on the site of the old Eaton's store at Hastings and Seymour, and the conversion into housing of the old Woodwards Department Store at Hastings and Abbott.

In the remainder of this chapter we examine specific examples of Vancouver's physical transformation at the local level. These examples highlight the different restructuring experiences of particular city precincts and the resulting contrasts in urban form, social structure and the built environment.

Concord Pacific's Pacific Place: Vancouver's Urban Mega-project

Concord Pacific's Pacific Place is Vancouver's (and Canada's) largest urban redevelopment project. Situated on the southern margins of the downtown peninsula (Figure 4.5, district A), the project involves the building of residential accomodations for approximately 15,000 people, 650,000 square feet of retail space, 600,000 square feet of hotel space and almost two million square feet of office space over a period of 12 to 15 years. Constructed on the former site of Expo 86, in a district previously given over to industrial and distribution uses, Pacific Place is an example of reconstruction of urban space on a grand scale.[27]

But the significance of the Pacific Place project goes well beyond its scale, as impressive as this may be in the context of Vancouver's overall development. The project also vividly illustrates the globalization of urban development, specifically the influence of Asian-Pacific multinationals and overseas Chinese in Vancouver's redevelopment; the role of mega-projects in urban restructuring; and the critical interdependency of capital, culture and technology in late twentieth-century metropolitan growth and change.

Concord Pacific Developments Ltd. purchased the former Expo 86 site on the north shore of False Creek in 1988. Nominally a Canadian company, Concord Pacific is in effect a subsidiary of Cheung Kong Holdings of Hong Kong. The principal shareholder is Li Ka-Shing, acknowledged to be Hong Kong's wealthiest individual. Other significant shareholders include Hong Kong billionaires Lee Shau Kee and Cheng Yu-Tung.[28] This ownership profile establishes an Asia-Pacific (and more specifically a Hong Kong) context for the project. In important respects the Pacific Place project is analogous to other urban mega-projects in various Asia-Pacific locations. In a review of some three dozen urban mega-projects in Europe,[29] Asia, Australia and North America, Olds observed that such projects are:

> (1) modelled on each other; (2) often developed and planned by architects, financiers, engineers and planners who have experience working on

> and/or knowledge of previous or ongoing mega-projects in other cities around the world; (3) often developed with both explicit and implicit internationalization strategies in mind; (4) marketed to overseas firms and high-net-worth individuals for subsequent lease or purchase; and (5) designed to symbolize a global urban "utopia" for the 21st century.[30]

Comparable urban mega-projects in the Pacific Rim region include the Darling Harbour Project in Sydney, the Minato Mirai development in Yokohama and the Mission Bay project in San Francisco.

In this context, we can readily identify the transformational impacts of the Pacific Place project. First, several years into the implementation phase the Pacific Place project is manifestly the centrepiece in the comprehensive reconstruction of the north shore of False Creek and the southern margins of the downtown peninsula. Within a relatively short time span (15 years), this 80 hectare site has been completely transformed from an industrial/distribution district into the site for Vancouver's world exposition in 1986 and then into a high-rise, high-density residential community (Figure 4.12).

Second, in many ways Pacific Place also represents an acceleration of Vancouver's socio-economic transformation process. The redevelopment of former industrial lands for residential and commercial uses is the most visible aspect of economic transition and land use shifts. However, the particular appeal of high-end condominiums to elite service workers constitutes another facet of the restructuring process. Also, the ethnicity of the developers (and that of many of the new residents) reflects the rise of a new Asia-Pacific entrepreneurial class in Vancouver.

Third, Pacific Place is not only a highly visible manifestation of Vancouver's connectivity with Asia-Pacific capital and corporate power, but also a symbol of the reorientation of Vancouver from a regional service centre to a city-region of international status. As Olds observes, the profile, scale and pace of urban mega-projects can "quickly reorientate the international imagery of a city."[31] This "international imagery" is reinforced in the Pacific Place example by an active sales and marketing effort that has sought potential buyers in Hong Kong, as well as in Vancouver and the rest of Canada.[32]

Finally, the Pacific Place project represents a prime example of the new mix of exogenous and local factors in metropolitan transformation in the late twentieth century, in particular the strategic interdependencies among capital, culture, environment and technology. While the substantial capital resources of Concord Pacific and its principal shareholders are seen as crucial to the feasibility of the project, local and domestic factors are significant as well.

figure 4.12
The Reconstruction of the North Shore of False Creek: Concord Pacific's Pacific Place Urban Mega-Project

With respect to technology, Pacific Place is promoted as North America's first residential development served by a comprehensive fibre-optic system developed by BC Tel, one of Canada's largest telecommunications corporations. The project also has several local design influences. Concord Pacific assembled a team of Vancouver-based architects (the Pacific Place Design Consortium) to prepare the plans. In addition, City planning staff were seconded to work with Concord staff in the preparation of plan broadsheets. These broadsheets were then used to convey design and land-use options to the Vancouver public in over 300 meetings.[33] The City insisted that Pacific Place plans respect the local environmental context (e.g., proximity to False Creek, views of the North Shore mountains) and complement existing and planned development patterns in the downtown as a whole.

The Pacific Place project thus reinforces the overall transformation of Vancouver. This and other large redevelopment mega-projects, such as the Coal Harbour development on Vancouver's central waterfront, provide support for Hall's view of urban mega-projects as one of four strategic preconditions for successfully negotiating the transition to more advanced stages of economic development (see chapter 1). The infusion of capital, technology and entrepreneurship generated by Pacific Place will clearly facilitate Vancouver's restructuring process. At the same time, the very success of Pacific Place implicitly underscores, on the one hand, the ascendancy of the professional and entrepreneurial elites in this advanced service economy and, on the other, the emergence of a new local identity and a more prominent international image for Vancouver.

Yaletown: The Reconstruction of an Inner-City Industrial Landscape

The inner city district of Yaletown, situated immediately to the north of Pacific Place (Figure 4.5, district 4), is only a fraction of the size of Pacific Place, but it offers a particularly rich example of urban transition and reconstruction in a post-industrial society. Yaletown's evolution provides insights into the broader processes of obsolescence, succession and reconstruction in the inner city. More recent developments also reflect the linkages between economic restructuring, occupational change and urban housing market preferences.

In 1886, the year of the City of Vancouver's incorporation, the Canadian Pacific Railway moved its BC base of operations from Yale, in the Fraser Canyon, to the north shore of False Creek.[34] In short order, the new Yaletown grew from a primitive settlement on the edge of the city into a substantial industrial community, complete with rail yards, repair and maintenance facilities, family housing and rooming houses.

With the expansion of resource processing on the north shore of False Creek around the turn of the century, Yaletown was transformed "from a frontier boomtown to an established working class community, complete with a school and a church."[35] As Vancouver expanded, however, Yaletown became part of the broader inner-city industrial district without a distinct identity of its own. In an editorial in the *Province* newspaper in 1924, Cecil Cotton observed that "Yaletown is today never heard of...Most Vancouverites are probably not aware that a district of the city was known by that name."[36]

By the 1970s, heavy industrial activity on the north shore of False Creek had fallen into decline as a result of market factors (plant obsolescence and a growing preference for suburban locations) and local government policies, in particular, the rezoning of False Creek South. The Yaletown industrial district shared in this general decline, evolving into a general warehousing and wholesaling district with relatively high vacancy rates. By the late 1970s and 1980s, however, new users began to locate in Yaletown (and other older industrial precincts in the inner city). Among these new tenants were architects, graphic artists, designers and others who tended to specialize in creative or applied design services (Figure 4.13).

The concentration of creative service firms in Yaletown can be interpreted either as a case of marginal users seeking relatively inexpensive space in the metropolitan core, or (more positively) as the outcome of creative professionals' and artisans' natural preference for environments with "character." The latter

figure 4.13
Cluster of Creative Service Firms in Yaletown

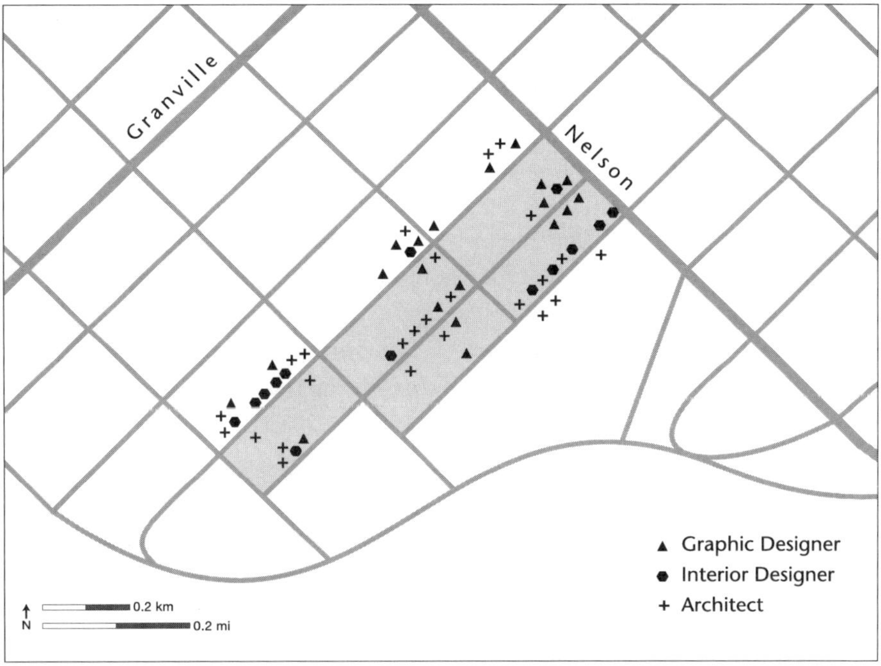

interpretation is supported by a survey that revealed that many design professionals in Yaletown and other inner-city precincts "expressed the desire to locate in an area with character and convenience – to lunching places, distinctive shops and other services."[37] For many, the somewhat gritty environment of a vestigial inner-city industrial district, together with coffee houses and other amenities, makes for a uniquely sympathetic and stimulating milieu.

Closer examination of the structure and function of industrial activity in the Yaletown district suggests that the clustering of applied design and creative firms also has considerable economic significance. Indeed, it can be seen as an example of "the internal specialization of the production spaces of the large metropolis" described by Scott.[38] What characterizes Yaletown as a "new production space" are the linkages to suppliers and clients, the types of enterprises involved and the availability of skilled labour. First, the majority of these firms were found to cater at least in part to other businesses and industries, many of which are situated in the metropolitan core, as well as to the general public.

Second, many of these creative service firms provide design inputs to various goods and services industries. One of the important features of advanced industrial production systems in the late twentieth century is a growing reliance on innovative design to add value, increase efficiency and differentiate products in increasingly competitive consumer markets.[39] The value of these design inputs is enhanced by flexible production regimes in which product cycles tend to be condensed and a high premium placed on the ability of producers to deliver new, design-enhanced goods and services to consumer markets quickly.

Third, creative service industries in Yaletown depend on other firms in the Central Area for key inputs. A survey of Central Area creative services indicated that design firms require an average of four service inputs for each service provided in-house, and that they obtain the majority of these inputs from firms in the metropolitan core.[40] For example, creative service firms in Yaletown rely on commercial photographers and printers in the Downtown South district, immediately to the north-west of Yaletown. Indeed, a more recent survey of design firms in Yaletown found that, in the majority of cases, location was determined more by proximity to suppliers (backward linkages) than to clients (forward linkages).[41]

Finally, the studies also revealed a strong link between the locational preferences of Yaletown design firms and the supply of skilled labour. Many of the professional and technical staff employed in the applied design and creative service firms were found to reside in the broadly defined metropolitan core, in areas such as False Creek, Kitsilano and the West End, which are at the upper end of the housing market, and in areas like Strathcona and Mount Pleasant in the east, which are less expensive.

Housing itself has become a factor in the most recent phase of Yaletown's transformation. As more amenities (e.g., restaurants, shops and recreational facilities) are established in the area, and as the Pacific Place project proceeds immediately to the south, Yaletown is an increasingly attractive residential location. The new cohort of residents, however, bears little resemblance to the typical occupants of older stock housing elsewhere in Vancouver's inner city. They tend to belong, instead, to what Ley describes as the "new middle class," that is, the well-educated, highly paid service workers or "service elite" that occupies the upper echelons of a restructured and highly tertiarized workforce.[42]

Recycling old industrial buildings has antecedents in the United States, namely New York's loft housing and brownstones, and also in Canada, notably in Toronto. The developer of a $16 million loft-housing project in Toronto described his market in this way: "This is the type of place that will appeal to people who go to Africa and stay at the Four Seasons. They are the ponytailed, Porsche crowd."[43] The Toronto developer of the Gotham Lofts project (New York allusions abound both in Toronto's and in Vancouver's loft conversions) identifies

figure 4.14
Reconstructed Heritage Building in Yaletown: The Percival Building

his target market as "active professionals, single or childless, who want high ceilings, doorless spatial flow, and no lawns...They eat out a lot; the kitchens are concise."[44] These tend to be some of the defining attributes of well-paid service professionals engaged in the business, finance, knowledge industries and creative services that are at the leading edge of occupational restructuring in post-industrial urban society.

In the Vancouver case, new Yaletown housing generally takes the form of high quality conversions of three- to eight-storey brick industrial buildings, originally constructed in the first few decades of this century. The Percival Building, designated as a heritage building by the City of Vancouver (Figure 4.14), and a conversion on Mainland Street (Figure 4.15) that also features street-level retail premises, are some examples.

This short history of the evolution of Yaletown over the last century depicts the various phases of this area's transformation as: (1) an administration and distribution centre for the initial CPR base of operations in 1886; (2) an integrated production district featuring industry, workers' housing and shops around the turn of the century; (3) a general warehousing and wholesaling

figure 4.15
Recycled Industrial Building in Yaletown: The Del Prado, Mainland Street

location in a period of decline in the 1960s and 1970s; (4) a "new production space" specializing in creative and applied design services in the 1980s; and (5) its current status as a new residential and retail district with fashionable restaurants and shops. Some of these uses co-exist; Yaletown is becoming a desirable residential address for urban professionals, but it is still a reconstructed production landscape with creative services firms that have strong (backward and forward) linkages to other firms in the metropolitan core.[45] Recent developments in Yaletown illustrate the specificity of change at the micro-level in a dynamic city as well as the convergence of economic change, occupational restructuring and urban reconstruction at the local level.

Culture, Public Policy and the Reconstruction of Residential Landscapes

As the cases of Yaletown and Pacific Place indicate, the reconstruction of Vancouver's *built form* is not simply a matter of market-driven redevelopment; a complex mix of social, economic, technological and policy influences is involved. The processes of transformation of Vancouver's *physical form* are also instructive. Changes in residential development, for instance, reflect (among other things) competing social visions, values, experiences and preferences.

The question of housing supply and affordability has assumed great importance in Vancouver as a result of demand pressures caused by demographic trends, shrinking household units, immigration levels and the income profiles of the market. Housing in Vancouver is the most expensive in Canada.[46] On the supply side, general access to housing must be assessed in the context of reduced federal involvement (e.g., CMHC's shrinking role in the supply of new housing) and efforts by the local and provincial governments to more effectively bridge the gap between supply and demand, in rental markets especially. In metropolitan Vancouver, approximately 20 percent of households are defined as in "core need," that is, as having to pay 30 percent or more of their gross income to obtain "suitable and adequate" housing.[47]

The housing debate is a particularly instructive example of the competing values and visions of a post-industrial urban society. At one level, of course, the issue of housing (and other competing uses) in districts zoned for industrial uses can be seen strictly in terms of optimal land use. That is, local authorities have an interest in deploying scarce urban land resources in such a way as to maximize their utility according to fiscal and economic criteria. Following the logic of this argument, local authorities may respond to changes in demand for land resulting from structural change by rezoning obsolescent industrial lands to housing, commercial development and other alternative "best" uses. However, in Vancouver, the residential reconstruction of industrial land involves choices based on more than cost-benefit considerations. For example, the rezoning of False Creek South from heavy industrial uses to medium-density housing in the late 1960s implied not only a utilitarian choice about land use, but also an important acknowledgement of Vancouver's emergence as a post-industrial urban society.[48]

During the Harcourt administration (1980-1986), Vancouver City Council adopted a somewhat different position by reaffirming the value of a plural urban society, emphasizing employment choice (blue-collar as well as white-collar occupations) and a more explicit valuation of industrial or blue-collar jobs. To be sure, this statement reflected in part Mayor Harcourt's affinity with blue-collar groups that represented important elements of his political constituency, but the decision to retain most of the city's industrial lands through zoning and land use controls was based on a broader, more inclusive vision of Vancouver's society.

With the election of Gordon Campbell as mayor in 1986, the debate over the future of Vancouver's industrial lands was reopened. Campbell, who was a member of the Phillips administration that initiated the rezoning of False Creek South, was clearly sceptical about Vancouver's viability as an industrial production centre. He instructed the City's Planning Department to revisit the question of Vancouver's industrial lands (an exercise that has proceeded intermittently since the late 1970s) and, more specifically, to identify further opportunities for residential development in obsolescent industrial districts.

In March of 1995, after extensive public consultation and debate, Council approved a new policy that effectively preserves the status of most of Vancouver's industrial precincts. The Planning Department found that the city's industrial sector did not fit the profile of urban industrial decline observed in so many other cities in the advanced economies. The planners discovered that the 686 hectares of city land zoned industrial (about six percent of the total city land base) has considerable vitality. The area contains over 2000 businesses and about 46,500 jobs, and it has low vacancy rates (in the three percent range) and significant re-investment.

While Council's decision in the spring of 1995 appeared to resolve the question of Vancouver's industrial lands, subsequent events suggest otherwise. The ongoing debate about whether to allow artists' live-work studios in areas zoned for industrial uses provides a good illustration of the complexity of choices in the contemporary urban landscape. On the one hand, the introduction of live-work studios can be seen as an appropriate response to housing affordability problems.[49] At the same time, however, the integrity of the City's industrial land use policy approved just three years ago is clearly at stake.

The notion of artists' live-work studios in industrial districts also recalls Jane Jacobs' well-known preference for mixed-use rather than exclusionary zoning to promote a more vital, interactive and stimulating urban society and built environment. Those involved in the debate – the City Council, staff and neighbourhoods – are divided on the question, suggesting that the issue of housing in Vancouver's industrial lands will not be decisively resolved, but will instead be reopened and reinterpreted as different visions of the city, its form and built environment are articulated over time.[50]

Preferences in the reconstruction of Vancouver's built environment can also be examined from the perspective of ethnicity and culture. In Vancouver, the redevelopment of residential areas over the past decade or so has generated intense public debate involving issues of taste and aesthetics but with distinct overtones of race. Coinciding with a period of high and increasing immigration from Asia-Pacific societies, the last decade has been marked by a series of neighbourhood struggles over the design, the scale and even the landscaping of new or reconstructed houses.

At one level, conflicts over the introduction (and in some areas, dominance) of new housing styles can be viewed simply in terms of urban land economics, as relatively small dwellings on large, expensive lots are demolished in order to make way for new structures that more fully utilize the site. Residential real estate prices in many parts of Vancouver have experienced sustained periods of inflation, making Vancouver the most expensive housing market in Canada. New buyers may, justifiably, want to construct housing that more fully realizes the development potential of the site, both for personal use and for higher resale value.

But these large (or "monster") new houses – associated in the public mind chiefly with Asian or Asian-Canadian residents – also represent a stark departure from traditional Vancouver houses, not just in scale, but also in style and design. For much of Vancouver's history, tastes in housing design were strongly influenced by the dominant English (or at least Anglophile) elite and were expressed most frequently in the mock Tudor or Georgian styles. Although these were most dramatically exemplified in Shaughnessy's grand, baronial mansions, originally the homes of captains of industry and railroad magnates around the turn of the century, they were also replicated on a smaller scale in many West Side neighbourhoods, complete with generous landscaping in the form of trees and shrubbery (Figure 4.16).

Later, the introduction of a distinct West Coast style inspired an indigenous Vancouver residential style (or architectural vernacular) that has many variations, but whose main characteristics are clean building lines, wooden

figure 4.16
Tudor-Style House, West-Side Vancouver (McKenzie Heights)

siding and extensive landscaping. One example is the classic "Kits" style of large, wood-sided house with peaked roofs (influenced by the craftsman residential style) prominent in Vancouver's Kitsilano district (Figure 4.17).

With the arrival of a growing number of non-British immigrants after the Second World War, new residential tastes began to emerge. In the 1960s and 1970s, German and Italian immigrants favoured the so-called "Vancouver specials," box-shaped buildings with wrought-iron railings, aluminum-frame windows and stuccoed exteriors which, at the time, also generated some criticism. These houses typically incorporated secondary suites, which could accommodate relatives or be used to generate rental income.

Today's so-called monster houses are in some ways the architectural descendants of the Vancouver specials,[51] although they are often built on larger lots and on a correspondingly (often much) larger scale. With their generic fake-brick fronts, frosted glass, bulging bay windows, two-story columns, street-visible chandeliers and flat, red-tile roofs, they have become a focus of neighbourhood conflicts about the desirability of encouraging housing forms that are compatible with traditional Vancouver residential styles. Some of these new, large

figure 4.17
Reconstructed Kitsilano-Style House, Point Grey Road

houses (Figure 4.18) are seen as a pastiche of design features that contrast starkly with the more conventional styles.

Because many of the owners of these houses are of Asian (principally Chinese and South Asian) ethnicity, debates about the suitability of new housing styles in Vancouver typically have a racial component. While many criticize Asians (directly, or more often, indirectly) for constructing homes that they perceive to be inimical to the design values of existing neighbourhoods, others blame the builders who create the over-sized "cookie cutter" houses. And it must be said that the typical Vancouver "monster house" bears little relation to the residential vernaculars prevalent in places like Hong Kong or the Punjab region of India, the originating homelands of many of Vancouver's recent immigrants. A Vancouver example of a more authentic Hong Kong residential style is the striking white-and-cream colonial style mansion shown in Figure 4.19 which would by no means look out of place in Hong Kong's Mid-Levels or Peak districts.

In response to the public outcry against monster houses and their perceived "desecration" of established Vancouver neighbourhoods, the City Planning Department has introduced "RS-6", a new residential zoning designation. While

figure 4.18
New House in "non-Traditional" Style, West-Side Vancouver

it is not in the City's powers to legislate housing tastes, even presuming such a thing were possible, the RS-6 zoning code has been designed (with the input of neighbourhood advisory committees) to at least discourage the most "detrimental" features, "things like excessive yard paving, flat roofs, bare windows and doors with no trim, cheap-looking wall coverings, coloured roofs, grandiose-looking entrances, and box-shaped houses."[52] The RS-6 zoning guidelines are being introduced initially in eastern Kerrisdale, where the monster house phenomenon is rampant, but it may be adopted in other West Side neighbourhoods. This would be consistent with the idea of greater devolution of residential development control proposed in the current *CityPlan.*

Interpretations of the monster house debate in Vancouver, vary according to individual perspective and experience. It has been ascribed to differences in tastes and aesthetics, to race and to neighbourhood concerns about the pace and nature of change in contemporary Vancouver. At least one expert has also suggested that the building of monster houses by recent immigrants and the vigorous resistance on the part of established neighbourhoods favouring traditional housing vernaculars can be viewed more broadly as a manifestation

figure 4.19
New House in Colonial Style

of a new socio-economic hegemony.[53] In this interpretation, the imposition of new, obtrusive, unsympathetic housing styles by recent Asian immigrants has a direct antecedent in the supplanting of First Nations settlement patterns by the mainly British settlers and immigrants earlier in this century. What is incontestable, however, is the clear influence of culture on the present-day reconstruction of Vancouver's urban form and built environment. It also illustrates, more generally, the interplay of local and external factors in the transformation of cities on the threshold of the twenty-first century.

Notes

1. "Post-industrial" describes a major phase of economic development in which service industries and "flexible" manufacturing processes (rather than mass or Fordist production) lead growth, output and labour formation. "Post-modernism" is a broader and more elusive term that rejects the elitist formalism of the modernist paradigm and a single world view, instead favouring cultural and political pluralism, eclectic architectural styles, regions and supranational bodies over nation-states as the dominant spatial-political units, and ecological and feminist values. See C. Jencks, "The Postmodern Agenda," in C. Jencks (ed.), *The Postmodern Reader* (London: Academy Editions, 1992), pp. 10-39.

2. For example, Vancouver's CBD is not in the centre of the metropolitan region but in the north-west quadrant.

3. T.A. Hutton and D.F. Ley, "Location, Linkages and Labour: The Downtown Complex of Corporate Activities in a Medium Size City, Vancouver, British Columbia," *Economic Geography*, Vol. 63 (1987), pp. 126-41.

4. D.F. Ley, "Liberal Ideology and the Post Industrial City," *Annals of the Association of American Geographers*, Vol. 70 (1980), pp. 238-58.

5. T.A. Hutton and H.C. Davis, "The Role of Office Location in Regional Town Centre Planning and Metropolitan Multinucleation: The Case of Vancouver," *The Canadian Journal of Regional Science*, Vol. 8 (1985), pp. 17-34.

6. A. Sancton, *Governing Canada's City-Regions: Adapting Form to Function* (Montreal: Institute for Research on Public Policy, 1994), p. 66.

7. D. Baxter, *Commercial and Industrial Floor Space in the Greater Vancouver Regional District* (Vancouver: Development Services, Greater Vancouver Regional District, December 1992).

8. C. DeMarco, *Industrial Lands Review. Part 2: Industrial Activity in the City of Vancouver* (Vancouver: Planning Department, City of Vancouver, September 1993).

9. Baxter, *Commercial and Industrial Floor Space.*

10. The exceptions are the Roberts Bank facility of the Port of Vancouver, a major coal port currently being expanded (and diversified with the addition of a container facility), and the less mature outer-suburban RTCs, which are endeavouring to build new agglomerations of service sector activities to serve local business needs and provide functional and physical definition and focus for the local commercial sector.

11. T.A. Hutton, *A Profile of Vancouver's Service Sector* (Vancouver: Department of Finance, Economic Development Division, City of Vancouver, 1989).

12. City of Vancouver, *Central Area Plan* (Vancouver: Planning Department, Central Area Division, 1991).

13. G. Bohn, "Fast Growth Spurs Output of New Apartment Towers," *The Vancouver Sun*, January 10, 1996, pp. B1, B2.

14. Bohn, "Fast Growth Spurs Output of New Apartment Towers."

15. Confirming the strategic importance of metropolitan structure to the success of planning in Greater Vancouver, the GVRD Board of Directors approved in October of 1995 *The Livable Region Strategic Plan,* which incorporates the nine regional centres (the CBD and eight RTCs) as its cornerstones. *The Livable Region Strategic Plan* was subsequently recognized as a "regional growth strategy" by the provincial Ministry of Municipal Affairs in February, 1996.

16. *Community* can have different meanings depending on whether it is defined (for example) by geography, ethnicity, class or other social constructions. It is used here as a basic element of urban social organization and a fundamental building block of local planning policy.

17. Bourne has observed that although national income inequalities in Canada as a whole have not increased, social polarization "both in and between neighbourhoods" has increased. See L.S. Bourne, "Polarization and the Redistribution of Income in Cities," paper presented at the 92nd annual meeting of the Association of American Geographers, Charlotte, North Carolina, April 9-13, 1996.

18. D.F. Ley, "Gentrification in Recession: Social Change in Six Canadian Inner Cities, 1981-1986," *Urban Geography*, Vol. 13, no. 3 (1993), pp. 230-56.

19. This important building has recently been converted to residential use. The decision to undertake this conversion may reflect concerns about the suitability of the former building configuration for modern office use, but it may also be the beginning of a trend toward the conversion of older office buildings on the fringe of the CBD's corporate complex.

20. R. Windsor-Liscombe, *The New Spirit: Modern Architecture in Vancouver 1938-1963* (Vancouver: Douglas and McIntyre/Montreal: The Canadian Centre for Architecture, 1997).

21. As quoted in R. Mason Lee, "The Grandeur of Rome Lives on in Vancouver," *The Globe and Mail*, August 12, 1995, p. D2. Mason Lee, a well known social critic and observer of Vancouver's development, offers the more charitable view that the new public library is a manifestation of Vancouver's cultural affinity with Italy.

22. City of Vancouver, *The Vancouver CorePlan: A Proposal for Discussion* (Vancouver: Planning Department, City of Vancouver, 1983).

23. In fact, distinct precincts can be discerned within some of these 34 Central Area districts; for example, sub-area 1 (the CBD) and sub-area 18 (the West End) feature highly differentiated uses, building types and social profiles.

24. City of Vancouver, *Victory Square Concept Plan* (Vancouver: Planning Department, Central Area Projects Division, June 1995).

25. City of Vancouver, *Victory Square Concept Plan*, p. 7.

26. J.S. Chanen, "In Chicago's Loop, Conversion to Condos," *New York Times*, July 27, 1997, p. 24.

27. The Mission Bay redevelopment project in San Francisco is currently the only urban megaproject in North America on a scale similar to Pacific Place.

28. Very few local interests were involved in the bidding for the Expo site, due to the very large capital requirements associated with the initial purchase price and the likelihood of a lengthy payback process. The revenues accruing to the provincial government from the sale of these lands were constrained by the conditions of the local market, the lack of serious bidders, the phasing of purchase payments and the fact that it was the vendor's responsibility to cover the cost of soil contamination clean-up for the site.

29. *La Défense* in metropolitan Paris and the Docklands redevelopment in Greater London are two of the most important urban megaprojects in Europe. *La Défense* involved commitments from private interests and all levels of government to promote a major new commercial centre some four kilometres downstream from central Paris, while the Docklands redevelopment resulted in huge public costs and the bankruptcy of the developer, Olympia and York of Toronto.

30. K. Olds, "Globalization and the Production of New Urban Spaces: Pacific Rim Megaprojects in the late 20th Century," *Environment and Planning A*, Vol. 27 (1995), pp. 1713-43. Many of these urban mega-projects are situated on waterfront, on disused central city port areas (Mission Bay), riverside docklands (Canary Wharf), obsolescent transportation zones (Pacific Place) and even reclaimed land (Minato Mirai).

31. Olds, "Globalization and the Production of New Urban Spaces," p. 1713.

32. The units in Pacific Place's first condominium tower were bought by Canadian and Hong Kong residents in equal numbers. Sales and marketing efforts directed at potential Hong Kong buyers are conducted at the Vancouver Information Centre in Cheung Kong's offices (Olds, "Globalization and the Production of New Urban Spaces").

33. For a critical analysis of the public role (and its limitations) in the planning of Pacific Place, see M. Beazley, *Public Participation in Urban Mega-project Planning: A Case Study of Pacific Place*, Vancouver, BC, Ph.D. dissertation, School of Community and Regional Planning, University of British Columbia, Vancouver, 1994.

34. As an inducement to the CPR to relocate its principal base of operations, the City offered a substantial quantity of land and exemption from municipal taxes for 20 years. P. Muir, "Industrial District Goes Cosmo," *Big City*, November 29-December 12, 1993.

35. Muir, "Industrial District Goes Cosmo."
36. C. Cotton, as quoted in Muir, "Industrial District Goes Cosmo."

37. Design Vancouver, *British Columbia Design Service Sector: 1990 Survey* (Vancouver:

Ministry of Regional and Economic Development, 1990), p. 21.

38. A.J. Scott, *Metropolis: From the Division of Labour to Urban Form* (Berkeley, California: University Press, 1988), p. 63.

39. K. O'Connor, "Utilization of Industrial Design Services by Firms: A Case Study of Producer Service-Industrial Linkages," paper presented at the 92nd annual meeting of the Association of American Geographers, Charlotte, North Carolina, April 9-13, 1996.

40. M. Shaughnessy, *Vancouver by Design: A Profile of the Applied Design Sector in Vancouver's Central Area*, MA thesis, Department of Geography, Simon Fraser University, 1988.

41. S.G. Brail, *Creative Services in Vancouver: A Case Study of Yaletown and Victoria Square* (Vancouver: MA thesis, School of Community and Regional Planning, UBC, 1994).

42. D.F. Ley, *The New Middle Class and the Remaking of the Central City* (Oxford: Oxford University Press, 1996).

43. As quoted in S. Bourette, "Developers Tap Lofty Ambitions," *The Globe and Mail*, October 15, 1995, pp. B1, B2.

44. J.B. Mays, "Lofty Visions for Hip Urbanites," *The Globe and Mail*, October 25, 1995, p. A15.

45. T.A. Hutton, *Reconstructed Production Landscapes in the Postmodern City: Applied Design, Intermediate Services, and Flexible Specialization*, Working Paper on Producer Services, WP 37, University of Bristol, and SSRU, University of Birmingham, 1996).

46. According to CMHC, the average (i.e., based on all residential categories) house price in Vancouver in June 1997 was $288,892, compared with $210,917 in Toronto, $144,330 in Ottawa, $142,603 in Calgary and $110,989 in Montreal.

47. C. Gray, *State of Social Housing in Vancouver–Report to Council* (Vancouver: Housing and Properties Department, City of Vancouver, May 17, 1994), pp. 2-3. Of course, many Vancouver residents among the middle class are certainly allocating more than 30 percent of gross income for housing, but this allocation represents a measure of choice as well as need.

48. Ley, "Liberal Ideology and the Post Industrial City."

49. R. Francis, "Painted into a Corner," *The West Ender*, June 1, 1995, p. 4.

50. Similar debates have taken place in other major Canadian cities, notably Toronto. In a recent Toronto mayoralty campaign, leading candidates expressed opposing views on the desirability of preserving (or rezoning and converting) industrial lands, reflecting sharply competing visions of the city's future and, more specifically, the value of social pluralism and occupational diversity.

51. F. Bula, "How Design Affects Taste," *The Vancouver Sun*, November 10, 1995, p. B2.

52. F. Bula, "Building a Better Big House" ("Vancouver is looking at new zoning to minimize the bad effects"), *The Vancouver Sun*, November 10, 1995, p. B1.

53. D.F. Ley, "Between Europe and Asia: The Case of the Missing Sequoias," *Ecumene*, Vol. 2, no. 2, pp. 185-209.

5

Structural Change and the Post-Industrial City-Region: Implications of the Vancouver Experience

This study describes Vancouver's emergence as a particularly dynamic city-region that is increasingly disengaged from national markets and the Canadian urban system, less reliant on British Columbia's resource-based economy and undergoing comprehensive structural change. It is a classic post-industrial city, where service industries are playing a leading role in economic and social development and in the transformation of the metropolitan structure and built form. Moreover, much of the growth in tertiary industry and employment has been associated with intermediate demand (i.e., providing services to other firms), rather than consumer demand. Over the past two decades, the expansion of business (or producer) services has generated strong growth in employment, output and trade. This process of tertiarization has contributed to the restructuring of the metropolitan economy into an advanced-services production centre. It has also been a leading agent of urban transformation.

When compared with the fluctuating fortunes of Canada's other major cities since the mid-1980s, Vancouver emerges as the national growth leader. In contrast with cities that have experienced decline or recessions for a variety of reasons – contractions in manufacturing (Winnipeg and Hamilton), a narrow resource base and limited hinterland market (Edmonton, and during the 1980s, Calgary) or the combined effects of political uncertainty and other structural factors (Montreal) – Vancouver's economy has greatly benefited from the growth of a broad range of specialized service industries and from its rapidly evolving association with the dynamic Asia-Pacific region. Over the past decade,

Vancouver has been alone, even among the ascendant service-oriented metropolitan economies of Toronto, Ottawa, London and more recently Calgary, in achieving consistently high levels of population and employment growth.

As we have seen in the Vancouver case, urban growth and change are demonstrably interdependent. While high levels of growth are providing the momentum for economic, social, spatial and physical transformation, change in all its manifestations – including technological innovations, socio-cultural factors, sectoral shifts and new regulatory and policy regimes – is also having a direct impact on urban growth.

In this concluding chapter we extend our analysis of Vancouver's development trajectory by referring to broad trends in urban growth, transition and transformation and drawing upon the experiences of other cities. First, Vancouver's distinctive transformational experience is examined within the context of emerging dynamics, that is, the new mix of exogenous and local factors that are influencing urban development. These factors are significant, as they underpin the international roles of city-regions while reasserting the importance of place and locality.

This general discussion sets the stage for an examination of urban competitive advantage. Although nation-states remain significant economic entities with important regulatory and policy levers, city-regions have clearly become key players within the global economy. In advanced economies especially, metropolitan regions perform strategic functions not only as gateways for trade and exchange, but also as centres for technological innovation and the diffusion of specialized knowledge, and as key nodes in extended production networks. This underscores the need to better understand the defining elements of urban competitive advantage in a context of economic globalization and market integration. It also suggests that the prospects for Canada's cities are highly differentiated.

Finally, we examine some of the policy issues raised by this study. The discussion highlights the need for a stronger policy response to the restructuring of Canada's city-regions. We consider various Canadian and international models and conclude with specific recommendations on policy directions for Vancouver.

The New Mix of Urban Development Factors: Lessons from the Vancouver Experience

As we have seen in this study, macro-level forces are playing a leading role in the transformation of city-regions. The rise of multinational enterprises (MNEs), corporate restructuring, the internationalization of most commodity markets, the diffusion of new production and communication technologies, the liberalization of financial markets and the emergence of new continental trading blocs are all having an impact on the development trajectories of national, regional and urban economies not only in the more advanced economies of the OECD, but also in newly industrialized and developing countries. Due to their pervasive influence, these macro-level forces have tended to impose common structural changes on city-regions. These include the contraction of traditional Fordist industries and expansion of tertiary activity and technology-intensive production, and the resulting changes in the division of labour favouring knowledge- or information-related occupations.

However, as powerful as these structural forces are, they are mediated and mitigated by national and regional factors. This explains the important differences observed among various cities' growth and transformational experiences. At the national level, the mediating influences are primarily a function of distinctive public policies and regulatory regimes (e.g., tariff and trade policies), fiscal and monetary policies and regional development programmes. Evidence suggests that these factors still play a significant role. As Helliwell and McCallum[1] observed, interprovincial trade in Canada remains many times higher than province-to-state trade, suggesting that we have not yet reached the state of the "borderless world" envisioned by Kenichi Ohmae.

In Canada, however, the role of the federal government in shaping urban growth and development has declined considerably. The progressive offloading of fiscal responsibility, the greatly attenuated role of the CMHC in the provision of urban housing and the retrenchment in regional development policies all bear witness to the decreasing federal influence. Apart from specific, one-off initiatives, the federal infrastructure programme may be the last major national urban development programme. While this programme entails substantial federal and provincial capital expenditures, it is hardly a decisive factor in the development prospects of most Canadian cities.[2]

While the federal (and in many cases the provincial[3]) government's influence on urban development may be waning, local and regional factors are increasingly important in urban development. These factors include not only *in situ* characteristics and attributes, but also new external relationships that are the result of changes in trade patterns and the structure of capital markets; reconfigured city-hinterland relationships; and the role of immigrants in enhancing inter-city networks of market intelligence, communications, investment and trade.

Changing City-Hinterland Relationships and Dynamics

The economic performances of Canadian cities have, to a large extent, depended on the relative fortunes of their resource-based hinterlands. Cities are linked to their hinterlands by complex networks of commodity exchange, production and consumption patterns, flows of specialized services and other sociocultural relationships (see chapter 2). As Coffey observes, "the 'regional factor' often exerts an important influence in the Canadian context."[4] This appears to have been the case for Vancouver, whose growth relative to other CMAs during the 1980s paralleled British Columbia's leading position among Canadian provinces in employment growth.[5]

However, these city-hinterland relations are not immutable. Indeed, rapidly changing relationships between metropolitan centres and their broader regions may be contributing to both the differentiation of growth patterns in the Canadian urban system and the increasing divergence between metropolitan economies and their provincial territories. Urban areas in Canada are generally faring better than their resource-dependent hinterlands, giving way to what has been described as a "two-track growth pattern: reasonable growth in and around the major urban areas and slow growth elsewhere."[6] Urban, and particularly metropolitan areas possess overwhelming structural economic advantages in terms of market scale and concentration, industrial mix, and access to capital, technology and skilled labour.

Beyond the traditional concept of hinterland in the regional, provincial and national contexts, changing hinterland relationships can also be identified in terms of linkages between cities and extended international and global markets. Figure 5.1 depicts some aspects of changing hinterland relations and dynamics in the cases of Toronto, Montreal and Vancouver. In each of these cities important changes are occurring, but in response to different sets of factors and with very different outcomes. The Montreal case is distinctive in that it has suffered (in Mario Polèse's words) a "lost empire," a reference to its former status as a key gateway to the West.[7] There has also been some penetration of its provincial market by firms based in Toronto and New York, but the city has been able to maintain some measure of economic dynamism as a result of extensive linkages with international markets.

Toronto, on the other hand, has become dominant in the provincial and the national markets, supplanting Montreal as Canada's principal financial and industrial centre. Over the past two decades, the growth of its corporate, financial and head office sectors has positioned Toronto as a second-tier global city, along with urban centres such as Sydney, Frankfurt and San Francisco.

Vancouver's relationships with its provincial hinterland and external markets are in many ways unique and contribute to its distinctive position within the Canadian urban system. As we have seen, the relative importance of Vancouver's traditional links with the province's natural-resource sector is diminishing as

figure 5.1
Changing Hinterland and External Market Relations in Canada's "Big Three" Metropolises: Toronto, Montreal and Vancouver

	TORONTO	MONTREAL	VANCOUVER
Regional level	Provincial capital and corporate control centre Centre of southern Ontario production sector (notably auto production and related industries); "overspill" growth beyond Toronto Metro to Greater Toronto Area (GTA)	High-order service centre for "linguistically defined" hinterland Montreal's "territory" subject to penetration from higher-order business centres (e.g., Toronto and New York); provincial political power increasingly concentrated in Quebec City	Command and control functions for BC's staple sector eroded by acquisitions, buy-outs and corporate restructuring Deepening linkages (economic, cultural, recreational) with Pacific Northwest and Cascadia bioregion
National level	Emerged as leading national business centre (banking, finance, head offices) in the 1970s Dominant Canadian "industrial metropole" (largest manufacturing sector)	Loss of corporate control functions to Toronto over the last quarter-century Diminution of its western gateway role (banking, transportation) since the 1970s	Disengagement from national markets and Canadian urban system Increasing cyclical divergence between Vancouver and other major Canadian city-regions
International/ global level	Established as second-tier world city (banking, finance, stock exchange and producer services) Linkages with cities and industries in US heartland (e.g., auto sector) Strong relationships with overseas societies (e.g., Asia, Caribbean, Europe) enhanced by having Canada's most diverse ethno-cultural population	Strong links to *la francophonie* (trade, culture, academia) Significant trading relationships with Southeast Asia, South America (engineering, aerospace, transportation industries) International image as cosmopolitan city and society	Integration with Asian-Pacific markets and societies Multifaceted relationships with Asian-Pacific cities (e.g., Hong Kong, Guangzhou) Role of diasporas in enhancing connectivity between Vancouver and major Asian city-regions

the city's command and control functions in this sector gradually erode. Its economy has nevertheless remained as vigorous (if not more so), mostly as a result of its increasing engagement with Pacific Rim markets, societies and cities. In a sense, Vancouver's hinterland has expanded beyond the confines of the provincial territory to encompass strong and increasingly defining relationships with the Asia-Pacific, the world's most dynamic economic and trading zone over the past decade.

Recent trends in British Columbia illustrate the changing city-hinterland rapport. As a number of analysts have observed, there are many indications of the deterioration of the provincial economy over the past two years or so – per capita GDP has fallen, business investment is lagging behind that in other provinces and competitiveness (as measured by unit labour costs) has declined over the 1990s.[8] These aggregate trends, which reflect significant structural adjustments and cyclical problems in the hinterland's resource sector, stand in marked contrast with the situation in Vancouver. For instance, employment in Vancouver CMA continues to increase annually, unemployment (at 8.1 percent in February 1997) is significantly lower than in the rest of the province and most other Canadian cities, and building permits remain in the $3.25-$3.50 billion range on an annual basis, as they have been throughout the 1990s.[9] Also, metropolitan Vancouver, with just under one-half of British Columbia's population, accounts for about 70 percent of provincial business incorporations annually.[10] These figures are an indication of both the entrepreneurial dynamism of the Vancouver economy and the increasing divergence between city and hinterland in British Columbia.[11]

International Connectivity and Global Networks

These complex and evolving city-hinterland relationships are to a great extent based on and facilitated by elaborate connecting systems and networks – telecommunications systems, financial linkages and institutions, transportation infrastructure, international air connections, and inter- and intra-cultural relations – which differ from one area to another, and produce distinctive patterns of urban growth and development. For instance, Vancouver's external networks and its connections with markets and cities in the Asia-Pacific can be seen as determining elements of the city's distinctive development path and its divergence from the growth patterns of other Canadian city-regions.

The quality of a city's links to external markets and major international business centres largely determines its capacity to (1) engage in international commodity trade; (2) participate in global financial markets and attract foreign capital; (3) interface with institutions and networks of specialized information, knowledge and expertise; (4) facilitate international tourism and convention activity; and (5) function as an intermediary for a wide range of international transactions and brokerage activities. There are, of course, potential costs as well as benefits associated with having closer links to international markets and trading systems. These include increased exposure to the vagaries of international and global business cycles, exogenous shocks and stresses (particularly those related to changes in financial and commodity markets) and the inflationary impact of foreign investment on local residential real estate and other consumer markets.

The size of the city is, of course, an important factor. World cities such as New York, London and Tokyo not only participate in international business, finance and trade, they can also shape developments and influence global markets due to their concentrations of financial corporations and head offices.[12] These world cities are the loci of control of the global economy.

Vancouver does not by any means approach the status of a world city. However, as a result of its relatively strong ties with these key foreign markets and systems of exchange, Vancouver has emerged as a significant node within the Asia-Pacific urban system and a major national (and even North American) gateway to Asia. This new role is reflected in a wide range of functions and activities, including sea-borne commodity trade, air travel and tourism, producer services (e.g., real estate development, engineering and management consulting) and education.

International and global connectivity are facilitated by what Peter Rimmer describes as "multi-layered" inter-city global networks.[13] In Vancouver's case, the principal channels of connectivity include:

- Trans-Pacific sea-borne cargo routes, specializing in bulk cargo and resource commodities, with regular connections to major Pacific Rim deep-sea ports;
- Trans-Pacific air connections, including direct flights by most of the major Asia-Pacific carriers (e.g., Japan Airlines, Cathay Pacific and Singapore Airlines) as well as daily flights by Canadian Airlines International and Air Canada, which connect Vancouver to other Pacific Rim business centres;
- Advanced telecommunications systems, including fibre optic and satellite feeds, which link Vancouver to other nodes of the Asia-Pacific urban network;
- Corporate networks created by the hundreds of Vancouver-based firms engaged in Asia-Pacific trade, commerce, investment and tourism;
- Strategic networks linking Vancouver to the Asia-Pacific created by major foreign firms and subsidiaries engaged in key sectors of activity, for example (1) in finance, the Hongkong Bank of Canada, which has its headquarters in Vancouver; (2) in aviation, Cathay Pacific, for which Vancouver serves as the North American operations centre; (3) in real estate development, Concord Pacific, a subsidiary of Cheung Kong Holdings of Hong Kong; (4) in business services, international firms such as the legal firm Stikeman Elliott; and (5) in trading, the subsidiaries of companies such as Mitsubishi and Sumitomo;

- Networks of public institutions, such as those involving UBC and the Asia-Pacific Foundation of Canada, which are engaged in many joint programmes and exchanges with Asia-Pacific partners (UBC's exchange programme with Ritsumeikan University of Kyoto is a prominent example);
- Socio-cultural networks established by immigrant groups that enable the transmission and exchange of significant business, financial and market intelligence.

This last element merits further elaboration. Immigrants can contribute to urban and regional economic growth not only through direct and indirect spending, business formation and job creation, but also by participating in the complex networks that link new immigrant communities with their societies of origin and other diasporas. These networks can play a number of important roles:

- *Enhanced international connectivity* – Immigrant networks provide another channel of connectivity among cities through which capital, information, business communications and even social values can be transmitted. In the Vancouver case, immigrants have played a significant role in enhancing Vancouver's ties with the high-growth economies of East and Southeast Asia and the global overseas Chinese network.
- *Market intelligence* – While not all information exchanges among members of immigrant networks are explicitly commercial in nature, they often relay market intelligence to the new community. This additional *information capital* enables network members to respond to change and opportunities, which can be of benefit to the host community.
- *New opportunities for external trade and investment* – Immigrants may learn about particular opportunities for trade and investment in external markets from other network members who possess specialized knowledge.
- *Inward trade and investment* – New immigrants may convey information about trade and investment opportunities in their new communities to network members residing in the originating society, which could generate new flows of investment capital and trade and foster local economic development.
- *Diffusion of the entrepreneurial culture* – The arrival of entrepreneurial immigrants and their continued contacts with colleagues in their country of origin (and in other nodes of the diaspora) may produce an entrepreneurial "spread effect" in the new community (e.g., through business and social institutions, business partnerships and special seminars).

- *Indirect spin-off effects* – Communication between new immigrants and residents in the society of origin may encourage additional immigration.

The presence of these networks greatly facilitates Vancouver's association with the Asia-Pacific and reinforces its role as Canada's gateway to the Pacific Rim. While Vancouver's capacity to establish its presence in overseas markets may be constrained by other factors (as discussed later in this chapter), these networks provide important channels of connectivity to the high-growth Asia-Pacific sphere and enhance Vancouver's status as an intermediary between distant markets, societies and cultures.

Urban Culture and Economic Development

Socio-cultural factors are playing an increasingly significant role in urban economic development. *Culture* in this context is broadly defined to include the distinctive mix of values, preferences and behaviours observed in cities as well as the more visible aspects of urban culture found in a city's built environment, language (or dialect), visual and graphic arts and other art-related activities (e.g., theatre, literature and music).

While this definition of culture incorporates local and more universal elements, it is the local elements that contribute most directly to the distinctive development patterns of various cities. The relationship between urban culture and development may take several forms:

1. *Culture of indigenous development* – This refers to the effect of social beliefs (including religion) on development. An often-cited (perhaps over-stated) example is the potential link between Confucianism and the high levels of growth experienced in East and Southeast Asia.
2. *Culture of political economy* – Social attitudes toward economic development may be *indigenous*, as described above, or *induced* by the introduction of particular ideologies (the prominent example in this century is Marxian economics and social thought).
3. *Culture of social organization* – As is the case in some Italian cities and regions (see chapter 1), the quality of civic organization can have a strong influence on development. It has a bearing on a society's ability to form regional production networks and to cooperate in the interest of collective welfare.
4. *Culture as economic capital* – Certain cities such as Paris, London, Rome and Beijing, are endowed with a unique "stock" of cultural capital that becomes a major engine of economic activity (e.g., tourism and conventions) and a defining element of local (and even national) identity.

5. *Culture as an input into production* – Cities like Paris and Milan (fashion and apparel), London (industrial design) and Munich and Los Angeles (automotive design) are renowned for excellence in design used in manufacturing distinctive, high-value-added consumer and capital goods.
6. *Culture of amenity* – Some cities are well known for a high quality of life that stems from their recreational amenity and makes them an attractive location for firms and skilled workers (e.g., Seattle and Vancouver).

Culture can also interact with other factors (such as technology) to produce a distinctive urban and regional development *milieu*. Anna Lee Saxenian's work provides a good example. She compared the formal, corporate mindset of high-technology firms on the "Route 128" region of Massachusetts with the more casual, lifestyle-oriented technology culture of California's Silicon Valley. She discovered important contrasts in the behaviour and creativity of technology entrepreneurs in the two regions, which have also produced quite different regional development cultures.[14]

With respect to Vancouver's economic development, we have identified a distinctive urban cultural base that includes at least three different influential groups. The first is the established resource-based corporate elite that is in relative decline due to the erosion of Vancouver's head office role and the contraction of BC's resource extraction sector. The other two groups are the workers in high-order services and the knowledge sector and the highly entrepreneurial urban contingent of recent immigrants. These two groups are clearly ascendant.

High-order service occupations are associated with the rise of specialized, information-intensive tertiary and quaternary industries. In Vancouver, the significance of tertiarization and the growth of the advanced service sector is, to a great extent, related to the formation of a new dominant social class and its role in the "remaking of the central city."[15] For instance, the development of high-rise residential buildings in Vancouver's Central Area, the appearance of new cultural, recreational and professional sports enclaves in the metropolitan core and the city's new identity as a *service city* stem from the location, housing and lifestyle preferences of this "new middle class."

The rise of new immigrant entrepreneurs in Vancouver may be even more significant for the city's development. Although entrepreneurs are present in large numbers among South Asian, Latin American and European immigrants, they are especially well represented among Vancouver's quarter-million Chinese-Canadians. By establishing new businesses and providing employment opportunities, Chinese-Canadians have had a major impact on Vancouver's economy. As Diana Lary and Roslyn Kunin have observed, high levels of entrepreneurship are found not only among immigrants admitted under the much-publicized investor and entrepreneurial categories, but also among those admitted under other categories (i.e., the family reunification and individual classes).[16] This is a key element of Vancouver's new *entrepreneurial* as opposed to *corporate* development culture.

Chinese-Canadians also contribute to Vancouver's economic growth and development through the workings of complex diaspora networks. At a recent UBC conference on the significance of "bamboo networks," it was observed that the networks of Chinese overseas are comparatively recent and are subtly different from European networks. In particular, they are based on "long-standing links of family, kinship, village neighbours and regional linguistic groups."[17] Vancouver has a particularly large Cantonese population with origins in Hong Kong and mainland China's Guangdong Province as well as a substantial cohort of Mandarin-speaking Taiwanese (in the order of 40,000)[18] and smaller but significant Shanghainese and Chiuchow contingents. Each of these groups contributes distinctively to Vancouver's ties within Asia-Pacific networks and to its global connectivity.

The cultural influence of Chinese-Canadians (and other immigrants) on Vancouver's development is also evident in the emergence of a new multicultural urban social identity. The contribution of Asian writers, artists, film-makers, designers and architects to Vancouver's economy has now attained critical mass, moving beyond the familiar sequence of cultural events and festivals to become an inherent component of Vancouver's society. In the words of *The Globe and Mail*'s arts correspondent for the West, "Vancouver seems finally ready to see itself as an Asian-Pacific city: geographically, economically and, more belatedly, culturally."[19]

Industrial Structure and the Propulsive Role of Advanced Services

Vancouver's exceptional growth performance over the past decade naturally leads us to consider the role of its industrial structure (i.e., its sectoral organization and industrial mix) in this context and relative to that of other large Canadian city-regions.

At the aggregate industry level, Vancouver's industrial mix is, in some respects, similar to those of the two other CMAs at the top of Canada's urban hierarchy, Toronto and Montreal, but there are also some striking contrasts (Table 5.1). The three CMAs have roughly comparable shares of employment in business services (around 17-18 percent); transportation, communications and utilities (7.7-8.1 percent); and public administration (4.7-5.1 percent). However, manufacturing employment is far more important in Toronto and Montreal than in Vancouver, whereas construction employment is considerably larger in Vancouver. This reflects the city's economic dynamism in recent years (employment in construction can fluctuate rapidly and is notoriously cyclical), as well as the extent of the building boom associated with this period of sustained growth.

Vancouver's business-service sector is slightly smaller than either Toronto's or Montreal's in relative terms, but the proportion of workers employed in the key FIRE (finance, insurance and real estate) category in Vancouver ranks just behind Toronto and ahead of Montreal. Moreover, employment growth in both business services and FIRE has been considerably higher in Vancouver than in Toronto and Montreal over the past decade, underscoring Vancouver's considerable gains in this area and its rapidly improving status as a financial and business services centre.

table 5.1
Distribution of Employment by Sector
for Montreal, Toronto and Vancouver CMAs, 1994

	Montreal	Toronto	Vancouver
Sector		(%)	
Primary/extractive	0.7	0.7	1.7
Manufacturing	19.0	17.0	10.9
Construction	3.9	5.2	8.7
Transport, communications & other public utilities	8.1	7.7	7.7
Business services	17.8	18.2	16.8
Finance, insurance & real estate	6.4	9.0	8.2
Services	39.2	37.6	40.9
Public administration	4.9	4.7	5.1
Total	100.0	100.0	100.0
Total employment (000s)	1,523.0	2,043.0	900.0

Source: Statistics Canada, Labour Force Survey [adapted from IRPP, 1996]

The significant expansion of financial and business services has important developmental implications. As William Coffey observed, "all services are not created equal"[20] in their potential to lead growth. It is not simply a matter of generating new employment. He argues that "if development is measured in a more rigorous manner involving considerations of structural change, productivity increase, market-earned income and so forth, business services occupy the pre-eminent position among service activities."[21]

The importance of services relative to manufacturing has also been the subject of much debate, although the co-dependence of specialized tertiary activities and manufacturing in advanced production systems is now widely acknowledged. And while the concentration of manufacturing industries may vary among individual cities within a national urban system, as it does in Canada, virtually all dynamic cities in developed economies are now highly tertiarized, with upwards of 75 percent of their labour forces employed in services and considerable growth recorded in specialized, knowledge-intensive service industries.

The growth of specialized service industries and the impact of this growth on urban transformation and the evolution of advanced production systems is an important aspect of the development of East and Southeast Asian city-regions in the Pacific Basin urban network (Figure 5.2). This is true of cities of all different sizes and at various stages of development.[22] The case of Hong Kong dramatically illustrates the potential for specialized services to transform city-regions in this dynamic Pacific area. Although some still describe Hong Kong as newly industrialized, it has in fact a highly tertiarized economy, with services representing approximately 77 percent of GDP.[23] While much of the manufacturing industry has relocated to Guangdong Province in China, service industries in Hong Kong remain closely involved in manufacturing activity. The city is thus viewed as having made the transition from a manual economy to a knowledge economy that directs some five million workers in China, and is positioned to "help China produce the high-value 'service-enhanced' manufactures that will define manufacturing in the coming century."[24]

Vancouver's service industries are also involved in production in distant markets, albeit on a much smaller scale. However, the most distinctive feature of the city's service economy is its diversity. A wide range of specializations has developed. In addition to rapidly growing financial and business services and international transportation, Vancouver's tertiary and quaternary sectors include a large tourism and convention industry, film production and post-production, software development, biomedical research, higher education, applied design and creative services and specialized retail activities. These industries account for much of the city's economic dynamism over the past decade.

Environmental Factors and Quality of Life

The natural environment was a major determinant of urban development during the era of the classic "industrial city." Environmental considerations included physical location (for example, on deep-water ports or the confluence of major rivers) as well as proximity to the natural resources essential for industrial production, notably coal and iron.

Environmental factors are still of considerable significance for urban development, but the particular role of natural assets has changed in some respects.

figure 5.2
Typology of Tertiarization among APEC City-Regions

First-order world or global cities: Tokyo and Los Angeles	Dominant corporate centres of the Pacific Basin economy World-scale banking and financial sectors Large (but slow-growing) manufacturing sectors
NIC city-states: Hong Kong and Singapore	Entering post-industrial phase of development Major regional (and second-order global) centres of banking, finance and business services Service elites prominent within urban social morphology and political institutions
Major East Asian industrial metropolises: Osaka, Nagoya, Yokohama, Seoul, Taipei	Rapid growth of services on base of world-scale manufacturing industry Specialization in producer services, information industries and technology Increasing engagement with the global economy
Chinese mega-urban regions: Beijing, Shanghai, Guangzhou	Dynamic but relatively small service sector on large industrial base Policy support for tertiarization as part of overall economic modernization programmes Service industries to complement production and international trade functions
Southeast Asian primary cities: Jakarta, Bangkok, Manila, Kuala Lumpur	Tertiarization an agent in socio-economic dualism Receiving areas for FDI, increasing integration into global economy *Desakota*[1] structure of urban-rural linkages
Highly tertiarized Western city-regions: Sydney, Melbourne, Brisbane, Auckland, San Francisco, San Diego, Portland, Seattle, Vancouver	Growth led by knowledge sector and advanced-technology production industries Professional and information-industry occupations emerging as dominant social and political groups within urban societies Growth in service exports and trade enhances status in APEC urban system (complemented by recent immigrants and diaspora networks)

[1] Describes densely populated regions with a mix of traditional agriculture, modern factories, commercial activities and suburban development.

First, while location and siting remain crucial factors, a city's position relative to metropolitan development corridors, new regions of dynamic production and trade and recreational facilities may be as decisive as proximity to resources and large consumer markets. As telecommunications and air travel networks continue to enhance connectivity, distance becomes less of an obstacle. For example, it can be argued that Vancouver's status both as the northern pole of the Vancouver-Seattle-Portland north-west agglomeration or "Cascadia corridor" and as part of the Asia-Pacific urban network has largely mitigated the disadvantages of its peripheral location in Canada.

Second, certain aspects of the natural environment, such as those related to recreational opportunities and the quality of the "stock" of natural capital (e.g., water quality, agricultural land), are now widely recognized as important factors in attracting new firms and skilled workers. With the globalization of markets and the emergence of industries that are intensive users of technology and human capital, firms can afford to be more selective in their choice of location. In the "sunrise" (knowledge and informational) industries, and especially in the advanced-technology sector, decision-makers have become much more sensitive to natural capital and the quality of life as factors that have a bearing on the work environment and as assets in attracting key personnel.

Third, the integrity of the environment, notably the quality of air and water, has a direct effect on the health of the urban population and workforce, and therefore on the economy. Healthy communities enjoy higher levels of social welfare and tend to be more productive than those whose environment is seriously degraded.

The natural environment has played a crucial role in Vancouver's development. The city's location in the Cascadia bioregion and its siting on a major deep-water port and riverine estuary have certainly enhanced its role as a gateway. At the same time, its proximity to recreational facilities and wilderness areas is often cited as a positive quality-of-life factor. However, these advantages cannot be taken for granted: other cities, such as Seattle and Calgary, which are in some ways competing centres, also have high levels of natural amenity. In addition, there is growing concern about the degradation of air and water quality in Vancouver and the Lower Mainland. The emphasis on environmental policies in the 1996 regional planning strategy is a response to these concerns.

The Competitive Advantage of City-Regions

Economists have studied the comparative advantage of nations in relation to economic growth and export specialization since Ricardo's (1772-1823) classic study of England and Portugal, which emphasized the relationship between production costs and external trade advantage. A century later, Eli Heckscher (1879-1952) introduced a significant refinement by proposing that the relative concentration of key endowments such as capital and labour determines comparative advantage among trading nations. More recently, the rise of nations possessing limited natural resources, such as Japan, Singapore and Hong Kong, and the developmental problems of some resource-rich nations, such as Russia and many African and South American countries, have encouraged a broader view of comparative advantage that includes human capital, socio-cultural attributes, "induced" (i.e., policy-driven) factors and market dynamics.

Similarly, the new mix of urban development factors and the growing role of cities in extensive production and trading networks suggest that a more comprehensive framework is also required to truly evaluate the relative capacity of individual city-regions to compete within globalized markets and international urban systems and hierarchies. A comparative analysis in this case would need to include all the factors that influence a city-region's overall competitive position: the broad range of elements that determine its ability to (1) compete for capital, skilled labour and market share; (2) develop a mix of "sunrise" industries in a period of (potentially destabilizing) restructuring; (3) maintain a position at or near the leading edge of transformational change; and (4) achieve a measure of sustainability to overcome shocks and stresses.

Of course, this type of assessment of the competitive advantage of city-regions raises some problematic methodological issues. In addition to problems of data availability and reliability, there is the difficulty of attempting to determine the development prospects of dynamic city-regions by means of static data that may not capture changing circumstances, and the limitations inherent in assuming that major influences on contemporary development will be equally decisive for urban growth and change in the future.[25] There is also the issue of comparability. For instance, cities may compete at different levels (regional, national and international) depending on the sphere of activity being examined. Except in the most specialized cases, cities may enjoy significant competitive advantage at one geographical level, but not at others. The question is whether the cities being compared are meaningfully competing. For instance, can Vancouver really be considered as competing with cities such as London, Miami or Atlanta? In most cases, competition is likely to be both sector- and city-specific, and this may be difficult to capture in a table of comparative indices.

An example of conventional analysis of inter-city competitiveness is presented in Table 5.2, which includes 10 comparative indices for Vancouver, Montreal, Toronto and 12 other international business centres. Eight of the 10 are cost factors for businesses. Of the remaining two, one (public security) is statistically derived, leaving only one qualitative factor (quality of life). In general, the three Canadian cities fare well in comparison with the 12 foreign cities in terms of business and related costs. For most of these variables, the US and other international cities are considerably (in some cases, massively) more expensive than the three Canadian cities (e.g., housing costs in Tokyo, corporate

table 5.2

Business Costs and Related Indices for Selected Cities (for the years 1994 and 1995)

	Cost of R&D	Corporate tax	Cost of telecommunications	Cost of prestige office space	Housing costs[1]	Cost of industrial construction	Cost of electricity	Index of public security[2]	Cost of living index	Quality-of-life index[3]
Montreal	100	100	100	100	100	100	100	100	100	1000
Toronto	111	115	100	112	105	98	173	75	104	1002
Vancouver	**104**	**125**	**101**	**112**	**149**	**107**	**93**	**125**	**99**	**1003**
New York	111	150	175	188	311	166	272	665	128	953
Boston	118	133	175	202	249	144	263	445	115	973
Chicago	127	123	178	141	218	116	155	763	121	967
Atlanta	130	125	178	135	100	99	122	1288	104	961
Los Angeles	120	132	180	119	311	148	249	771	119	950
Paris	151	107	153	367	250	146	169	160	158	983
Milan	108	168	142	192	272	133	182	125	126	936
London	152	106	88	494	238	129	217	61	141	986
Brussels	136	129	147	195	169	134	169	13	156	993
Frankfurt	132	135	177	317	468	166	288	265	155	989
Stockholm	163	90	135	164	163	147	98	40	141	985
Tokyo	110	166	350	798	3615	327	253	28	282	975

Source: Communauté urbaine de Montréal, *Décision: Montréal* (Montreal: Office de l'expansion économique, 1996).

[1] Upper-middle-class suburban house

[2] Calculated on the basis of homicides per 100,000 population

[3] Montreal = 1000

taxes in Milan, and office space costs in Tokyo, London, Paris, Frankfurt, Boston and New York).

The three Canadian cities also rank high on the quality-of-life index, each scoring at least 1000, a level unmatched by any of the other cities in the sample. This result is similar to those of surveys produced by the UN and other organizations, which consistently rank the major Canadian cities among the world's leaders in terms of quality of life. However, two caveats should be registered here: first, the range of results based on the quality-of-life index is relatively narrow compared with that obtained for the other nine indices; second, while the index includes certain statistically comparable elements (e.g., mortality, health indices and educational levels), it may also encompass more subjective judgements related to lifestyle preferences.

As might be anticipated, the differences among the three Canadian cities are relatively small, compared with those between the Canadian and foreign cities. The quality-of-life ratings and telecommunications costs are almost identical, and office space costs and the cost of living are not dissimilar. There are, however, some significant contrasts, notably in housing costs, with Vancouver estimated to be almost 50 percent more expensive than Toronto and Montreal, and in the cost of electricity, where Toronto is clearly at a major disadvantage relative to Vancouver or Montreal. Toronto is also rated as much safer (as measured by homicides per 100 thousand inhabitants) than Montreal, which in turn is deemed safer than Vancouver by a similar margin.

Comparisons of this kind may be useful to the extent that they reveal significant cost advantages among the cities in a given sample and assuming that such differentials do influence the behaviour of footloose firms (as well as the commitment of existing firms). However, while no firm can be insensitive to cost factors, overemphasizing costs to the exclusion of other attributes provides an unacceptably reductionist profile of competitive advantage among urban areas.

A more comprehensive (but by no means exhaustive) framework of the determinants of urban competitiveness is depicted in Figure 5.3. This framework consists of 10 categories of variables representing various forms of urban "capital" and important systems in city-regions. Conventional cost factors are included, but the importance of other elements is also acknowledged, including quality-of-life and amenity attributes as well as other institutional and socio-cultural factors. While the importance of *human capital* (labour force) and *technological capital* in the metropolitan economy – and the fact that the quality of these assets varies significantly from one city to another – is increasingly recognized, the influence of other factors is often neglected in this type of exercise. *Social capital*, which is defined in this framework as the socio-cultural attributes

figure 5.3
The Structure of Urban Competitive Advantage: Representative Capital Stocks and Systems

Environmental capital	Location and siting Integrity of environmental capital stock Supply/quality of land Environmental amenity
Economic capital	Stock of production capital (factories, offices) Propulsive sectors, industries and firms (including advanced services) Agglomerative clusters Indigenous multinational corporations and firms Supply of commercial and industrial land Local market conditions (efficiency, openness) Local income levels and savings rates
Physical capital (infrastructure)	Roads, railways and other transportation systems Seaports and airports Public buildings Quality of the housing stock
Technological capital	Quality of local technological base Costs of technology Technology diffusion mechanisms
Human capital (labour force)	Labour productivity Embodied skills and expertise (including literacy and numeracy) Entrepreneurship Adaptability and attitudes
Social capital (population and community as a whole)	Quality of social organization (tolerance, equity, etc.) Community networks (socio-cultural agglomeration) Culture (beliefs, values, behaviours and cultural capital) Leadership capital Strength of non-governmental organizations (NGOs) Health indices
Connectivity and communications	Air connections to international business centres Niche within trade networks (commodities, services) Diaspora networks Communications infrastructure and systems Internal metropolitan circulation (efficiency of transit systems)
Institutions, governance and policy systems	Quality of educational institutions Efficiency of public institutions and agencies Integrity and openness of public institutions Responsiveness of policy systems Condition of local democracy
Quality-of-life and amenity capital	Access to health services Access to cultural and recreational amenity Personal security and safety Vitality of urban/community life
Identity capital and image	International image Uniqueness/distinctiveness of local culture, identity Community self-image and confidence

of the entire urban community, is a case in point. *Connectivity* and *communications* also feature prominently, as these are key elements that determine the ability of cities to function effectively in global capital, production and trading systems. Finally, urban *identity* and *image* are included in the framework since they constitute important factors for certain kinds of firms and economic activities.[26]

Although this type of inventory of urban competitive advantage clearly has limitations, it is a more accurate reflection of the range of factors that determine the capacity of city-regions to compete for capital, labour and market share and to negotiate the transition to more advanced stages of economic development. Unlike the statistically derived indices presented in Table 5.2, the elements included in Figure 5.3 require informed judgement and intuitive evaluation. This framework could be applied by establishing the ranking in each category for two or more cities in a given sample and weighing those factors perceived to be most critical to the type of inter-city competition at issue. Alternatively, one could assign a maximum value of (say) 10 for the highest ranking city in each category and then assign relative scores (of nine or less) to the other cities in the sample. As a further refinement, it might be appropriate to rank cities within broad urban categories, based on a composite typology of (1) metropolitan scale (population in millions); (2) stage of development; and (3) position in the hierarchy of international and global cities. Competitive advantage could then be evaluated among first-tier global cities such as Tokyo, New York and London, second-tier cities such as Toronto and Sydney, and specialized third-tier cities such as Vancouver and Seattle.

Although space precludes a comprehensive assessment here, we can examine briefly what this type of analysis indicates about Vancouver's competitive advantage within the Canadian metropolitan system. First, Vancouver appears to enjoy a strong competitive advantage over most Canadian cities with respect to environmental capital, in particular its deep-water port, its proximity to wilderness and ecological amenities and its strategic location on the Pacific Rim.

Vancouver also rates highly among Canadian cities in infrastructural capital. A decade of sustained private and public capital investment, starting with the Expo 86 building boom, has produced major new port facilities, a new international terminal and runway for Vancouver International Airport, a major convention centre (and a second one pending), a downtown professional hockey arena and public facilities such as the new municipal library.[27] These new facilities are generating considerable economic activity and revenues for both the public and the private sectors well beyond the construction phase.

Our assessment of Vancouver's competitive advantage in economic capital produces mixed results. On the positive side of the ledger, Vancouver's advantages include: (1) the overall dynamism of the service sector; (2) the presence of specialized service industry clusters; and (3) the strong performance of key service categories including business services, finance, international transportation and communications. In a report on Vancouver's "comparative advantage as an international city" for the Asia-Pacific Initiative, Craig Davis and Michael Goldberg concluded, on the basis of location quotients and export performance, that Vancouver possesses a significant comparative advantage among North American cities in producer services and communications. They added, however, that initiatives should be undertaken to enhance Vancouver's export-related services.[28]

Metropolitan Vancouver also has an adequate supply of commercial and industrial land, although land costs are high relative to most other Canadian cities. More importantly, however, there are significant long-term constraints on Vancouver's land development due to topography, political borders and the Agricultural Land Reserve. These constraints are such that by the second decade of the twenty-first century, other Canadian cities will likely be able to accommodate growth and development more easily than Vancouver (assuming there is no significant change in development densities).[29]

Vancouver is also clearly at a disadvantage (relative to Toronto and Montreal) with respect to its lack of large indigenous multinational corporations and major head offices. Indeed, Calgary has a greater concentration of "top 500" Canadian corporate head offices than Vancouver. On the other hand, Vancouver enjoys a significant competitive advantage in the Canadian urban system with respect to firms exporting to the Asia-Pacific, especially small to medium-sized firms.

The city also possesses competitive advantages in other spheres of activity. In addition to its enviable position within key international networks, Vancouver ranks highly in terms of connectivity and communications, and it has an efficient local government. The City of Vancouver's triple-A status with the major bond-rating agencies in New York, for instance, is an important advantage for municipal borrowing.

However, Vancouver also has weaknesses in a number of important areas. The city's notoriously high housing costs may reflect strong demand resulting from growth, but they have become an impediment to recruitment in some occupations. In addition, its high-technology sector is still relatively weak. Although telecommunications, transportation, aerospace, subsea and energy industry firms are located in Vancouver, the sector lacks truly propulsive enterprises on the scale of those found in Montreal, Toronto and Ottawa (e.g., Northern Telecom, Bell Northern Research and Corel).

In summary, Vancouver's most important competitive advantages appear to be in the areas of environmental capital, connectivity and communications, social and infrastructural capital and advanced service industries. These elements support the city's strategic role as a gateway and intermediary as well as its brokerage, tourism, cultural and knowledge-based functions. The lack of indigenous MNEs, corporate head offices and propulsive technology firms, however, represents a significant disadvantage for Vancouver, especially in terms of its capacity to project itself decisively in global markets. Nevertheless, the city is, on balance, well positioned to develop as an active participant in Asia-Pacific markets and in niche-type activities in global markets.

Metropolitan Transformation and Emerging Urban Policy Issues

The role of local governments in Canada (and in many other countries) has traditionally been limited to the provision of local services and infrastructure, land development regulation and public education at the primary and secondary levels. This narrow range of activities reflects not only a long-established culture of local administration, but also the limits of local government powers. Local governments in this country function almost entirely within the purview of provincial authorities, as they lack "full government" status under the Canadian constitution. In the current regime, local authorities are both "lower" and "lesser" levels of government.[30]

This emphasis on regulation, provision of basic services and administrative efficiency has served Canada's communities well, but it seems appropriate to question whether, with such a restricted role, local governments can address adequately the complex local issues raised in the context of economic restructuring, comprehensive socio-cultural transformation and concern for competitiveness and sustainability. Expanding the role of local government may seem radical, but it can be persuasively argued that far-reaching changes in the responsibilities of local government will become inevitable as a result of market-driven events and the actions of higher levels of government. The restructuring of local authorities recently initiated by the Ontario provincial government can be seen as evidence of this.[31] As Davis and Goldberg observe, the "time has passed in which cities can be complacent and passively await the outcomes of federal and provincial programmes...they must actively pursue economic strategies, land use policies, and marketing programmes that allow them to position themselves in this global system to take maximum advantage of emerging trends and opportunities."[32] It thus seems reasonable to propose that, at the very least, local governments adopt a more proactive policy stance, rather than merely reacting to external pressures.

This study has described the growing importance of city-regions as national and global centres of production, finance, knowledge, culture and technology.

Local governments have clearly lagged behind in these developments. Over the past two decades, local governments in Canada have undertaken sporadic economic development programmes consisting mainly of industrial and business parks, marketing and information services and incentive measures such as local tax reductions and land write-downs. These types of initiatives may help create some new jobs, but it is by no means clear that they provide a net benefit to the community (once foregone tax revenues and other related public costs are taken into account). Also, they hardly qualify as strategic responses to the challenges and issues identified in this study.

As we have seen, some of the most important influences on urban growth and change are local, which suggests that there are important entry points for local policy. These include human and social capital, environmental assets, physical infrastructure, community identity and quality of life. Intervening constructively in these areas, however, does present some difficulties, not the least of which is the wide range of issues involved and the need to coordinate the actions of disparate institutional players. Also, the fact that policy initiatives in these areas will probably only yield results over the medium to long term implies a planning horizon that may be difficult to sustain given short local electoral cycles and an often volatile public agenda. The quality of leadership is clearly crucial here, but scholars of urban development and policy researchers can also play an important role in bringing these issues to the attention of elected officials and communities at large.

For instance, Donald Lidstone, a well-known Canadian expert on municipal law and local development, has proposed that local authorities adopt a *sustainability contract*, based on the principles of "Agenda 21" and the Habitat II proclamation, which would guide strategic policy.[33] He also recommended that provincial governments grant new powers to local authorities to enable them to effectively assume these new responsibilities. The implementation of sustainable development policies at the local level may require much more than a new approach to metropolitan and municipal planning; it represents a new paradigm for local governance and policy making.

Sustainable development can be viewed as successor to the more tactical *growth management* plans of the 1980s and the *containment* model of the post-World-War-Two period (see Figure 5.4). The containment model was responsible for an impressive legacy of green belts as well as new towns, communities and housing in the immediate post-war period and in the 1970s, when it inspired many second-generation containment strategies. Yet, the containment model is too narrowly focused on spatial/physical planning and too inward-looking, and is therefore inadequate for the current and future needs

figure 5.4
The Evolution of Strategic Planning Models for City-Regions

MUNICIPAL DEVELOPMENT CONTROL	REGIONAL CONTAINMENT STRATEGIES	SECOND-GENERATION METROPOLITAN CONTAINMENT PLANS	GROWTH MANAGEMENT POLICIES	SUSTAINABLE DEVELOPMENT PARADIGM
Early 20th century to the present	Early post-World-War-Two period	1970s	1980s	1990s
Response to pollution and other negative externalities	Response to congestion in the urban core, suburban sprawl, over-concentration of industry in large cities, need for housing and social reconstruction	Response to resurgence of metropolitan growth and sprawl, over-concentration of commerce in the core	Response to costs of suburban sprawl, dispersed patterns of development and environmental degradation	Response to perceived ecological limits to growth, need for inter-generational perspective and integration of environmental, social and economic imperatives (influence of Rio "Agenda 21" and Habitat II Conference)
Introduction of zoning and land use controls, height and other building envelope guidelines	Development of regional plans incorporating (a) controls in the central area, (b) green belts, (c) new and expanded towns on metropolitan periphery, and (d) major public housing development	Emergence of "MK II" containment plans, with (a) controls on CBD office development, (b) decentralization strategies, and (c) regional town centres and metropolitan "multi-nucleation" policies	Updated metropolitan plans, focusing on livability, quality of life and the urban environment; experimentation with use of pricing mechanisms, densification, focus on public transit, delimitation of urban-rural boundaries	Experimentation with more holistic planning: (a) industrial ecology, (b) housing NGOs, (c) compact and complete communities (influence of neo-urbanism and neo-traditional planning and design), and (d) integrated planning for city-regions encompassing bioregions
Regulatory emphasis	Regulatory and distributive components	Regulatory emphasis with some developmental and distributive aspects	Largely regulatory emphasis	Attempts to combine regulatory, distributive and developmental aspects
Early applications in the US and Germany; now pervasive	Seminal influence of London plans 1944; influence of Abercombie, Geddes, Unwin	Examples of London-South-East (UK) plan, Delouvrier plan for Paris; many similar plans for Canadian, Australian, European, Japanese cities, Hong Kong, etc.	Many applications in US, Canada and other developed urban societies	Sustainable development in an incipient, rather than established, planning mode: growing number of experiments (including transitional urban sustainability plans) in Europe, Canada and other jurisdictions

of urban development. In contrast, the sustainability model is based on a developmental and integrative approach to local planning that extends well beyond the current narrow emphasis on regulation.

Some of the more progressive urban societies have responded to the pressures of restructuring by promoting sustainability and the integrity of major capital stocks (human, economic and ecological) within an intergenerational policy framework. This bold approach is still very experimental, but it is gaining acceptance in a growing number of communities, municipalities and metropolitan regions (e.g., in Scandinavia and Northwestern Europe), reflecting an increased awareness of and support for urban sustainability principles.

In summary, while market forces exert powerful and seemingly immutable influences on urban development trajectories, there is still an important role for policy in directing, reshaping or mitigating these forces and their outcomes. Even taking into account the important differences between Canada's and other countries' political and social cultures, it is clear that this policy role has by no means been fully assumed by Canadian city-regions.[34] Therefore, in the next decade, it should be a priority within the Canadian polity at large to provide local authorities with the necessary powers, territory and instruments to enable them to cope more effectively with the complex effects of urban restructuring. Explicit constitutional recognition of local authorities as an order of government and new powers sanctioned by provincial legislation would enable city-regions to better assume their increasingly important role in the nation's economic, social and cultural life. The future welfare of Canada as a whole will largely depend on the introduction of innovative policies that enhance city-regions' capacity to adapt to change and achieve long-term sustainability.

Policy Priorities and Directions for Vancouver

The challenges facing local policy makers vary from city to city, depending on a wide range of factors such as local factor endowments and overall competitive advantage, growth trends (or even decline, in some cases) and the specific mix of local values and priorities. In the Vancouver example, the broad emphasis on environmental policy over the past two decades seems to have been appropriate, given the deep community values associated with the region's natural amenities and ecological capital stock and the role of environmental capital in defining the city's competitive advantage. This policy emphasis notwithstanding, the cumulative effects of growth over the past decade or so have begun to significantly erode the integrity of Vancouver's environmental capital. More vigorous efforts, that is, better coordination of land use and transportation policies within the region and supporting regulatory instruments, will be required to preserve the region's quality of life and its competitive advantage in natural amenity.

There is also a need to renew Vancouver's economic development policy approach and programme. According to Coffey, the City of Vancouver ranked as a Canadian leader in this area in the 1980s, with an imaginative and forward-looking economic strategy initiated in 1983. This strategy, which emphasized the potential of the advanced service sector as well as the city's Pacific Rim gateway role and its economic and socio-cultural ties with the Asia-Pacific,[35] was in large part realized, but it has had no real successor.

The analysis presented in this study suggests some broad policy directions for Vancouver. First, the political executive in the City and the GVRD should articulate a fresh vision for the city that fully recognizes the importance of Vancouver's role in the Asia-Pacific and the Cascadia bioregion as well as the city's more limited future as command and control centre for BC's resource-based economy. One objective should be to develop ideas on how Vancouver can effectively build on its associations with the Asia-Pacific in strategic areas such as finance, producer services, tourism and education, and enhance its international and regional gateway functions.

Second, a new economic policy programme should be put in place to mobilize Vancouver's substantial corporate, institutional, human and socio-cultural resources. Considerable research and consultation[36] will be required to define the specifics of the new economic strategy, but the list of priorities should include: (1) carefully targeted marketing and information services; (2) support for Vancouver's export-oriented service industries and institutions; (3) land-use policies that actively facilitate the transition to advanced service and production industries and support crucial inter-sector and inter-industry linkages within the region; (4) active liaison and cooperation with immigrant groups to maximize the city's Asia-Pacific competitive advantage; and (5) recognition of Vancouver's status as a centre of higher education within the Pacific Rim and, in the Canadian context, as a teaching and research centre specializing in the Asia-Pacific.

Finally, there is a pressing need for a more explicit and cohesive *regional* economic policy. Over the last decade, there have been sporadic efforts by the GVRD to establish an economic strategy for metropolitan Vancouver. However, these attempts have been seriously compromised by the parochial attitudes of many of the region's municipalities as well as a general assumption that higher levels of government and the private sector can adequately serve local interests. Also, with most of the GVRD's resources being allocated to transportation planning and environmental policy, there is relatively little funding left to undertake social and economic policy initiatives.

This choice of policy priorities can be justified on planning grounds: the preservation of natural amenity and maintenance of efficient transportation systems are essential elements of Vancouver's economic well-being. But there is also a persuasive case for more forward-looking economic programmes at the metropolitan level. After all, the metropolitan area incorporates a large portion of the region's space-economy, production networks, labour market and commuter zone; even the largest of the GVRD's municipalities encompass only segments of these. More active municipal development policy initiatives, as welcome as they may be, are not a substitute for an effective regional strategy.

As discussed earlier, there is considerable complacency following more than a decade of relatively high growth in population, employment and investment,[37] but, as we have seen, the fortunes of individual city-regions can change very quickly in this era of economic globalization and market integration. Vancouver has acquired considerable economic strengths, but it also has significant weaknesses, notably the lack of indigenous MNEs, head offices of major corporations and propulsive high-technology firms. The GVRD should take the lead, with the support of its municipalities, to build a strategy that

- acknowledges the crucial interdependency between the environment and the economy;
- builds on the region's role in the transportation and communications sectors;
- facilitates the process of transition in the region's economy;
- capitalizes on the region's competitive advantages in environmental, human and social capital and its connectivity with the Asia-Pacific;
- enhances the region's resilience against the inevitable economic shocks and stresses.[38]

As the GVRD did with its progressive spatial planning initiatives, the regional economic plan should provide an effective framework for achieving metropolitan objectives and ensuring constructive coordination among municipalities. While local government in Vancouver operates, and will continue to operate in the foreseeable future, with important resource and jurisdictional constraints, local authorities can nevertheless intervene strategically and effectively to influence the trajectory of growth and change.

Concluding Remarks

This study has described Vancouver's ongoing transformation from "core metropole" in BC's resource economy into an increasingly significant node of the Pacific Basin urban system. Indeed, based on our assessment of Vancouver's multi-faceted association with the markets, trading systems, societies and cultures of the Asia-Pacific, it could even be argued that the city has attained "critical mass" as a Pacific Rim metropolis. This relationship will thus continue to be a defining element of Vancouver's development, and while it may at times be problematic – as the current turmoil in Asian currency and financial markets attests – it is, on the whole, much to Vancouver's benefit.

More uncertain is whether Vancouver can eventually transcend this growing international role within the Asia-Pacific region to assume the status of a world or global city. By the third decade of the third millennium, metropolitan Vancouver's population will exceed three million, which is roughly equivalent to the present population of Montreal – or, beyond Canada's boundaries, Singapore, Milan and Melbourne. However, attaining world-city status implies more than considerations of urban scale; it is a function of a city's particular role in the global economy and its level of activity in certain key areas. Thus, while Vancouver is unlikely to become a global banking or corporate control centre, it can realistically be considered an emerging world centre in certain specialized functions, notably as a gateway centre linking North America, Europe and the Asia-Pacific; as an international tourism and convention destination; and as an important node in global diaspora networks, in particular the overseas Chinese network.

There is, of course, considerable ambivalence on the part of Vancouver's population regarding its present growth trajectory, which reflects justifiable concerns about social and environmental impacts as well as current and pending changes in the city's identity and image. At the same time, the evidence of the last 20 years has shown that structural change inevitably implies profound shifts in the urban economic base, industrial structure and market orientation. The experience of cities such as Montreal, Pittsburgh and Manchester demonstrates this. Moreover, the severe recession that afflicted Toronto in the early 1990s shows that even the most robust and diversified urban economies are susceptible to sudden and severe downturns. In this light, the principal challenge is to develop policies for Vancouver that take advantage of the market forces and pressures of the new global economy in a constructive way, while recognizing and not compromising the value of the city's unique socio-cultural and environmental qualities.

Notes

1. J.F. Helliwell and J. McCallum, "National Borders Still Matter for Trade," *Policy Options*, Vol. 16, no. 5 (1995), pp. 44-48. The authors do point out, however, that preliminary trade data for the post-1989 period suggests that "the importance of the Canada-US border might have diminished substantially" (p. 44).

2. As the federal government gets its deficit under control there may be scope for new development initiatives, but these are not likely to be on the scale of the policies and programmes undertaken during the high-water mark of federal intervention in the 1970s.

3. Many provincial governments are themselves engaged in debt reduction and deficit control and are attempting to further offload spending responsibilities onto local authorities. The most dramatic example is the Harris government's plan to transfer a considerable share of social spending and public housing responsibilities to local government in Ontario. However, even NDP governments (notably Romanow's in Saskatchewan) are exercising fiscal restraint. Only British Columbia has an active public housing programme, but this has also been scaled down in recent years, partly as a result of the provincial government's revenue shortfalls and budgetary problems.

4. W.J. Coffey, *Employment Growth and Change in the Canadian Urban System 1971-94*, Working Paper no. W/02/1996 (Ottawa: Canadian Policy Research Networks, 1996), p. 71.

5. Coffey, *Employment Growth and Change in the Canadian Urban System*, p. 73.

6. J. Simpson, "Reform's Hard Line Against Quebec Exploits our Differences," *The Globe and Mail*, May 27, 1997.

7. M. Polèse, "Montreal, a City in Search of a Country," *Policy Options*, Vol. 17, no. 7 (1996), pp. 31-34.

8. B. Little, "The Hollow Sound of B.C.'s Boom," *The Globe and Mail*, May 26, 1997.

9. GVRD, *Greater Vancouver Key Facts: 1996 Edition* (Vancouver: GVRD, 1996).

10. GVRD, *Greater Vancouver Key Facts: 1996 Edition.*

11. T.A. Hutton, "The Innisian Core-Periphery Revisited: Vancouver's Changing Relationships with British Columbia's Staple Economy," *B.C. Studies*, no. 113 (1997), pp. 69-100.

12. Cities at the top of the global urban and corporate system also tend to play a role in all or most significant international markets, while second- and third-tier centres are characterized by more selective engagement, often concentrated in a smaller number of regional markets.

13. P. Rimmer, "Megacities, Multi-layered Networks and Development Corridors in the Pacific Economic Zone," in A. McNeil and T.A. Hutton (eds.), *Conference Papers on Transportation and Urban Development, Proceedings of the Third Annual Conference of the Pacific Rim Council on Urban Development*, pp. 6-56.

14. A. Saxenian, "Regional Networks: Industrial Adaptations in Silicon Valley and Route 128," presentation and panel discussion at the 90th Annual Meeting of the Association of American Geographers, San Francisco, March 29-April 2, 1994.

15. D.F. Ley, *The New Middle Class and the Remaking of the Central City* (Oxford: Oxford University Press, 1996).

16. R. Kunin and D. Lary, *Succeeding–Profiles of Chinese-Canadian Entrepreneurs* (Vancouver: The Asia-Pacific Foundation of Canada, 1997). Interestingly, the authors suggest that the success of Chinese-Canadian entrepreneurs is likely due to a propensity to work hard, rather than to other culturally determined values or behaviours.

17. G. Hamilton, "The Historical Evolution of Chinese Entrepreneur Networks," presentation for a panel discussion on *Bamboo Networks and Economic Growth in the Asia-Pacific Region*, Research Workshop on Chinese Entrepreneur Networks, UBC, Vancouver, April 11-12, 1997.

18. Vancouver attracted approximately 70 percent of the 7647 Taiwanese immigrants to Canada in 1996, according to a recent report by Jennifer Hunter, *Report on Business Magazine* (November 1996) p. 127.

19. C. Dafoe, "East Heats West," *The Globe and Mail*, May 3, 1997, p. C4.

20. Coffey, *Employment Growth and Change in the Canadian Urban System*, p. 123.

21. Coffey, *Employment Growth and Change in the Canadian Urban System.*

22. T.A. Hutton, "Service Industries, Economic Restructuring and the Reconfiguration of APEC City-Regions," paper presented to the Annual Meeting of the Western Regional Science Association (special session on service industries within APEC), Kamuela, Hawaii, February 20, 1997.

23. *Hong Kong 1995* (Hong Kong: Census and Statistics Department, Government of Hong Kong, 1995), p. 66.

24. "Hurrah the Middleman!" *Far Eastern Economic Review*, April 24, 1997, p. 5.

25. To these we can add the problem of separating purely local factors from national influences.

26. Certain urban centres have become strongly associated with specialized activities. Thus, they continue to attract new (or relocating) establishments because of the *identity* and *image* they project and the advantages they offer due to agglomeration factors. This is the case in Manhattan and the City of London for international banking, Los Angeles for film-making and Paris and Milan for *haute couture.*

27. The City of Vancouver pursues a policy of replacing about 1-1.5 percent of the city's infrastructure annually, which reflects the approximate life span of major public physical infrastructure and is consistent with prudent fiscal stewardship.

28. H.C. Davis and M.A. Goldberg, *Determination of the Comparative Advantages of Vancouver as an International City* (Vancouver: Asia-Pacific Initiative, 1988). The Asia-Pacific Initiative was funded by the municipal, provincial and federal governments.

29. There are benefits associated with land constraints: (1) they may encourage more efficient use of land, (2) higher population densities can lead to economies in public infrastructure and services (such as transit service), and (3) a more compact urban structure may enhance agglomeration effects.

30. It can also be argued that some local governments have been reluctant to use the powers they have. During the Harcourt administration, the Minister of Municipal Affairs introduced housing legislation to enable and encourage municipalities to exercise more vigorously the powers they already possessed in relation to housing.

31. See E. Slack, "Finance and Governance: The Case of the Greater Toronto Area," in P.A.R. Hobson and F. St-Hilaire (eds.), *Urban Governance and Finance: A Question of Who Does What* (Montreal: Institute for Research on Public Policy, 1997), pp.113-32.

32. Davis and Goldberg, *Determination of the Comparative Advantages of Vancouver as an International City*, p. 28.

33. D. Lidstone, "How We Live, Where We Live, If We Live," in M. M'Gonigle (ed.), *Urban Green Governance*, Report Series R96-2 (Victoria: University of Victoria Faculty of Law and Environmental Studies, 1996). "Agenda 21" was the statement of principles and recommendations for action produced at the United Nations Conference on the Environment and Development, Rio de Janeiro, 1992. "Habitat II" was the second world summit of the United Nations Centre for Human Settlements, convened in Istanbul, Turkey, in May of 1996.

34. This point was made by William Coffey in the first volume of this series. Coffey documented the inadequate local response to the challenge of structural change in Canada's city-regions and the outdated regional policies of the federal government. These policies emphasized primary industries and manufacturing to the disadvantage of growth-oriented service industries, which clearly represent the new economic base of Canadian cities. He concluded his monograph by exhorting all three levels of government "to develop a new consciousness concerning the nature and functioning of metropolitan economies." W.J. Coffey, *The Evolution of Canada's Metropolitan Economies* (Montreal: Institute for Research on Public Policy, 1994), p. 109.

35. Coffey, *The Evolution of Canada's Metropolitan Economies*, p. 102.

36. In this context, it is instructive to note that very little economic policy research is conducted among the local governments of the GVRD, a situation that seriously inhibits the task of policy development and implementation.

37. While growth in these areas is evident, as documented by this study, there are inadequate empirical data on regional GDP, trade and productivity. The lack of such data at the CMA level is a major impediment to a fuller understanding of the true growth of city-regions in Canada.

38. The example of Toronto, reported in chapter 2, vividly illustrates the vulnerability of even the largest and most diversified city-regions in an era of accelerated globalization and integration. In the Vancouver case, potential economic *stresses* include a protracted decline in the provincial staple or resource sector, while *shocks* might include natural disasters (such as a major earthquake), the break-up of the Canadian confederation and, as recent events have suggested, a prolonged crisis in Asian financial markets.

Note on Contributors

Thomas A. Hutton is Acting Director of the Centre for Human Settlements and Associate Professor in the School of Community and Regional Planning at UBC. He is one of Canada's leading specialists on the role of service industries in urban growth and change, and in this capacity has contributed to previous IRPP conferences and publications, as well as to an extensive range of Canadian and international books and periodicals. In addition to this current volume on Vancouver for IRPP, Dr. Hutton is presently engaged in a number of other research projects and initiatives on service industries and the transformation of Asia-Pacific city-regions.

France St-Hilaire has been a Research Director at IRPP since 1992. She currently directs and coordinates the Institute's research programs on public finance, city-regions, labour market and human capital. Her own research and publications are in the area of public sector economics, in particular, public finance, social policy and fiscal federalism. Recent publications include a book (with co-author, Paul Hobson) on reforming fiscal arrangements and a study of the incidence and redistributive impact of federal personal income tax expenditures.

Recent IRPP Publications

City-Regions

Paul A.R. Hobson and France St-Hilaire (eds.), *Urban Governance and Finance: A Question of Who Does What*

Andrew Sancton, *Governing Canada's City-Regions: Adapting Form to Function*

William Coffey, *The Evolution of Canada's Metropolitan Economies*

Education

Derek Hum and Wayne Simpson, *Maintaining a Competitive Workforce: Employee-Based Training in The Canadian Economy*

Thomas T. Schweitzer, *The State of Education in Canada*

Stephen B. Lawton, *Busting Bureaucracy to Reclaim our Schools*

Bruce Wilkinson, *Educational Choice: Necessary But Not Sufficient*

Peter Coleman, *Learning About Schools: What Parents Need to Know and How They Can Find Out*

Edwin G. West, *Ending the Squeeze on Universities*

Public Finance

Paul A.R. Hobson and France St-Hilaire, *Toward Sustainable Federalism: Reforming Federal-Provincial Fiscal Arrangements*

Governance

Guy Laforest and Roger Gibbins, *Beyond the Impasse: Toward Reconciliation*

Guy Laforest and Roger Gibbins, *Sortir de l'impasse : les voies de la réconciliation*

Peter Aucoin, *The New Public Management: Canada in Comparative Perspective*

F. Leslie Seidle, *Rethinking the Delivery of Public Services to Citizens*

Kirk Cameron, Graham White, *Northern Governments in Transition: Political and Constitutional Development in the Yukon, Nunavut and the Western Northwest Territories*

G. Bruce Doern, *The Road to Better Public Services: Progress and Constraints in Five Canadian Federal Agencies*

Donald G. Lenihan, Gordon Robertson, Roger Tassé, *Canada: Reclaiming the Middle Ground*

F. Leslie Seidle (ed.), *Seeking a New Canadian Partnership: Asymmetrical and Confederal Options*

F. Leslie Seidle (ed.), *Equity and Community: The Charter, Interest Advocacy and Representation*

F. Leslie Seidle (ed.), *Rethinking Government: Reform or Reinvention?*

Social Policy

Adil Sayeed (ed.), *Workfare: Does it Work? Is it Fair?*

Monique Jérôme-Forget, Joseph White and Joshua M. Wiener (eds.), *Health Care Reform Through Internal Markets: Experience and Proposals*

Ross Finnie, *Child Support: The Guideline Options*

Elisabeth B. Reynolds (ed.), *Income Security: Changing Needs, Changing Means*

Jean-Michel Cousineau, *La Pauvreté et l'État : Pour un nouveau partage des compétences en matière de sécurité sociale*

Telecommunications

W.T. Stanbury (ed.), *Perspectives on the New Economics and Regulation of Telecommunications*

Yves Rabeau, *Les télécommunications : problématique d'une industrie en évolution rapide*

Recent IRPP Publications

Telecommunications cont'd

Charles Sirois, Claude E. Forget, *The Medium and the Muse: Culture, Telecommunications and the Information Highway*

Charles Sirois, Claude E. Forget, *Le Médium et les Muses : la culture, les télécommunications et l'autoroute de l'information*

Choices / Choix

Public Finance:

Technology, Taxation and Canada's Competitiveness: Policies for the New Global Economy
Les pensions de retraite dans une société vieillissante
Bad Tasting Medecine: Removing Intergenerational Inequity from the CPP
The Taxing Question of Savings: Should Retirement Savings be Taxed?
A qui profitent les avantages fiscaux ? / For Whom the Tax Breaks
Restoring Generational Balance in Canada
Répartition régionale des dépenses fiscales touchant les corporations / Regional Distribution of Federal Corporate Tax Expenditures

Governance:

Les agences britanniques, source d'inspiration des modernisations administratives
Operational Agencies: From Half-Hearted Efforts to Full Fledged Government Reform

Family Policy:

Subsidizing Child Care for Low-Income Families: A Good Bargain for Canadian Governments?
La politique familiale: ses impacts et les options
Comment accroître le soutien public en faveur des enfants ?

Social Policy:

La sécurité du revenu au Québec: une critique de la réforme proposée
IRPP prend position / The IRPP Position
Commentaries on the Axworthy Green Paper

Health:

Les marchés internes dans le contexte canadien

Série Québec-Canada :

Un Québec souverain et l'union économique Québec-Canada
L'évolution du fédéralisme canadien
La monnaie d'un Québec souverain
The Future of the Anglophone Community in Quebec / L'avenir de la communauté anglophone au Québec
Les peuples autochones et l'avenir du Québec
Les implications économiques d'un Québec souverain
L'accession du Québec à la souveraineté : aspects juridiques

These and other publications are available from:

Renouf Publishing 5369 Canotek Road, Ottawa, Ontario K1J 1J3
Tel.: (613) 745-2665 Fax: (613) 745-7660

To order copies of the *Choices/Choix*,
please contact IRPP directly or visit our website at www.irpp.org

IRPP 1470 Peel Street, Suite 200, Montreal, Quebec H3A 1T1
Tel.: (514) 985-2461 Fax.: (514) 985-2559 E-mail: irpp@irpp.org